40 Days
Through
REVELATION

40Days Through REVELATION

RON RHODES

HARVEST HOUSE PUBLISHERS
EUGENE, OREGON

Cover by Dugan Design Group, Bloomington, Minnesota

Cover photos © iStockphoto / Model-la, IgOrZh

40 DAYS THROUGH REVELATION
Copyright © 2013 by Ron Rhodes
Published by Harvest House Publishers
Eugene, Oregon 97402
www.harvesthousepublishers.com

Library of Congress Cataloging-in-Publication Data
    Rhodes, Ron.
    40 days through Revelation / Ron Rhodes.
        p. cm.
    Includes bibliographical references (p.   ).
    ISBN 978-0-7369-4827-2 (pbk.)
    ISBN 978-0-7369-4828-9 (eBook)
    1. Bible. N.T. Revelation—Devotional use. I. Title.
    BS2825.54.R49 2013
    228'.06—dc23

                                                            2012026063

To Kerri
with love and appreciation

Acknowledgments

After I became a Christian, I read one prophecy book after another. I could not get enough, gravitating toward those written by professors at Dallas Theological Seminary—John F. Walvoord, J. Dwight Pentecost, Charles Ryrie, and others. I found their books to be intelligently and persuasively written.

Little did I know then that in the not-too-distant future, I would actually enroll at Dallas Theological Seminary and take courses under these men, obtaining master's and doctoral degrees in theology. As I now write about the prophetic book of Revelation, I want to acknowledge my personal indebtedness to these teachers of the Word. Their work continues to bear fruit in my life.

I also want to offer continued praise to God for the wonderful family He has blessed me with—my wife, Kerri, and my two grown children, David and Kylie. With every year that passes (much too quickly!) I grow in appreciation for these three.

Thank You, Lord! I am grateful.

Contents

Introduction

Thank you for joining me in this exciting journey through the book of Revelation. You are in for a spiritually uplifting time! My hope and prayer is that as you read *40 Days Through Revelation*, you will attain...

- a thorough understanding of God's sovereignty and control over human history,

- an assurance that God will one day providentially cause good to triumph over evil,

- a yearning for the soon coming of Jesus Christ at the rapture,

- a joyful anticipation of our future in heaven, where we will not only be reunited with Christian loved ones but also dwell face to face with God Himself,

- an exalted view of the true majesty and glory of Jesus Christ,

- a deep appreciation for the wondrous salvation we have in Jesus Christ,

- and an increased conviction of the trustworthiness of the Bible in general and the prophecies in the Bible in particular.

The book of Revelation is the only book in the Bible that promises a special blessing to those who read it and obey its message: "Blessed is the one who reads aloud the words of this prophecy, and blessed are those who hear, and who keep what is written in it, for the time is near" (Revelation 1:3). "Blessed is the one who keeps the words of the prophecy of this book" (Revelation 22:7). So be encouraged. Blessing awaits you as you study this fascinating prophetic book.

As we begin our journey together, I want to address a few things that will lay a foundation for better understanding the book of Revelation. Let's look at the big picture first, and then we will zoom in on the details in subsequent chapters.

The Author and Recipients of Revelation

The author of the book of Revelation is the apostle John (see Revelation 1:1,4,9; 22:8). This is confirmed by second-century witnesses, such as Justin Martyr, Irenaeus, Clement of Alexandria, and Tertullian.

John had been imprisoned on the isle of Patmos, in the Aegean Sea, for the crime of sharing the message about Jesus Christ (Revelation 1:9). This island is where John received the revelation. The book was apparently written around AD 95.

The original recipients of the book were Christians who lived some 65 years after Jesus had been crucified and resurrected from the dead. Many of these were second-generation Christians, and the challenges they faced were great. Their lives had become increasingly difficult because of Roman hostilities toward Christianity.

The recipients of the book were suffering persecution, and some of them were even being killed (Revelation 2:13). Unfortunately, things were about to get even worse. John therefore wrote this book to give his readers a strong hope that would help them patiently endure amid relentless suffering.

At the time, evil seemed to be prevailing at every level. However, Revelation indicates that evil will one day come to an end. Sin, Satan, and suffering will be forever banished. Believers will no longer know sorrow or death, and fellowship with God will be perpetual and uninterrupted. This was good news for the suffering church in John's day.

A Contextual Outline of Revelation

John provides a contextual outline of his prophetic book in Revelation 1:19: "Write therefore the things that you have seen, those that are and those that are to take place after this."

• The "things that you have seen" is a reference to Revelation 1, where we find a description of Jesus in His present majestic glory and an introduction to the book of Revelation.

- "Those that are" relates to the then-present circumstances of the seven churches of Asia Minor recorded in Revelation 2–3. John directed his book to these seven churches.

- "Those that are to take place after this" refers to the futuristic prophecies of the tribulation period, the second coming, the millennial kingdom, the great white throne judgment, and the eternal state, which are described in Revelation 4–22.

The book closes by informing God's people that they will enjoy His presence forever in a new heaven and a new earth (Revelation 21:1). Jesus promises, "I am coming soon" (22:20). Such wonderful promises regarding the future empower suffering believers to patiently endure the present.

Approaches to the Book of Revelation

Scholars throughout the ages have taken four primary interpretive approaches in studying the book of Revelation.

1. The historicist view. This approach to Revelation holds that the book supplies a prophetic panorama of church history from the first century to the second coming of Christ. This approach emerged in the fourth century when some interpreters saw parallels between current events and biblical prophecy. Later, Joachim of Fiore (AD 1135–1202) developed the approach by dividing history into three ages. The Reformers were attracted to historicism and viewed the pope as the antichrist.

But a comparison of Revelation with other prophetic Scriptures (for example, Daniel 9:25-27; Matthew 24–25, 2 Thessalonians 2:1-12; Titus 2:13-14) reveals that these prophecies point to the future tribulation period, antichrist, second coming, millennial kingdom, great white throne judgment, and eternal state.

2. The idealist view. This view holds that the book of Revelation is primarily a symbolic description of the ongoing battle between God and the devil, between good and evil. However, it is hard to see how the idealist approach to Revelation could bring any genuine comfort to the original recipients of the book, who were undergoing great persecution.

Moreover, this view ignores specific time markers within the book. For example, it refers to 42 months in Revelation 11:2 and 1260 days in Revelation 12:6. Further, the many symbols in the book of Revelation point to real people and real events in the future tribulation period—the antichrist, Christ's second coming, Christ's millennial kingdom, the great white throne judgment, and the eternal state.

3. *The preterist view.* This approach holds that the prophecies of Revelation were fulfilled in AD 70 when Titus and his Roman army overran Jerusalem and destroyed the Jewish temple. So in this scheme, the book of Revelation does not deal with the future.

A primary problem with this view is that Revelation claims to be prophecy (see Revelation 1:3; 22:7,10,18-19). Further, multiple events described in Revelation bear no resemblance to the events of AD 70. For example, a third of mankind was not killed, as is predicted in Revelation 9:18.

Moreover, substantive evidence indicates that the book of Revelation was written about AD 95, far after the destruction of Jerusalem. Writing in the second century, Irenaeus declared that Revelation had been written toward the end of the reign of Domitian (AD 81–96). Later writers, such as Clement of Alexandria, Origen, Victorinus, Eusebius, and Jerome affirm the Domitian date. This being the case, the book of Revelation must refer to events that had not yet happened.

4. *The futurist view.* The futurist approach to interpreting the book of Revelation—the view we will follow in this book—holds that most of the events described in the book will take place in the end times, just prior to the second coming of Jesus Christ. This view honors the book's claim to be prophecy. It also recognizes that just as the Old Testament prophecies of the first coming of Christ were fulfilled literally (more than 100 of them!), so the prophecies of the second coming and the events that will lead up to it will be fulfilled literally.

The early church took a futurist view of the book, seeing the tribulation, second coming, and millennium as yet-future events. Later writers who took a futurist approach include Francisco Ribera (1537–1591) and John Nelson Darby (1800–1882). As we examine specific prophecies throughout Revelation, we will see that a futurist approach makes very good sense.

How to Use This Book

As you begin each chapter, pray something like this:

> *Lord, I ask You to open my eyes and enhance my understanding so that I can grasp what You want me to learn today* [Psalm 119:18]. *I also ask You to enable me, by Your Spirit, to apply the truths I learn to my daily life, and be guided moment by moment by Your Word* [Psalm 119:105; 2 Timothy 3:15-17]. *I thank You in Jesus' name. Amen.*

Following this short prayer, read the assigned section of the book of Revelation using your favorite Bible. With your Bible still in hand, you can then go verse by verse through your Bible again, but this time, after reading each verse, also read the appropriate notes in this book.

You'll notice that some of the biblical phrases I comment on are in quote marks and some aren't. Whenever John is speaking, quote marks are not used. Whenever someone else is speaking (such as Jesus or an angel), quote marks are used.

After the insights on each verse in the passage, I provide four brief summaries:

- *Major Themes.* These topical summaries will help you learn to think theologically as you study the Bible.

- *Digging Deeper with Cross-References.* These will help you discover relevant insights from other books of the Bible.

- *Life Lessons.* This is where you learn to apply what you have read to your daily life. You will find that the book of Revelation will transform you!

- *Questions for Reflection and Discussion.* Use these for your own journaling or for lively group interactions.

Lord, by the power of Your Spirit, please enable my reader to understand and apply truth from the book of Revelation. Please excite him or her with Your Word and instill a sense of awe for the person of our Lord Jesus Christ. I thank You in Jesus' name. Amen.

John's Introductory Prologue

Revelation 1:1-8

Scripture Reading and Insights

Begin by reading Revelation 1:1-8 in your favorite Bible. Read with the anticipation that the Holy Spirit has something important to teach you today (see Psalm 119:105).

In the introduction, we noted the outline of Revelation in 1:19: "Write therefore the things that you have seen, those that are and those that are to take place after this." In this chapter, we will begin to examine "the things that you [John] have seen." With your Bible still accessible, consider the following insights on Revelation 1:1-8, verse by verse.

Revelation 1:1-3

The revelation of Jesus Christ (1:1): The word "revelation" carries the idea of "uncovering" or "revealing." The book of Revelation uncovers and reveals prophetic truth. "Revelation *of* Jesus Christ" can mean either revelation that comes from Christ or revelation that is about Him. Both senses are probably intended in this verse.

Which God gave him (1:1): The Father gave this revelation to Jesus Christ.

Things that must soon take place (1:1): This should not be taken to mean that the events described in Revelation would all take place within a few years of the time John saw them. John recorded Revelation in Greek, and the Greek word translated "soon" can mean "quickly, swiftly, speedily, at a rapid rate" (see Luke 18:8). In Revelation 1:1, the term indicates that when the predicted events first start to occur in the end times, they will then progress rapidly.

He made it known by sending his angel (1:1): God the Father gave this revelation to Jesus Christ, and Christ then communicated it to John using an angel as an intermediary. The specific angel is not mentioned by name, but some speculate that it might be Gabriel, who delivered notable revelations from God to Daniel, Mary, and Zechariah (Daniel 8:16; 9:21-22; Luke 1:18-19,26-31).

To his servant John (1:1): The angel was an intermediary between Christ and John. Elsewhere in Revelation John receives communications directly from Christ (Revelation 1:10-16), from an elder (7:13), and from a voice in heaven (10:4). John was commissioned to pass this revelation on to the seven churches of Asia Minor (2–3).

Witness (1:2): John faithfully testifies to and vouches for all he witnessed in this divine revelation of Jesus Christ.

Blessed (1:3): The word "blessed" means "spiritually happy." This is the first of seven pronouncements of blessing in the book of Revelation (see 14:13; 16:15; 19:9; 20:6; 22:7,14).

The one who reads aloud (1:3): Revelation is the only book in the Bible that promises a blessing to the person who reads it aloud and the person who listens to it, responding in obedience. John's contemporaries did not own copies of Scripture. They had to go to church, where they listened to Scripture being read aloud.

Blessed are those who hear, and who keep what is written in it (1:3): Obedience brings blessing. We should not just be hearers of God's Word, but doers of it (James 1:22-25).

For the time is near (1:3): This should not be taken to mean that the events in this book will necessarily happen soon. After all, Scripture elsewhere indicates that there will be enough of a delay in the second coming that some people will begin to wonder if it will ever occur (see Matthew 24:36-39; 2 Peter 3:3-4). "Near" communicates imminence. The next event in God's prophetic calendar—the rapture of the church—could occur at any time.

Revelation 1:4-6

John to the seven churches that are in Asia (1:4): These seven churches were experiencing severe persecution. They were called to shine as lights in the midst of the darkness (see Matthew 5:14-16; Philippians 2:15). Revelation 2–3 reveals that five of these seven churches needed to make some internal corrections. One reason the book of Revelation was written was to encourage and motivate these suffering believers.

Grace to you and peace (1:4): "Grace" refers to God's unmerited favor to those who believe in Jesus. "Peace" refers to the believer's standing and experience in relation to God. It is rooted in Christ's work of salvation on the cross.

From him who is and who was and who is to come (1:4): This is the eternal Father.

Seven spirits (1:4): In the Bible, seven is often associated with completion, fulfillment, and perfection (see, for example, Genesis 2:2; Exodus 20:10; Leviticus 14:7; Acts 6:3). The number seven occurs often in the book of Revelation. In addition to the seven spirits, we find seven...

churches (1:4)

lampstands (1:12)

stars (1:16)

torches before the throne (4:5)

seals on the scroll (5:1)

horns and eyes of the Lamb (5:6)

spirits of God (4:5; 5:6)

angels and trumpets (8:2)

thunders (10:3)

heads of the dragon (12:3)

heads of the beast (13:1)

golden bowls (15:7)

kings (17:10)

Some scholars suggest that the seven spirits are seven angels that are before the throne of God in heaven. Others suggest the seven spirits are the seven angels mentioned in conjunction with the seven churches of Revelation 2–3.

Still others understand the seven spirits to be a metaphorical reference to the Holy Spirit in His fullness. If this is correct, a possible cross-reference is Isaiah 11:2, which speaks of the sevenfold ministry of the

Holy Spirit as related to the divine Messiah: "The Spirit of the Lord shall rest upon him, the Spirit of wisdom and understanding, the Spirit of counsel and might, the Spirit of knowledge and the fear of the Lord."

From him who is and who was and who is to come…the seven spirits… Jesus Christ (1:4-5): If the seven spirits represent the Holy Spirit, we witness each person of the Trinity in verses 4-5.

Jesus Christ the faithful witness (1:5): Jesus is a faithful and reliable source of the revelation being communicated to John. John could thus trust what he was being told.

The firstborn of the dead (1:5): This could mean that Christ was the first to be permanently raised from the dead. More likely, however, the term indicates that Christ is the supreme or preeminent One among those who have been or will be raised from the dead (see Psalm 89:27; Colossians 1:15).

The ruler of kings on earth (1:5): Christ is absolutely sovereign. He rules over all. He is the King of kings and Lord of lords (Revelation 19:16). Though Christ is the absolute ruler of the kings of the earth, He will not fully exercise this authority until His second coming, when He sets up His millennial kingdom (Revelation 19–20).

Freed us from our sins (1:5): Jesus saves His people from sin, as His name proclaims. "Jesus" means "Yahweh saves" or "Yahweh is salvation."

Made us a kingdom, priests to his God and Father (1:6): All Christians become a part of God's kingdom and submit to Christ's rule. As priests, Christians have the privilege of entering God's presence and serving Him forever.

To him be glory and dominion forever and ever (1:6): This is the yearning and utterance of praise of Christians of all generations who recognize that our God is an awesome God.

Revelation 1:7

He is coming with the clouds (1:7): Clouds are often used in association with God's visible glory (Exodus 16:10; 40:34-35; 1 Kings 8:10-11; Matthew 17:5). Just as Christ was received by a cloud in His ascension (Acts 1:9), so He will return again in the clouds of heaven (Matthew 24:30; 26:64; Mark 13:26; 14:62; Luke 21:27). Just as Jesus left with this visible manifestation of the glory of God, so He will return at the second coming with the same visible manifestation of the glory of God. (Note that the second coming is different from the rapture. I'll address this when I discuss Revelation 3:10.)

Every eye will see him (1:7): The second coming of Christ might not be an instantaneous event. It may be visible for a full day or more so that as the earth rotates, every eye on earth can witness the coming of Christ with the armies of heaven. Of course, television broadcasts and the Internet will likely play a role.

Even those who pierced him (1:7): This is a reference to Christ's crucifixion (John 19:34) and to the Jews living on the earth at the time of the second coming (see Zechariah 12:10). These Jews will represent those who crucified Christ in the first century (see Acts 2:22-23; 3:14-15).

All tribes of the earth will wail on account of him (1:7): They will wail and mourn for fear of punishment from the divine Messiah, the Judge of humankind (Revelation 20:4; see also Matthew 24:30).

Revelation 1:8

"I am the Alpha and the Omega" (1:8): This is a powerful confirmation of Jesus' divine identity (compare with Revelation 22:13). "Alpha and Omega" is used exclusively of God in the Old Testament (Isaiah 44:6; 48:12-13). The title expresses eternality and omnipotence. Jesus is the all-powerful One of eternity past and eternity future. He is the eternal God who has always existed in the past and who will always exist in the future.

"Who is and who was and who is to come" (1:8): Christ, as God, is an eternal being.

"The Almighty" (1:8): This depicts absolute deity. Christ is supreme and sovereign over all things, including the unfolding of events in the book of Revelation (see Revelation 4:8; 11:17; 15:3; 16:7,14; 19:15; 21:22).

Major Themes

1. *God is a revealer.* God takes the initiative in revealing Himself and His will (Hebrews 1:1-2). The ultimate revelation came in the person of Jesus Christ (John 1:18).

2. *God is a Trinity.* The doctrine of the Trinity is based on three lines of evidence:

- There is only one true God (Isaiah 44:6; 46:9; John 5:44; 17:3; Romans 3:29-30; 16:27; 1 Corinthians 8:4; Galatians 3:20; Ephesians 4:6; 1 Timothy 2:5; James 2:19).

- Three persons are recognized as God—the Father (1 Peter 1:2), Jesus (John 20:28; Hebrews 1:8), and the Holy Spirit (Acts 5:3-4).

- There is three-in-oneness within the one God (Matthew 28:19; 2 Corinthians 13:14).

Digging Deeper with Cross-References

Angels—2 Kings 6:17; Psalm 91:11; Matthew 25:31; Luke 15:7-10; Colossians 1:16; Hebrews 1:14; 13:2.

God is Almighty—Genesis 17:1; Psalm 91:1; 2 Corinthians 6:18; see also Matthew 19:26; Mark 10:27.

Life Lessons

1. *You can trust the Bible.* The Bible is God's revelation to you. It is God's voice to you. It is God speaking to you (see Psalm 119; 2 Timothy 3:15-17).

2. *Obedience brings blessing.* Obedience to God brings blessing (Luke 11:28), long life (1 Kings 3:14), happiness (Psalms 112:1; 119:56), peace (Proverbs 1:33), and a state of well-being (Jeremiah 7:23; see also Exodus 19:5; Deuteronomy 4:40; 12:28; 28:1-14; Joshua 1:8; 1 Chronicles 22:13; Isaiah 1:19).

Questions for Reflection and Discussion

1. Christ is the Alpha and the Omega. What difference does that make in the way you live your daily life?

2. Christ is coming again. What difference does that make in the way you live your daily life?

3. You have been freed from your sins. Does that motivate you to live for Christ? How?

4. Revelation 1:3 promises that obedient Christians will be blessed. Does this motivate you to obey God's Word? How?

John's Awesome Vision

Revelation 1:9-20

Scripture Reading and Insights

Begin by reading Revelation 1:9-20 in your favorite Bible. Read with the anticipation that the Holy Spirit has something important to teach you today (see Psalm 119:105).

In yesterday's reading, Christ was described as the Alpha and the Omega and as the One who is and who was and who is to come. In this chapter we will focus on John's description of the glorified Christ in heaven and on Jesus' intimate familiarity with churches on earth. With your Bible still accessible, consider the following insights on the biblical text, verse by verse.

Revelation 1:9-11

I, John, your brother and partner in the tribulation (1:9): John and his readers were persecuted by Roman authorities for their faith in Christ. Jesus had affirmed, "In the world you will have tribulation" (John 16:33). The apostle Paul taught the same (Acts 14:22).

Patient endurance (1:9): The trials John and his readers faced called for patient endurance amid conflict. The prophecies in the book of Revelation were intended to empower them to patiently endure, for God assured them of victory in the end.

That are in Jesus (1:9): Jesus gives us His strength and peace in the midst of the storm. Recall what He had told His followers: "Peace I leave with you; my peace I give to you. Not as the world gives do I give to you. Let not your hearts be troubled, neither let them be afraid" (John 14:27).

On the island called Patmos (1:9): Patmos is a mountainous and rocky desert island on the Aegean Sea with an area of about 60 square miles. It lies off the southwest coast of Asia Minor—modern Turkey. People were banished and exiled to this desolate and barren island for crimes committed on mainland Rome and were usually forced to engage in hard labor in mines. Patmos was a Roman penal colony.

The testimony of Jesus (1:9): John gave relentless testimony for and about Jesus. This is why he was persecuted by Rome.

I was in the Spirit (1:10): This refers to the state of spiritual ecstasy in which John received a vision containing a revelation from the Lord. The Lord supernaturally "pulled back the veil" so John could see things to come (see Acts 10:10-11).

On the Lord's day (1:10): Some scholars take this as Sunday, the first day of the week, on which Christians gathered to worship and celebrate the Lord's Supper (1 Corinthians 11:20). This may be the case, or John may have been saying, "I was in the Spirit on a Lord-glorifying and Lord-manifesting day."

I heard behind me a loud voice like a trumpet (1:10): John probably had not heard the voice of his beloved Savior for more than 60 years. Now he hears it again, this time "like a trumpet"—loud, majestic, and otherworldly.

"Write what you see in a book" (1:11): "Book" indicates a scroll made of parchment. God often directed people to write down His revelations for future generations (Exodus 24:4; Joshua 24:25-26; 1 Samuel 10:25; Isaiah 8:1).

"Send it to the seven churches" (1:11): These churches are addressed in Revelation 2–3. The order of mention of these seven churches forms a geographical half-moon, beginning with Ephesus, going north to Smyrna and Pergamum, and moving east and south to Thyatira, Sardis, Philadelphia, and Laodicea. John had apparently been like a spiritual father to these churches.

Revelation 1:12-16

I saw seven golden lampstands (1:12): Jesus reveals in Revelation 1:20 that "the seven lampstands are the seven churches"—that is, the ones addressed in Revelation 2–3. The churches are symbolized as lampstands because they bear God's light in a dark world (see Matthew 5:16).

A son of man, clothed with a long robe and with a golden sash around his chest (1:13): "Son of man" is a messianic title derived from Daniel 7:13. It was Jesus' favorite title during His three-year ministry (it occurs 81 times in the Gospels).

Jesus, the Son of Man, is in the midst of the churches—that is, He is intimately acquainted with all that is going on in each of them. Revelation 2:1 tells us that Jesus walks among the churches. The long robe and sash designate Christ as a priest (see Exodus 28:4; Leviticus 16:1-4; Hebrews 2:17).

The hairs of his head were white, like white wool, like snow (1:14): This points to the infinite wisdom and purity of Christ, the divine Messiah. The white hair may also symbolize eternity, much like "Ancient of Days" (Daniel 7:9,13,22).

His eyes were like a flame of fire (1:14): This description points not only to Christ's absolute holiness but also to His penetrating scrutiny in seeing all things as they truly are. For example, He accurately diagnoses the strengths and weaknesses of the seven churches in Revelation 2–3. Christ's eyes of scrutiny will also play a key role at the future judgment (see 1 Corinthians 3:13).

His feet were like burnished bronze, refined in a furnace (1:15): The polished brass feet may symbolize divine judgment. Fire consumed sin offerings on the bronze altar. Seen in this light, Christ the divine Judge moves among the seven churches to judge what is right and what is wrong.

His voice was like the roar of many waters (1:15): No one would dare challenge One with such a voice!

In his right hand (1:16): Scripture always portrays the right hand as a place of honor and distinction (see Ephesians 1:20).

He held seven stars (1:16): Revelation 1:20 reveals that the seven stars are the angels of the seven churches. This could indicate that each church has a guardian angel assigned to it. Or "angels" could refer to the pastors of each of the seven churches, because the Greek term for "angel" literally means "messenger" (see Luke 9:52; James 2:25). If this is correct, then the fact that Christ holds the stars in His hand demonstrates Christ's providential control over each church and its leaders.

From his mouth came a sharp two-edged sword (1:16): This is apparently a reference to the Word of God. Ephesians 6:17 refers to "the sword of the Spirit, which is the word of God." Hebrews 4:12 tells us that "the word of God is living and active, sharper than any two-edged sword." Christ stands against His enemies with the sword of His Word (see Revelation 2:16; 19:19-21).

His face was like the sun shining in full strength (1:16): Christ's bright white appearance here is similar to Christ's appearance on the Mount of Transfiguration, where "his face shone like the sun, and his clothes became white as light" (Matthew 17:2). Christ is the God of glory (see John 17:5).

Revelation 1:17-18

I fell at his feet as though dead (1:17): Falling before the Lord was a common response among those who saw the Lord in Bible times (Genesis 17:3; Numbers 16:22; Ezekiel 1:28; Acts 9:4). This too reminds us of the Mount of Transfiguration, where the disciples "fell on their faces and were terrified" (Matthew 17:6).

"Fear not" (1:17): The Lord comforted and reassured John by touching him and speaking to him. Just as Christ had exhorted His followers not to fear during His three-year ministry (Matthew 10:31; Luke 8:50; 12:7,32), so He encouraged John.

"I am the first and the last" (1:17): The phrase "the first and the last" is used of Almighty God in the Old Testament (Isaiah 44:6). Christ's use of this title here (and Revelation 2:8; 22:13) demonstrates His equality with God.

"The living one" (1:18): Christ was crucified, and then He defeated death by rising from the dead (John 2:19; Revelation 1:5).

"I have the keys of Death and Hades" (1:18): In the New Testament, a key implies authority to open a door and give entrance to a place or realm. Jesus' words here imply that as God, He has the authority to grant entrance and exit from the realms of death and Hades (John 5:21-26; 1 Corinthians 15:54-57; Hebrews 2:14; Revelation 20:12-14). Jesus sovereignly decides who lives, who dies, and when.

Revelation 1:19

"Write therefore..." (1:19): Here we find a three-part outline of the book of Revelation. "The things that you have seen" points to the things John saw and recorded in chapter 1. "Those that are" points to the current state of the seven churches (chapters 2–3). "Those that are to take place after this" points to future events (chapters 4–22).

Revelation 1:20

"As for the mystery" (1:20): A biblical mystery is a truth that cannot be discerned simply by human investigation and that requires special revelation from God. Generally, this word refers to a truth that was unknown to people living in Old Testament times but explained in the New Testament (Matthew 13:17; Colossians 1:26).

"The seven stars...the seven golden lampstands" (1:20): Jesus is apparently referring to the seven pastors of the seven churches.

Major Themes

1. *Names and titles.* In the ancient world, names and titles were not mere labels as they are today. A name revealed important characteristics about a person. That is why we learn much about Jesus Christ in Revelation 1.

2. *The glory of God and Jesus.* God's glory is the luminous manifestation of His person. Brilliant light consistently accompanies His glory (Matthew 17:2-3; 1 Timothy 6:16). The word "glory" is often linked with verbs of seeing (Exodus 16:7; 33:18; Deuteronomy 5:24; Isaiah 40:5) and appearing (Exodus 16:10).

3. *The kingdom.* Scripture uses the word "kingdom" in two primary senses. Presently, God spiritually rules over His people from heaven (Colossians 1:13; see also 1 Corinthians 4:20). In the future, after His second coming, Christ will reign on earth in the millennium (Revelation 20:1-6; see also Isaiah 65:17–66:24; Jeremiah 32:36-44; Zechariah 14:9-17).

Digging Deeper with Cross-References

Fear—Psalms 27:1; 56:11; Proverbs 3:25; Isaiah 51:12; John 14:27; Romans 8:31; 2 Timothy 1:7; 1 John 4:18.

Death—Psalms 23:4; 116:15; Ecclesiastes 3:1-2; 7:2; 8:8; Isaiah 25:8; Ezekiel 33:11; Romans 14:8; 1 Corinthians 15:26; Philippians 1:21; Hebrews 9:27; Revelation 21:3-4.

Being a witness of Christ—Acts 2:32; 3:15; 4:18-20; 10:39-40; 2 Peter 1:16; 1 John 1:1.

Life Lessons

1. *Strength from other Christians.* Each of us is a "brother and partner" for every other Christian (Revelation 1:9). Remember that "a threefold cord is not quickly broken" (Ecclesiastes 4:12). We gain strength from each other, especially during trials.

2. *Trusting God with the future.* We may not know every single detail of what the future holds, but we do know the One who does. Let's trust Him (Psalm 37:5; Proverbs 3:5-6).

3. *A worshipful attitude toward Jesus.* Though Jesus is our Savior and Friend, let's not forget that He is also our glorious and majestic Lord and sovereign God who deserves our utmost reverence (Revelation 1:17; see also Exodus 3:5).

Questions for Reflection and Discussion

1. What evidence do you see in Revelation 1 that Revelation is a Christ-centered book? Be specific. What implications might this have for your own life being Christ-centered?

2. John refers to "patient endurance" in Revelation 1:9. What does James teach us about this (James 1:2-4)?

DAY 3

The Churches at Ephesus and Smyrna

Revelation 2:1-11

Scripture Reading and Insights

Begin by reading Revelation 2:1-11 in your favorite Bible. As you read, remember that the Word of God is alive and working in you (Hebrews 4:12).

In yesterday's reading, we were introduced to seven churches and their pastors in Asia Minor. John was apparently their general overseer. In today's lesson, we will focus our attention on the strengths and weaknesses of two of these churches—those in Ephesus and Smyrna. With your Bible still accessible, consider the following insights on the biblical text, verse by verse.

Revelation 2:1-3

"To the angel of the church" (2:1): This could be either an angel assigned to protect the church in Ephesus or, more likely, the pastor (literally, "messenger") of the church.

"In Ephesus" (2:1): Ephesus was well known for its temple of the Roman goddess Diana (in Greek, Artemis). Many pagans lived here. During his third missionary tour, the apostle Paul spent about three years in Ephesus building up the church (Acts 19). When he left, Paul's young associate Timothy pastored there for another year (1 Timothy 1:3). Paul later wrote his epistle to the Ephesians while a prisoner in Rome in AD 61.

"'The words of him who holds the seven stars in his right hand'" (2:1): That Christ holds the stars (apparently the pastors of the churches) in His hand symbolizes His sovereign and providential control over each church and its leaders.

"'Who walks among the seven golden lampstands'" (2:1): Jesus was intimately acquainted with all that was going on in each of the churches. He walks among them, observing what is right and was is wrong in each.

"'I know your works, your toil and your patient endurance'" (2:2): In Revelation 2–3, Jesus reveals that the churches are often in need of correction. Still, He commends them if they have done something commendable.

"'You cannot bear with those who are evil'" (2:2): The believers in Ephesus refused to compromise by participating with pagans, whose immoral acts indicated they had no fear of God.

"'Have tested those who call themselves apostles and are not, and found them to be false'" (2:2): These Ephesian believers tested false apostles against the clear teachings of Scripture (compare with Acts 17:11; 1 Thessalonians 5:21). Decades before Revelation was written, the apostle Paul warned the Ephesian elders that false teachers would seek to lead them astray (Acts 20:28-31; see also 2 Corinthians 11:13). The discerning believers at Ephesus remembered this and rejected the teachings of the false apostles.

"'You are enduring patiently'" (2:3): At the time of the writing of Revelation, the church at Ephesus had patiently remained faithful to the Lord for some 40 years.

"'Bearing up for my name's sake'" (2:3): It was for the sake of the Savior that these Ephesians were willing to suffer. They took up their cross and followed Christ (Matthew 16:24).

"'You have not grown weary'" (2:3): These believers had not given up. Their commitment to Christ kept them unbendingly faithful, even amid great suffering.

Revelation 2:4-5

"'I have this against you'" (2:4): Despite their faithfulness and commitment to sound doctrine, they were still in need of correction.

"'You have abandoned the love you had at first'" (2:4): Thirty years earlier, the church at Ephesus had been commended for the love it had shown to others and to the Lord (Ephesians 1:15-16). Their love had since waned. They needed to renew their love (Matthew 22:37-38; John 14:21,23; 1 Corinthians 16:22).

"'Remember therefore from where you have fallen'" (2:5): The Greek word translated "remember" literally means "keep on remembering." They were never to forget from where they had fallen.

"'Repent, and do the works you did at first'" (2:5): To repent is to change one's thinking and behavior (Matthew 4:17; Luke 24:47; Acts 3:19). These believers in Ephesus were to change by increasing their love for Christ.

"'If not, I will come to you and remove your lampstand from its place'" (2:5): This may mean that the Lord would remove the church from its place of service and usefulness. Or it may mean that God would bring an end to the church.

Revelation 2:6-7

"'Yet this you have'" (2:6): Despite their lack of love, something was still very much in their favor.

"'You hate the works of the Nicolaitans'" (2:6): The Nicolaitans condoned license in Christian conduct, ate food sacrificed to idols, and engaged in idolatry. Christians at Ephesus were commended for their stand against the Nicolaitans.

"'He who has an ear, let him hear'" (2:7): In Bible times, hearing often implied obedience.

"'What the Spirit says to the churches'" (2:7): Ultimately, the Holy Spirit inspires all Scripture (2 Timothy 3:15-17; 2 Peter 1:21). The Holy Spirit is God (Acts 5:3-4) and the Spirit of truth (John 15:26; 16:13), so this Scripture containing prophecy is trustworthy (John 10:35).

"'The one who conquers'" (2:7): Jesus promised a blessing for conquering or overcoming Christians (Revelation 2:11,17,26; 3:5,12,21). "Conquering" and "overcoming" are essentially synonyms for "faithfulness" and "obedience." Christians who fail to conquer (those who are unfaithful and disobedient) suffer a loss of rewards but not a loss of salvation (Romans 14:10-12; 1 Corinthians 3:10-15; 2 Corinthians 5:10).

"'Eat of the tree of life'" (2:7): The tree of life is first seen in Eden. It bestows continuing life (Genesis 2:9,17; 3:1-24). It will appear again in the eternal city of heaven, the new Jerusalem (Revelation 22:2).

"'In the paradise of God'" (2:7): The word "paradise" literally means "garden of pleasure" or "garden of delight." It refers to heaven in 2 Corinthians 12:3.

Revelation 2:8-9

"To the angel of the church" (2:8): This is likely the pastor of the church.

"In Smyrna" (2:8): Smyrna was located about 35 miles north of Ephesus and was a prosperous commercial center. The Roman imperial cult severely persecuted Christians in this city who refused to say, "Caesar is Lord."

"'The first and the last'" (2:8): Christ indicates He is eternal God, who has always existed and who always will.

"'Who died and came to life'" (2:8): Christ was crucified (John 19:17-42) but was gloriously resurrected (Matthew 28:9-10,16-20; Luke 24:13-43; John 20:11-18,26-29; 1 Corinthians 15:3-6).

"'I know your tribulation and your poverty'" (2:9): Christ sees everything (Revelation 1:14), so He is aware of all circumstances of all believers (Matthew 11:27; John 2:25; 21:17; Acts 1:24; Hebrews 4:13). He was fully aware of the suffering of the Christians in Smyrna.

"'But you are rich'" (2:9): These believers actually had a large storehouse of eternal riches awaiting them in heaven (see Matthew 6:19-20).

"'The slander of those who say that they are Jews and are not'" (2:9): Because the apostate Jews in this city hated Christ, they also hated all who followed Christ. They slandered Christians, just as the devil does. They were Jews by physical lineage but did not hold to the religion of

their Jewish ancestors, such as Abraham. They had become paganized in a pagan culture.

"Synagogue of Satan'" (2:9): Because these apostate Jews were engaged in false religion, they were instruments of the devil, and the synagogue they attended was in reality a habitat of Satan.

Revelation 2:10-11

"'Do not fear what you are about to suffer'" (2:10): "Do not fear" in the Greek is literally "stop having fear." The believers in Smyrna were already experiencing fear. God knows in advance the sufferings His people will encounter (see Genesis 15:13; Acts 9:16). Christ knows in advance the suffering about to be experienced by the Christians in Smyrna. He thus exhorts them not to be fearful.

"'The devil'" (2:10): The devil is a fallen angel who is aligned against God and His purposes. The word "devil" carries the idea of "adversary" (1 Peter 5:8).

"'Is about to throw some of you into prison'" (2:10): It is not stated whether apostate Jews or pagans will accomplish this. But the devil will be the instigator behind it.

"'That you may be tested'" (2:10): The testing will show where their true loyalty lies.

"'For ten days you will have tribulation'" (2:10): This may refer to ten literal days of particularly intense persecution yet to come, or it may refer to ten short outbreaks of persecution under ten Roman emperors: Nero, Domitian, Trajan, Hadrian, Septimus Severus, Maximin, Decius, Valerian, Aurelian, and Diocletian.

"'Be faithful unto death, and I will give you the crown of life'" (2:10): In the second century, the pastor of the church in Smyrna, Polycarp (a pupil of the apostle John), was burned alive for refusing to worship Caesar.

All believers must face the judgment seat of Christ (Romans 14:8-10; 1 Corinthians 3:1-10; 2 Corinthians 5:10). Believers will either receive or forfeit rewards, such as the crown of life. The crown of life is given to those who persevere under trial and especially to those who suffer to the point of death (James 1:12).

"He who has an ear, let him hear'" (2:11): Hearing implies obedience to that which was heard.

"What the Spirit says to the churches'" (2:11): The Holy Spirit is ultimately behind these prophetic revelations (2 Timothy 3:15-17; 2 Peter 1:21).

"The one who conquers'" (2:11): This refers to faithful and obedient Christians.

"Will not be hurt by the second death'" (2:11): The "first death" is physical death, the separation of the spirit or soul from the body (as in Genesis 35:18). Virtually all people (except Christians who are raptured) will experience the first death. The second death is for unbelievers only and refers to eternal separation from God in the lake of fire, or eternal hell.

In this figure of speech, a positive idea is emphasized by negating its opposite. For example, "I am not amused" means "I am annoyed." The Lord's point is that faithful believers may eagerly anticipate a wonderful eternal life.

Major Themes

1. *True apostles.* The apostles were chosen messengers of Christ, handpicked by the Lord or the Holy Spirit (Matthew 10:1-4; Acts 1:26). They were the special recipients of God's self-revelation (1 Corinthians 2:13). They recognized their special divine authority (1 Corinthians 7:10; 11:23) and were authenticated by miracles (Acts 2:43; 3:3-11; 5:12-16; 9:32-42; 19:11-17).

2. *The resurrection of Christ (Revelation 2:8).* The resurrection of Christ is the foundation stone of the Christian faith. Paul wrote, "If Christ has not been raised, your faith is futile" (1 Corinthians 15:17). Jesus made many appearances to many people over many days to prove that He had been resurrected (see Acts 1:3; 1 Corinthians 15:6).

Digging Deeper with Cross-References

Love for God—Matthew 22:37; Mark 12:30; Luke 10:27; John 14:15,21,23; 21:15-17; James 2:5; 1 Peter 1:8.

Spiritual riches—Matthew 6:19-21; 19:21; Luke 12:13-21; Hebrews 10:34; 11:26; James 2:5; 1 Peter 1:3-4.

Satanic persecution—John 8:44; Acts 16:16-18; Revelation 2:10,13; 12:4,12.

Life Lessons

1. *Take up your cross.* Living as a committed Christian can be costly. As we continue to near the end times, the persecution of Christians will continue to increase. Regardless of what the world throws at us, however, our destiny is secure, and a glorious inheritance awaits us in heaven (Romans 8:18; 1 Peter 1:4). Never hesitate to take up your cross and follow Jesus on a daily basis (Matthew 16:24).

2. *Repentance.* True repentance shows itself in the way one lives. John the Baptist urged Jewish leaders to "bear fruit in keeping with repentance" (Matthew 3:8). People are urged to "repent and turn to God, performing deeds in keeping with their repentance" (Acts 26:20).

Questions for Reflection and Discussion

1. Do you test all religious teachings against the Scriptures, whether you hear them at church, on the radio, or on TV? (Meditate on Acts 17:11 and 1 Thessalonians 5:21.)

2. Is your love for the Lord as fervent as it was when you first became a Christian?

3. Do you pay more attention to building up eternal riches than accumulating material riches?

The Churches at Pergamum and Thyatira

Revelation 2:12-29

Scripture Reading and Insights

Begin by reading Revelation 2:12-29 in your favorite Bible. As you read, remember that the Word of God is alive and working in you (Hebrews 4:12).

In the previous lesson, we studied the messages to the churches in Ephesus and Smyrna. In today's lesson, we focus attention on the strengths and weaknesses of the churches in Pergamum and Thyatira. With your Bible still accessible, consider the following insights on the biblical text, verse by verse.

Revelation 2:12-13

"To the angel of the church" (2:12): This is likely the pastor of the church.

"In Pergamum" (2:12): Pergamum is in northwest Asia Minor. It featured large buildings and a library with more than 200,000 items. At one time, Pergamum was the capital city of the Roman province of Asia.

"'The sharp two-edged sword'" (2:12): This is apparently a reference to the Word of God (see Ephesians 6:17; Hebrews 4:12; Revelation 19:19-21).

"'I know where you dwell, where Satan's throne is'" (2:13): Satan is not omnipresent (only God is), so he can be in only one place at a time.

Perhaps at the time Christ spoke these words, Satan was localized in Pergamum.

Pergamum was the official center of emperor worship in Asia. It also featured a temple of Asclepius, a pagan god whose symbol was a serpent (like Satan—see Genesis 3:1; 2 Corinthians 11:3). A giant altar of Zeus overlooked the city. With this abundance of false religion, it is not surprising that Satan has a throne there.

"You hold fast my name'" (2:13): Citizens of Pergamum were expected to participate in the civil and pagan religion of emperor worship. A failure to comply was interpreted as disloyalty to the state. The Christians in Pergamum refused participation.

"You did not deny my faith even in the days of Antipas my faithful witness, who was killed among you'" (2:13): Antipas—perhaps a church leader—was a faithful defender of the truth who was burned to death inside a brass bull positioned over burning flames.

"Where Satan dwells'" (2:13): As a bastion of anti-Christian false religion, this area would have made Satan feel right at home.

Revelation 2:14-15

"I have a few things against you'" (2:14): Despite these believers' commitment to Christ, they were not faultless. Corrective action was required.

"The teaching of Balaam'" (2:14): In Old Testament times, Balaam had been hired by Balak, the king of Moab, to lure the hearts of the Israelites away from the Lord God by having Moabite women seduce Israelite men into intermarriage (Numbers 22–25; 31). The Israelites succumbed to fornication and idolatrous feasts.

"The teaching of the Nicolaitans'" (2:15): The Nicolaitans were open to license in Christian conduct, they ate food sacrificed to idols, and they engaged in idolatry.

Revelation 2:16-17

"Therefore repent'" (2:16): Repentance involves a change in one's thinking that yields changed behavior (see Matthew 4:17; Luke 24:47; Acts 3:19). Members of the church were called to repent of their openness to false teachings.

"I will come to you soon" *(2:16)*: This is not the second coming, but rather a coming in judgment. These church members would not be permitted to continue in sin.

"War against them with the sword of my mouth" *(2:16)*: Antipas had died by the Roman sword, but some members of this church would encounter Christ's "sword" if they did not repent.

"He who has an ear, let him hear" *(2:17)*: Hearing implies obedience to the message.

"What the Spirit says to the churches" *(2:17)*: The Holy Spirit inspires all Scripture, including prophecy (2 Timothy 3:15-17; 2 Peter 1:21).

"The one who conquers" *(2:17)*: This describes the Christian who is faithful and obedient. He will be rewarded at the judgment seat of Christ.

"Hidden manna" *(2:17)*: Just as manna sustained the Hebrews during the wilderness sojourn (Exodus 16:32-36; Hebrews 9:4), so Christ Himself, the bread of life, sustains believers (see John 6:33,35,48,51). Believers who refused to eat food sacrificed to idols would enjoy a much better banquet in heaven—the hidden manna, Jesus Christ Himself.

"A white stone" *(2:17)*: There are several viable interpretations of the significance of the white stone. Winning athletes in biblical times were given white stones that served as admission passes to a winners' celebration. The faithful believer's white stone may point to admittance into the ultimate winners' celebration: eternal life in heaven.

Roman gladiators who became favorites were granted retirement from life-endangering combat. A white stone was given to them to symbolize this retirement. Perhaps believers who are engaged in battle against sin and an ungodly world will be granted "retirement" to heaven, where they enjoy eternal rest (see Revelation 14:13).

Judges in Bible times indicated defendants' innocence by placing a white stone in a vessel. Perhaps the white stone represents the believer's assurance of being acquitted before God (see Romans 8:1).

"With a new name written on the stone" *(2:17)*: In the Old Testament, the high priest wore 12 stones on his breastplate that were inscribed with the names of the 12 tribes (God's chosen people). A new name on a stone may point to believers being included in God's chosen people.

Revelation 2:18-19

"To the angel of the church" (2:18): Apparently the pastor of the church.

"In Thyatira" (2:18): Thyatira was located about halfway between Pergamum and Sardis and had been under Roman rule for centuries. The city was a thriving commercial center. Its primary industries were wool and dye (see Acts 16:14).

"'The Son of God'" (2:18): This is a title of deity. Whenever Jesus claimed to be the Son of God, His Jewish contemporaries fully understood that He was making an unqualified claim to be God (see John 5:18; 19:7).

"'Eyes like a flame of fire'" (2:18): Christ has penetrating scrutiny and sees all things as they truly are—something He will demonstrate at the future judgment (see 1 Corinthians 3:13).

"'Whose feet are like burnished bronze'" (2:18): The polished brass feet may symbolize divine judgment. Fire consumed sin offerings on the bronze altar.

"'I know your works, your love and faith and service and patient endurance'" (2:19): Christ with His eyes "like a flame of fire" (Revelation 1:14) is aware of all the good things that characterize members of this church.

Revelation 2:20-23

"'I have this against you'" (2:20): Despite the love, faith, and patient endurance these believers had, they were nevertheless in need of corrective action.

"'You tolerate that woman Jezebel'" (2:20): This brings to mind the idolatrous queen who enticed Israel to engage in Baal worship (1 Kings 16–19). The evil woman of Revelation 2:20 may have been named Jezebel. Or Jezebel may have been her pseudonym or simply Christ's description of her—a Jezebel-like woman.

"'Seducing my servants to practice sexual immorality'" (2:20): This woman promoted the idea that people could engage in sins of the outer body (such as sexual immorality) without injuring the inner spirit (see Acts 15:19-29).

"'I gave her time to repent'" (2:21): God always provides people with ample time to repent (Genesis 15:16; Isaiah 48:9; Romans 2:4-5).

Recall that He gave the Ninevites 40 days to repent, which they did, thus averting judgment (Jonah 3:4; see also Jeremiah 18:7-10).

"She refuses to repent" *(2:21)*: Many people harden their hearts against God, refusing to repent (see 2 Kings 17:14; 2 Chronicles 28:22; 33:23; Nehemiah 9:29; Jeremiah 6:15; Daniel 9:13; Luke 16:31; Revelation 9:21). The false prophetess Jezebel was hardened against God.

"I will throw her onto a sickbed" *(2:22)*: Notice the irony. This woman promoted sexual immorality, a sin committed on a bed. In judgment, she would be thrown on a sickbed.

"I will throw into great tribulation" *(2:22)*: The Greek is literally, "throw into great distress." Severe judgment was imminent.

"Unless they repent" *(2:22)*: Only repentance can avert judgment (Jeremiah 18:7-10).

"I will strike her children dead" *(2:23)*: These are not literal offspring but rather her followers.

"I am he who searches mind and heart" *(2:23)*: Nothing escapes God's (Christ's) notice. He has a perfect knowledge of what transpires in every human heart (see Psalm 7:9; Proverbs 24:12).

"I will give to each of you according to your works" *(2:23)*: God's (Christ's) judgment is just, commensurate with one's deeds (Matthew 16:27; Romans 2:6; Revelation 20:12).

Revelation 2:24-29

"The rest of you" *(2:24)*: Not everyone in the church had been unfaithful to the Lord, and He provides a special word for them.

"The deep things of Satan" *(2:24)*: This apparently refers to the seductive false teachings that led to eating food sacrificed to idols and sexual immorality. (Contrast this with the deep things of God—1 Corinthians 2:10.)

"I do not lay on you any other burden" *(2:24)*: Christ did not wish to make their already difficult lives any more difficult.

"Hold fast what you have" *(2:25)*: Jesus urges these faithful believers to not give up in resisting evil.

"Until I come" *(2:25)*: Believers are to remain faithful until Christ's second coming, at which time He will reward all of them for their faithfulness (Revelation 3:3; 16:15; 22:7,17,20).

"The one who conquers" *(2:26)*: The Christian who is faithful and obedient.

"Who keeps my works until the end" *(2:26)*: God's people are to perpetually remain faithful.

"I will give authority over the nations" *(2:26)*: Faithful believers will reign with Christ during His future millennial kingdom (Revelation 20:6; see also 1 Corinthians 6:2-3; 2 Timothy 2:12; Revelation 3:21). Believers who do not remain faithful apparently forfeit participation in this reign.

"He will rule them with a rod of iron" *(2:27)*: Christ will rule in the millennial kingdom with unbending and relentless righteousness, justice, and equity (see Psalm 2:9).

"Even as I myself have received authority from my Father" *(2:27)*: Christ received His authority from His Father (see John 5:22). Faithful believers will have authority under Christ.

"I will give him the morning star" *(2:28)*: Christ Himself is the morning star (see Revelation 22:16). Though this morning star has already dawned in the hearts of believers (2 Peter 1:19), they will one day encounter Him directly and in fullness.

"He who has an ear, let him hear" *(2:29)*: Hearing implies obedience to the message.

"What the Spirit says" *(2:29)*: The Holy Spirit inspires all Scripture, including prophecy Scripture (2 Timothy 3:15-17; 2 Peter 1:21).

Major Themes

1. *Satan.* Satan is called the ruler of this world (John 12:31) and the god of this world (2 Corinthians 4:4). He deceives the whole world (Revelation 12:9; 20:3). He has power in government (Matthew 4:8-9), health (Luke 13:11,16; Acts 10:38), spiritual forces (Jude 9; Ephesians 6:11-12), and religion (Revelation 2:9; 3:9).

2. *God doesn't want people to perish*. God typically delays judgment to give people time to repent and thus not perish. Second Peter 3:9 affirms, "The Lord is not slow to fulfill his promise as some count slowness, but is patient toward you, not wishing that any should perish, but that all should reach repentance."

Digging Deeper with Cross-References

Martyrdom—Matthew 10:39; 16:25; 24:9; Mark 13:12; Luke 9:24; Revelation 6:9; 11:7; 16:6.

Spiritual adultery—Hosea 3:1; Matthew 12:39; 16:4; James 4:4; 1 John 2:15-16.

Importance of correct doctrine—Romans 16:17; Ephesians 4:14; 1 Timothy 1:10; 4:1; 6:3; 2 Timothy 4:3-4; Titus 1:9; 2:1.

Life Lessons

1. *A failure to repent brings discipline*. A failure to repent of sin always brings God's discipline to believers (Psalms 32:3-5; 51; Hebrews 12:5-11). Developing a lifestyle of repentance before God therefore makes good sense. First Corinthians 11:31 affirms, "If we judged ourselves truly, we would not be judged."

2. *Avoid sexual immorality.* Christians are commanded to abstain from fornication (Acts 15:20). People should flee fornication (1 Corinthians 6:13,18). Fornication should not be named among Christians (Ephesians 5:3).

Questions for Reflection and Discussion

1. Is sexual purity a high priority in your life?

2. A failure to repent of sin can bring discipline from God. It is therefore wise to periodically examine yourself. Reflect for a few moments and consider whether there might be

any sin in your life, and experience the freeing power of repentance.

3. Does false doctrine bother you? Do you ever feel tempted to turn a blind eye toward false doctrine in order to avoid conflict with others?

The Churches at Sardis and Philadelphia

Revelation 3:1-13

Scripture Reading and Insights

Begin by reading Revelation 3:1-13 in your favorite Bible. As you read, remember that those who hear and obey the Word of God are truly blessed (Psalm 119:2; Luke 11:28; Revelation 1:3).

In yesterday's reading, we studied Jesus' message to the churches in Pergamum and Thyatira. In today's lesson, we focus attention on the strengths and weaknesses of the churches in Sardis and Philadelphia. With your Bible still accessible, consider the following insights on the biblical text, verse by verse.

Revelation 3:1

"To the angel of the church" (3:1): Apparently the pastor of the church.

"In Sardis" (3:1): Sardis is located about 30 miles southeast of Thyatira, at the foot of Mount Tmolus, on the river Pactolus. The primary business of this industrial city was harvesting wool, dying it, and making garments from it. This city featured extensive pagan worship.

"'The words of him who has the seven spirits of God'" (3:1): The seven spirits are apparently a metaphorical reference to the Holy Spirit in His fullness (seven is a number of completeness or fullness). Perhaps the Holy Spirit is mentioned because the Holy Spirit is the One who can bring new life to this lifeless church (see Galatians 5:22-23).

"And the seven stars'" (3:1): The seven stars are "the angels of the seven churches" (see Revelation 1:20). This likely refers to the pastors of the seven churches.

"I know your works'" (3:1): Christ, who has eyes "like a flame of fire" (Revelation 1:14), knows all the works of church members at Sardis.

"You have the reputation of being alive, but you are dead'" (3:1): This church had no spiritual vitality even though it still had a few genuine believers (verse 4). The church members were similar to the Pharisees: Outwardly they appeared spiritual, but they were actually spiritually dead (Matthew 23:27-28).

Revelation 3:2-3

"Wake up, and strengthen what remains and is about to die'" (3:2): Church members needed to awaken from their spiritual slumber and fan into a flame their dying embers of spiritual commitment (see Romans 13:11).

"I have not found your works complete in the sight of my God'" (3:2): The works of these believers fell short of what God required of them.

"Remember, then, what you received and heard'" (3:3): "Remember" is literally "keep in mind." They were to keep in mind their rich spiritual heritage and return to the attitudes and activities their teachers had taught them earlier.

"Keep it, and repent'" (3:3): Repentance involves a change in thinking with a subsequent change in behavior (see Matthew 4:17; Luke 24:47; Acts 3:19). Christ required immediate repentance.

"If you will not wake up, I will come like a thief, and you will not know at what hour I will come against you'" (3:3): If church members failed to rectify things, Christ would bring swift judgment at a time when they would least expect it.

Revelation 3:4-6

"Yet you have still a few names in Sardis, people who have not soiled their garments'" (3:4): Garments in the Bible often metaphorically refer to a person's character. Soiled garments indicate a polluted character.

This verse thus indicates that some people in the church had remained spiritually unstained (see Jude 23).

"They will walk with me in white, for they are worthy" *(3:4)*: The redeemed will be dressed in white (Revelation 6:11; 7:9,13; 19:8,14), indicating their imputed righteousness and purity.

"Will be clothed thus in white garments" *(3:5)*: This promise would have been especially meaningful to people who lived in a city where woolen garments were manufactured.

"I will never blot his name out of the book of life" *(3:5)*: The book of life is a heavenly record of the names of the redeemed who will inherit heaven (Revelation 3:5; 13:8; 17:8; 20:12,15; 21:27; see also Luke 10:20; Philippians 4:3). Believers will not have their names blotted out. This is a Hebrew literary device in which a positive truth is taught by negating its opposite.

"I will confess his name before my Father and before his angels" *(3:5)*: In the Gospels Christ promised, "Everyone who acknowledges me before men, I also will acknowledge before my Father who is in heaven" (Matthew 10:32).

"He who has an ear, let him hear what the Spirit says" *(3:6)*: Believers must hear and obey this prophetic Scripture inspired by the Holy Spirit (2 Timothy 3:15-17; 2 Peter 1:21).

Revelation 3:7-8

"To the angel of the church" *(3:7)*: Apparently the pastor of the church.

"In Philadelphia" *(3:7)*: Philadelphia was a city in Lydia, located in western Asia Minor, about 28 miles from Sardis. Its major industry was wine. Its chief deity was the god of wine, Dionysus.

"The words of the holy one" *(3:7)*: Only God is holy (Isaiah 6:3), and Jesus is "the holy one" (compare with Mark 1:24; Luke 4:34; John 6:69), so Jesus is here portrayed as God.

"The true one" *(3:7)*: Jesus is also called true. Unlike the false gods of paganism, Jesus was genuinely God.

"Who has the key of David" *(3:7)*: The key of David represents the authority to open and shut the door that leads to the Davidic kingdom—Christ's future millennial kingdom (see Isaiah 22:22; Matthew 1:1).

"'Who opens and no one will shut, who shuts and no one opens'" *(3:7)*: An open door is an opportunity for ministry (see Acts 14:27; 1 Corinthians 16:9; 2 Corinthians 2:12; Colossians 4:3).

"'I know your works'" *(3:8)*: Christ, who has eyes "like a flame of fire" (Revelation 1:14), knows all the works of church members at Philadelphia.

"'I have set before you an open door, which no one is able to shut'" *(3:8)*: Jesus sovereignly gave the church at Philadelphia an opportunity to serve in ministry, and no one can thwart this opportunity (see Acts 16:6-10).

"'I know that you have but little power'" *(3:8)*: God's strength is more than able to make up for human weakness (see 2 Corinthians 12:9).

"'You have kept my word and have not denied my name'" *(3:8)*: The Jews, who rejected Jesus Christ, probably tried to force church members to deny Christ's name. But these believers stood firm.

Revelation 3:9-11

"'I will make those of the synagogue of Satan who say that they are Jews and are not, but lie'" *(3:9)*: These were Jews by lineage, descendants of Abraham. Having rejected Jesus Christ (see John 8:31-59), however, they became tools of Satan.

"'I will make them come and bow down before your feet'" *(3:9)*: Eventually these Jewish antagonists would be forced to admit their error. This may take place at the great white throne judgment (Revelation 20:11-15).

"'They will learn that I have loved you'" *(3:9)*: Contrary to Jewish exclusivism, everyone will see that God has loved these Gentile believers who were faithful to Jesus.

"'You have kept my word about patient endurance'" *(3:10)*: Church members kept Christ's word—that is, they were obedient to it and patiently endured all the trials and persecutions they encountered.

"'I will keep you from the hour of trial that is coming on the whole world, to try those who dwell on the earth'" *(3:10)*: Many Bible expositors believe this verse looks beyond Philadelphia and is a promise to deliver the entire church from the tribulation period by means of the rapture.

Notice the definite article—"*the* hour." The church would be kept from the actual hour of testing, not just the testing itself.

The Greek preposition (*ek*) translated "from" carries the idea of separation from something. Believers will be kept *from* the hour of testing in the sense that they will be completely separated from it by being raptured before the period even begins. This makes sense because the church is not appointed to wrath (Romans 5:9; 1 Thessalonians 1:9-10; 5:9).

"*'I am coming soon'" (3:11)*: We do not know when this will occur, so we must always be ready, living in righteousness and purity (Titus 2:13-14).

"*'Hold fast what you have'" (3:11)*: Christ encouraged the believers to stand strong and not to give up or weaken in their resolve.

"*'So that no one may seize your crown'" (3:11)*: The rewards Christians will receive from Jesus at the judgment seat of Christ are often described as crowns (1 Corinthians 9:25; 2 Timothy 4:8; James 1:12; 1 Peter 5:4). Christ exhorts these believers not to act in such a way as to forfeit their reward at the judgment seat of Christ.

Revelation 3:12-13

"*'The one who conquers'" (3:12)*: Christians conquer by being faithful and obedient.

"*'I will make him a pillar in the temple of my God'" (3:12)*: Magistrates were honored in Philadelphia by having a pillar placed in a temple in their name. Jesus indicated that faithful believers would be honored (see Revelation 21:22).

"*'Never shall he go out of it'" (3:12)*: In contrast to earthly temples, in which pillars eventually decay and fall over, believers will continue forever in the temple in heaven—the new Jerusalem.

"*'I will write on him the name of my God'" (3:12)*: In Bible times, imprinting a name indicated ownership. God writes His name on Christians to show that they belong to Him, they are His redeemed property, and they are in His eternal family.

"*'The name of the city of my God, the new Jerusalem'" (3:12)*: The new Jerusalem is the heavenly city in which the saints of all ages will eternally dwell (see John 14:1-3; Hebrews 11:10).

"Which comes down from my God out of heaven" (3:12): After God creates the new heavens and new earth, the new Jerusalem—the eternal city where believers will dwell forever—will come down out of heaven and rest on the renewed earth (see Revelation 21:2,10).

"My own new name" (3:12): A person's name in the Bible often points to his or her character, so Christ's new name may indicate that believers in heaven will have the opportunity to behold the full wonder of Christ's glorious character.

"He who has an ear, let him hear what the Spirit says to the churches" (3:13): Believers must hear and obey this prophetic Scripture inspired by the Holy Spirit (2 Timothy 3:15-17; 2 Peter 1:21).

Major Themes

1. *The rapture (Revelation 3:10).* The rapture is that glorious event in which the dead in Christ will be resurrected, living Christians will be instantly translated into their resurrection bodies, and both groups will be caught up to meet Christ in the air and taken back to heaven (John 14:1-3; 1 Corinthians 15:51-54; 1 Thessalonians 4:13-17).

2. *Character and clothing.* Scripture often relates character to clothing (as in Revelation 3:4). For example, 1 Peter 5:5 exhorts, "Clothe yourselves, all of you, with humility toward one another." Colossians 3:12 exhorts, "Put on... compassionate hearts, kindness, humility, meekness, and patience" (see also Romans 13:14).

Digging Deeper with Cross-References

The rapture—John 14:1-3; Romans 8:19; 1 Corinthians 1:7-8; 15:51-53; 16:22; Philippians 3:20-21; 4:5; Colossians 3:4; 1 Thessalonians 1:10; 2:19; 4:13-18; 5:9,23; 2 Thessalonians 2:1,3; 1 Timothy 6:14; 2 Timothy 4:1,8; Titus 2:13; Hebrews 9:28; James 5:7-9; 1 Peter 1:7,13; 5:4; 1 John 2:28–3:2; Jude 21.

The second coming—Daniel 7:9-14; 12:1-3; Zechariah 12:10; 14:1-15; Matthew 13:41; 24:15-31; 26:64; Mark 13:14-27; 14:62;

Luke 21:25-28; Acts 1:9-11; 3:19-21; 1 Thessalonians 3:13; 2 Thessalonians 1:6-10; 2:8; 1 Peter 4:12-13; 2 Peter 3:1-14; Jude 14-15; Revelation 1:7; 19:11–20:6; 22:7,12,20.

Life Lessons

1. *The imminence of the rapture.* "Imminent" literally means "ready to take place" or "impending." The rapture is imminent—that is, no more prophecies must be fulfilled before the rapture can occur (1 Corinthians 1:7; 16:22; Philippians 3:20; 4:5; 1 Thessalonians 1:10; Titus 2:13; Hebrews 9:28; James 5:7-9; 1 Peter 1:13; Jude 21). This reality ought to motivate us to live in purity (Romans 13:11-14; 2 Peter 3:10-14; 1 John 3:2-3).

2. *Avoid hypocrisy.* Hypocrisy is the pretense of having a virtuous character, religious beliefs, or moral principles that one does not really possess (see Revelation 3:1). Jesus spoke sternly against the religious hypocrisy of His day (Matthew 23:28; Mark 12:15; Luke 12:1).

Questions for Reflection and Discussion

1. Is there any discrepancy between who you are on the inside and how you appear to others externally (Revelation 3:1)?

2. Does the fact that you will one day appear before the judgment seat of Christ motivate you in your spiritual life?

3. Just as Christ knows all that goes on in the churches, so He knows all that goes on in each of our lives. Does that reality please you or scare you? Why?

DAY 6

The Church at Laodicea

Revelation 3:14-22

Scripture Reading and Insights

Begin by reading Revelation 3:14-22 in your favorite Bible. As you read, remember that those who hear and obey the Word of God are truly blessed (Psalm 119:2; Luke 11:28; Revelation 1:3).

In yesterday's lesson, we looked at the letters to the churches in Sardis and Philadelphia. In today's lesson, we focus attention on the strengths and weaknesses of the church in Laodicea. With your Bible still accessible, consider the following insights on the biblical text, verse by verse.

Revelation 3:14

"To the angel of the church" (3:14): Apparently the pastor of the church.

"In Laodicea"' (3:14): Laodicea was a wealthy and commercially successful city that was east of Ephesus, west of Colossae. It had three primary industries: banking, wool, and medicine. Because of an inadequate water supply in the city, an underground aqueduct was built that carried water from hot springs into the city.

"The words of the Amen"' (3:14): Isaiah 65:16 refers to "the God of truth," which in Hebrew is "the God of amen." This was a title of God in the Old Testament. The title is applied to Jesus here, for Christ is the God of truth. He is now about to tell the truth about the condition of the church of Laodicea. Honesty is the first step in correcting a problem.

"'The faithful and true witness'" (3:14): He is the reliable source of the revelation being communicated to John (see John 14:6). John could thus trust what he was being told.

"'The beginning of God's creation'" (3:14): The Greek word *arche* has a wide range of meanings. Here it is translated "beginning," but the word also carries the important meaning of "one who begins," "origin," "source," "creator," or "first cause." This is the intended meaning of the word in this verse. Jesus is the Creator, the first cause of the creation. The English word "architect" is derived from *arche*. We might say that Jesus is the architect of all creation (see John 1:3; Colossians 1:16; Hebrews 1:2).

Greek scholars note that another possible meaning of *arche* is "ruler" or "magistrate." They observe that when *arche* is used of a person in Scripture, it is almost always used of a ruler (see Romans 8:38; Ephesians 3:10; Colossians 2:15). The English word "archbishop" is related to this sense of the Greek word *arche*. An archbishop is one who is in authority over other bishops. If "ruler" is the correct meaning for *arche* in Revelation 3:14, then it means that Christ has authority over all creation.

It may be that in the case of Christ, both senses are intended. Scripture portrays Christ as both the Creator (Hebrews 1:2) and Ruler (Revelation 19:16) of all things.

Revelation 3:15-17

"'I know your works'" (3:15): Christ has eyes "like a flame of fire" (Revelation 1:14). He sees all. Nothing escapes His all-knowing gaze. He knows all the works of church members at Laodicea.

"'You are neither cold nor hot. Would that you were either cold or hot!'" (3:15): This is an allusion to the underground aqueduct, in which water became lukewarm in transit to Laodicea. This contrasted with the hot springs in nearby Hieropolis and the pure, cold water in nearby Colossae.

Just as a resident of Laodicea recognized that the water that was piped in was neither cold nor hot, so Christ recognized that church members were neither cold nor hot. The church at Laodicea was not spiritually dead, but neither was it filled with spiritual zeal. Church members were neutral and even compromising. This needed to be rectified.

"Because you are lukewarm, and neither hot nor cold, I will spit you out of my mouth'" (3:16): Just as a person might be tempted to spit out the dirty, tepid water of Laodicea, so Christ wanted to spit out lukewarm church members. A neutral or compromising attitude of church members was unacceptable to the Lord. He calls for complete obedience and commitment. Partial obedience will not suffice. Spitting out is apparently a graphic metaphor representing divine discipline.

"You say, I am rich, I have prospered, and I need nothing'" (3:17): The three primary industries of the city—gold, clothing, and eye salve—made this a wealthy city. The residents had nice homes, nice clothes, and plenty of affluence. This outward wealth led the church to a state of spiritual complacency.

"Not realizing that you are wretched, pitiable, poor, blind, and naked'" (3:17): Church members were so enamored with material things that they were blind to their true condition. Words like "wretched" and "pitiable" paint a horrible picture of the spiritual state of this church.

Revelation 3:18-20

"Buy from me gold refined by fire...white garments...salve'" (3:18): The Lord alludes to the city's three main sources of income: banking, the production of wool cloth, and medicine. Jesus draws a powerful contrast in terms they understand. The Laodiceans' gold blinded them to their spiritual poverty. Their expensive garments hid their spiritual nakedness. They produced eye salve but were unaware of their spiritual blindness. Christ calls the church to repentance.

"Those whom I love'" (3:19): Despite the fact that these believers have some staggering problems to rectify—problems that were offensive to Christ—Christ nevertheless affirms His relentless love for them.

"I reprove and discipline'" (3:19): If the children of God sin and refuse to repent, God brings discipline (sometimes very severe) into their lives to bring them to repentance (Proverbs 3:11-12; Hebrews 12:4-11). Christians will respond either to God's light or to His heat.

"Be zealous and repent'" (3:19): "Be zealous" is a present imperative in the Greek. The imperative indicates that this is a command and not a mere option. The present tense indicates that the action is to be ongoing and perpetual. We might paraphrase this, "Keep on being zealous, moment by moment, day by day."

"Repent" is more literally from the Greek, "repent at once." The word "repent" means to change one's thinking with a subsequent change in behavior (see Matthew 4:17; Luke 24:47; Acts 3:19). These church members needed to immediately turn from their wrong thinking and behavior.

"I stand at the door and knock'" (3:20): Sometimes this verse is applied to evangelism. The idea is that Christ is knocking at the door of the unbeliever's heart and wants to come in. In context, however, these words were directed at a church, not unbelievers. Amazingly, Christ has to speak these words to a church because it was excluding Him. Christ reveals to them that He seeks intimate fellowship with them, and He takes the initiative by knocking at their hearts.

"If anyone hears my voice and opens the door'" (3:20): Notice that the Lord here speaks not to the church as a whole but rather to the individual. If more individuals develop a close relationship with Christ, the entire church will benefit.

Revelation 3:21-22

"The one who conquers'" (3:21): This refers to a Christian who is faithful and obedient.

"I will grant him to sit with me on my throne'" (3:21): Scripture promises that Christ will gloriously reign from the Davidic throne (2 Samuel 7:12-13). But Scripture also promises that the saints will reign with Christ. In 2 Timothy 2:12, for example, the apostle Paul explains, "If we endure, we will also reign with him." Those who faithfully endure trials will one day rule with Christ in His future kingdom.

This presents an interesting parallel between Jesus Christ and Christians. Christ Himself endured and will one day reign (1 Corinthians 15:25). In the same way—though obviously to a much lesser degree, and under the lordship of Christ—believers must endure and will one day reign with Him.

The idea of reigning with Christ is compatible with what we learn elsewhere in the book of Revelation. For example, Revelation 5:10 reveals that believers have been made "a kingdom and priests to our God, and they shall reign on the earth." Revelation 20:6 makes a similar affirmation: "Blessed and holy is the one who shares in the first resurrection! Over such the second death has no power, but they will be priests of God and of Christ, and they will reign with him for a thousand years."

This privilege of reigning with Christ continues beyond the millennial kingdom. Revelation 22:5 describes the eternal state, which follows the millennial kingdom: "Night will be no more. They will need no light of lamp or sun, for the Lord God will be their light, and they will reign forever and ever." What an awesome privilege and blessing!

"He who has an ear, let him hear what the Spirit says to the churches" *(3:22)*: The Holy Spirit inspires all Scripture (2 Timothy 3:15-17; 2 Peter 1:21). The entire book of Revelation constitutes "what the Spirit says to the churches." The Holy Spirit is God (Acts 5:3-4), and He is the "Spirit of truth" (John 15:26; 16:13), so this Scripture can be utterly trusted (see John 10:35). Every Christian is therefore called to hear these words and obey what is written.

Major Themes

1. *The Trinity and creation.* The Old Testament attributes the act of creation to God (Genesis 1:1; Psalms 96:5; 102:25; Isaiah 37:16; 44:24; 45:12; Jeremiah 10:11-12), sometimes through His Spirit (Job 26:13; 33:4; Psalm 104:30). The New Testament also attributes the act of creation to the Father in a broad, general sense (1 Corinthians 8:6) but names the Son as the actual agent or mediating cause of creation (John 1:3; Colossians 1:16; Hebrews 1:2).

2. *The danger of materialism.* A love of money and riches can lead to sure destruction. The apostle Paul stated that "those

who desire to be rich fall into temptation, into a snare, into many senseless and harmful desires that plunge people into ruin and destruction" (1 Timothy 6:9). Jesus warned His followers, "Take care, and be on your guard against all covetousness, for one's life does not consist in the abundance of his possessions" (Luke 12:15). He urged His followers to have an eternal perspective, laying up treasures in heaven instead of on earth (Matthew 6:19-20).

Digging Deeper with Cross-References

Self-deception—Psalm 36:2; Isaiah 44:20; Galatians 6:3; James 1:22,26; 1 John 1:8.

Christ's example in being zealous—Isaiah 59:17; Luke 2:49; John 2:17; 4:34; 9:4; Acts 10:38.

Fellowship with Christ—Matthew 18:20; 1 Corinthians 1:9; 1 John 1:3.

Life Lessons

1. *Being fervent for God.* Scripture reveals that people can be cold toward God (Matthew 24:12), warm toward God (Luke 24:32), and lukewarm toward God (Revelation 3:16). God desires that we be "fervent in spirit" (Romans 12:11). This ought to be our daily goal.

2. *Divine discipline motivated by love.* Revelation 3:19 reveals that even though Christians may have significant problems in their lives, Christ nevertheless loves them. In fact, Christ loves them so much that He will not idly stand by, allowing them to remain in sin. That's why He brings divine discipline. His discipline is designed to woo us to repentance and restored fellowship with Him (see Hebrews 12:5-11).

Questions for Reflection and Discussion

1. Has your attitude toward money ever been a hindrance to your spiritual life? Do you ever feel as if you need to "keep up with the Joneses"? What problems does that cause?

2. On a spectrum that runs from cold to hot, where would you place your own spiritual life?

3. God is the Creator (Revelation 3:14). What implications does this have for your sense of obligation to Him?

God's Majestic Throne in Heaven

Revelation 4

Scripture Reading and Insights

Begin by reading Revelation 4 in your favorite Bible. As you read, keep in mind that just as we eat food for physical nourishment, so we need the Word of God for spiritual nourishment (1 Corinthians 3:2; Hebrews 5:12; 1 Peter 2:2).

In the previous four lessons, we focused attention on seven churches in Asia Minor. In this chapter, we switch locations as we zero in on God's majestic throne in heaven. With your Bible still accessible, consider the following insights on the biblical text, verse by verse.

Revelation 4:1

A door standing open in heaven! (4:1): John was granted a visionary entrance into the heavenly domain to witness the awesome things of heaven and receive knowledge of the end times.

"Come up here, and I will show you what must take place after this" (4:1): John was transported to heaven in the Spirit. Once there, he was given revelation about the future, including the tribulation period (Revelation 4–18), the second coming (19), the millennial kingdom (20), and the eternal state (21–22).

Revelation 4:2-4

I was in the Spirit (4:2): This refers to a state of spiritual ecstasy in which John received a vision of the future. The Lord supernaturally "pulled back the veil" so John could see things to come (see Acts 10:11). Apparently John's physical body remained on the island of Patmos while this vision took place.

A throne stood in heaven, with one seated on the throne (4:2): This points to God's absolute sovereignty (Proverbs 19:21; 21:30; Ecclesiastes 7:13; Isaiah 14:24; 46:10; Lamentations 3:37; 1 Timothy 6:15).

He who sat there had the appearance of jasper and carnelian (4:3): Human language is inadequate to describe the actual glory of God and His throne room. John thus uses jewels to portray the matchless beauty of what he beheld.

Jasper is a glittering precious stone of various colors that was placed in the high priest's breastplate (Exodus 28:20). The walls of the new Jerusalem are built with this precious stone (Revelation 21:18-19). Sardius, or carnelian, is a fiery-bright, ruby-like jewel. God's appearance is characterized by the brilliance of these wondrous jewels. The sight must be even more glorious because God is clothed "with light as with a garment" (Psalm 104:2).

Around the throne was a rainbow that had the appearance of an emerald (4:3): An emerald is a light green jewel, and this light green hue permeates the multicolored rainbow surrounding God's throne (see Ezekiel 1:28).

Around the throne were twenty-four thrones, and seated on the thrones were twenty-four elders (4:4): The identity of the 24 elders has prompted much debate. Some suggest they are angelic beings—perhaps a heavenly ruling council (see Jeremiah 23:18,22). However, they seem to be glorified, crowned, and enthroned—characteristics that seem more in keeping with redeemed human beings. Scripture elsewhere reveals that believers will be judged (1 Corinthians 3:1-10; 2 Corinthians 5:10) and then rewarded with crowns (2 Timothy 4:8; James 1:12; 1 Peter 5:4; Revelation 2:10), unlike angels.

It makes good sense to view the 24 elders as representative of the church. This would coincide with the pretribulational view of the rapture, which holds that the church will be raptured and brought to heaven before the tribulation.

Why the number 24? First Chronicles 24:3-5 tells us there were

24 courses of priests in the Old Testament temple, and Revelation 1:6 refers to God's people as "a kingdom, priests" (compare with 1 Peter 2:9).

Revelation 4:5-11

From the throne came flashes of lightning, and rumblings and peals of thunder (4:5): Lightning and thunder point to the awesome majesty and glory of God. They also indicate that God's fiery and awesome judgments are about to be unleashed on the world (see Revelation 8:5; 11:19; 16:18).

Before the throne were burning seven torches of fire, which are the seven spirits of God (4:5): This is apparently a metaphorical reference to the Holy Spirit in His fullness (see Isaiah 11:2). The number seven denotes completeness or fullness.

Before the throne there was as it were a sea of glass, like crystal (4:6): The floor of God's throne room appears as a glistening sea, like crystal. This brings to mind Exodus 24:9-10 (NIV): "Moses...saw the God of Israel. Under his feet was something like a pavement made of lapis lazuli, as bright blue as the sky" (see also Ezekiel 1:22). Some suggest that the crystal sea may be indicative of God's holiness.

Around the throne...are four living creatures, full of eyes in front and behind (4:6): These angels are apparently cherubim (Ezekiel 1:18). Some believe there may be a connection with angels called "watchers" (Daniel 4:13).

The etymology of the word "cherubim" is not known for certain, though some have suggested that the word means "to guard." They guarded the entrance of Eden (Genesis 3:24). In Revelation 4:6, they are apparently guardians of God's holiness.

The first living creature like a lion (4:7): The creature is mighty and powerful.

The second living creature like an ox (4:7): Just as an ox is engaged in faithful and patient service to its owner, so this living creature is engaged in humble service to God.

The third living creature with the face of a man (4:7): Scripture often portrays men as intelligent and rational beings (Isaiah 1:18), so this creature is similarly intelligent and rational.

The fourth living creature like an eagle (4:7): Just as an eagle can fly swiftly and is considered the greatest of all birds, so this creature is a great being who is swift in service to God.

Each of them with six wings (4:8): Angels' wings are often mentioned in Scripture (for example, Exodus 25:20; Isaiah 6:1-5; Ezekiel 1:6). Other Bible verses don't mention wings on angels (for example, Hebrews 13:2).

"Holy, holy, holy" (4:8): God is the absolutely holy One of the universe. The threefold affirmation echoes Isaiah 6:3 and indicates the totality of God's holiness. It may also relate to the Trinity. God is absolutely righteous (Leviticus 19:2), majestic in holiness (Exodus 15:11), and separate from all that is morally imperfect (see Exodus 15:11; 1 Samuel 2:2; Psalms 99:9; 111:9; Revelation 15:4).

"The Lord God Almighty" (4:8): Some 56 times Scripture describes God as Almighty (Revelation 19:6). God is abundant in strength (Psalm 147:5) and has incomparably great power (2 Chronicles 20:6; Ephesians 1:19-21). No one can hold back His hand (Daniel 4:35), and no one can thwart Him (Isaiah 14:27). Nothing is too difficult for Him (Genesis 18:14; Jeremiah 32:17,27).

"Who was and is and is to come!" (4:8): God is eternal. He is from everlasting to everlasting (Deuteronomy 33:27; Psalm 90:2) and abides forever (Psalm 102:27; Isaiah 57:15). He is the King eternal (1 Timothy 1:17) who alone is immortal (6:16).

Glory and honor and thanks to him (4:9): This is the first of many hymns of praise in the book of Revelation (see also Revelation 4:8,11; 5:9-13; 7:12-17; 11:15-18; 12:10-12; 15:3-4; 16:5-7; 18:2-8; 19:2-6).

Seated on the throne (4:9): The fact that God is on a throne indicates His absolute sovereignty (Proverbs 19:21; 21:30; Ecclesiastes 7:13; Isaiah 14:24; 46:10; Lamentations 3:37; 1 Timothy 6:15).

Who lives forever and ever (4:9): God is eternal (Deuteronomy 33:27; Psalms 90:2; 102:12,27; Isaiah 57:15; 1 Timothy 1:17; 6:16).

The twenty-four elders fall down before him who is seated on the throne and worship him (4:10): The Hebrew (Old Testament) word for worship, *shaha*, means "to bow down" or "to prostrate oneself" (see Genesis 22:5; 42:6). Likewise, the Greek (New Testament) word for worship, *proskuneo*, means "to prostrate oneself" (see Matthew 2:2,8,11). In Old English, "worship" was rendered "worthship," pointing to the worthiness of the God we worship. Such worship is the creature's proper response to the divine Creator (Psalm 95:6).

They cast their crowns before the throne (4:10): All believers will one day stand before the judgment seat of Christ (Romans 14:8-10), where He will examine each believer's earthly actions. This judgment has nothing to do with whether or not the Christian will remain saved. Those who have placed faith in Christ *are* saved, and nothing threatens that (see Romans 8:30; Ephesians 4:30). Instead, this judgment determines only the reception or loss of rewards, based on how one lives as a Christian.

Scripture often describes these rewards as crowns that we wear (see 1 Corinthians 9:25; 2 Timothy 4:8; 1 Peter 5:4; James 1:12; Revelation 2:10). This verse pictures believers casting their crowns before the throne of God in an act of worship and adoration. Clearly the crowns (as rewards) are bestowed on us not for our own glory but ultimately for the glory of God (compare with 1 Corinthians 6:20).

"Worthy are you, our Lord and God, to receive glory and honor and power" (4:11): Rich Mullins reminded us, "Our God is an awesome God." Unlike the false pagan deities of ancient times, the true God is worthy of worship and praise.

"You created all things" (4:11): Scripture consistently points to God as the Creator of all things. He said in Isaiah 44:24, "I am the LORD, who made all things, who alone stretched out the heavens, who spread out the earth by myself." Other Scriptures reveal that all three persons of the Trinity were involved—the Father (1 Corinthians 8:6), the Son (John 1:3; Colossians 1:16; Hebrews 1:2), and the Holy Spirit (Job 26:13; 33:4; Psalm 104:30).

Because God is our Creator, a worshipful response is appropriate. "Oh come, let us worship and bow down; let us kneel before the LORD, our Maker! For he is our God, and we are the people of his pasture, and the sheep of his hand" (Psalm 95:6-7).

Major Themes

1. *The tribulation period.* Our passage describes a scene in heaven just before the tribulation period begins on earth. The tribulation will be a definite period of time at the end of the age that will be characterized by great travail (Matthew 24:29-35). The period will last seven years (Daniel 9:24,27). It will be characterized by...

wrath (Zephaniah 1:15,18)	destruction (Joel 1:15)
judgment (Revelation 14:7)	darkness (Amos 5:18)
indignation (Isaiah 26:20-21)	desolation (Daniel 9:27)
trial (Revelation 3:10)	overturning (Isaiah 24:1-4)
trouble (Jeremiah 30:7)	punishment (Isaiah 24:20-21)

2. *The source of the tribulation.* Scripture reveals that this is a time of satanic wrath and especially divine wrath. It is the "day of the wrath of the LORD" (Zephaniah 1:18; see also Isaiah 26:21; Revelation 6:16-17). Satan's wrath is evident in Revelation 12:4,13,17.

Digging Deeper with Cross-References

Heaven opened—Matthew 3:16; Acts 7:56; 10:11; Revelation 19:11.

Throne of God—Psalm 45:6; Isaiah 66:1; Revelation 20:11.

Worship of God—Exodus 20:3-5; 1 Samuel 15:22-23; Psalms 29:2; 95:6; 100:2; Isaiah 29:13; Hebrews 12:28; Revelation 14:7.

Life Lessons

1. *Be holy.* Revelation 4:8 tells us that God is "Holy, holy, holy." First Peter 1:16 quotes Leviticus 11:44: "You shall

be holy, for I am holy." You and I are called to be set apart from sin and set apart to God on a daily basis.

2. *A continual attitude of worship.* Revelation 4:8 reveals that the angelic creatures do not rest in their worship and praise of God. In Western culture we tend to worship God only on Sunday. Why not do it daily? One way we can do this is by daily giving ourselves to God. The apostle Paul encourages us, "I appeal to you therefore, brothers, by the mercies of God, to present your bodies as a living sacrifice, holy and acceptable to God, which is your spiritual worship" (Romans 12:1).

Questions for Reflection and Discussion

1. Are you satisfied with your worship life?

2. Is thanksgiving a regular feature of your prayer life?

3. Self-examination can be uncomfortable, but it can also be a helpful spiritual exercise. Does a particular sin in your life often trip you up as you seek to be holy before God?

Day 8

He Who Is Worthy: Jesus Christ

Revelation 5

Scripture Reading and Insights

Begin by reading Revelation 5 in your favorite Bible. As you read, keep in mind that just as we eat food for physical nourishment, so we need the Word of God for spiritual nourishment (1 Corinthians 3:2; Hebrews 5:12; 1 Peter 2:2).

In yesterday's reading, we focused attention on God's glorious throne in heaven. Now let's find out more about Jesus Christ, the only one worthy to open the sealed scroll. With your Bible still accessible, consider the following insights on the biblical text, verse by verse.

Revelation 5:1-4

I saw in the right hand of him who was seated on the throne (5:1): The throne points to God's absolute sovereignty (Proverbs 21:30; Ecclesiastes 7:13; Isaiah 14:24; 46:10; 1 Timothy 6:15). This sovereign One, God the Father, is in possession of the scroll.

A scroll written within and on the back, sealed with seven seals (5:1): People often used long strips of papyrus to write on in the first century. These sheets of papyrus were glued side by side to make the scrolls longer, though rarely would a scroll have more than 20 sheets or exceed 30 feet. After the writing was complete, the bulky scroll was rolled up and sealed to protect its contents.

People often wrote on both sides of the papyrus. The important details of the document were on the inside of the scroll. A summary of the inner contents was written on the outside. Important documents were often sealed seven times at the edge of each roll within the scroll.

I saw a mighty angel proclaiming with a loud voice (5:2): The name of the angel is not given. It may have been Gabriel, whose name means "mighty one of God" (see Daniel 8:16). Gabriel gave Daniel special revelations from God regarding the coming Messiah (Daniel 8:16; 9:21). More than 500 years later, he appeared to Mary with the news that she, a virgin, would give birth to the promised Messiah.

"Who is worthy to open the scroll and break its seals?" (5:2): This scroll contains the seven seal judgments to be unleashed during the tribulation period. No created being—human or angelic—was found worthy to open it.

No one in heaven or on earth or under the earth was able to open the scroll (5:3): This is a biblical way of indicating that no creature in the universe was qualified to open the scroll.

I began to weep loudly because no one was found worthy (5:4): The Greek word translated "weep" literally means "kept on shedding many tears." John wept in sorrow because God's sovereign plan would apparently remain hidden and postponed because no one had sufficient authority to open the scroll.

Revelation 5:5-7

One of the elders (5:5): The elder is not identified, but his identity is unimportant, for the center of attention is Jesus Christ.

"Weep no more" (5:5): John did not need to weep any further. God's sovereign plan would not remain hidden and postponed. Jesus is worthy to open the scroll, and once opened, the revelations would continue.

"Behold, the Lion of the tribe of Judah" (5:5): The tribe of Judah is the kingly tribe (Genesis 49:9). The term "lion" symbolizes dignity, nobility, sovereignty, strength, courage, fierceness, and victory. This term points to the Messiah, who is from the kingly tribe of Judah and who possesses all these attributes.

"The Root of David" (5:5): Jesus, the Messiah, is the promised One

who descended from David's line and fulfills the Davidic covenant (2 Samuel 7:12-16; Isaiah 11:1,10; see also Matthew 1:1).

"Has conquered" (5:5): Jesus Christ conquered Satan, sin, and death, so He is worthy to reveal and implement God's purposes for the future, which this scroll represents.

I saw a Lamb standing, as though it had been slain (5:6): The term "Lamb" refers to Christ's first coming and His death on the cross. Christ is called a Lamb some 27 times in this book. The phrase "as though it had been slain" indicates that the resurrected Christ still bears the scars of His crucifixion on His hands and feet (see Luke 24:40; John 20:20,27).

With seven horns (5:6): Animals use horns as weapons (see Genesis 22:13; Psalm 69:31), so horns became symbols of power and might. By extension, they signified dominion, representing kingdoms and kings, as in the books of Daniel and Revelation (see Daniel 7:8; Revelation 13:1,11; 17:3-16). In the Bible, the number seven indicates completeness or perfection. Christ's seven horns therefore symbolize His complete dominion and omnipotence.

With seven eyes (5:6): Christ, the omnipotent One, sees everything.

Which are the seven spirits of God sent out into all the earth (5:6): The "seven spirits of God" apparently points to the Holy Spirit (see Revelation 1:4; 4:5). That the Holy Spirit is sent out into all the earth may be a metaphor of His omnipresence (see Psalm 139:2-9).

He went and took the scroll from the right hand of him who was seated on the throne (5:7): This Lamb-Lion was found worthy, so the scroll was given to Him. This brings to mind Daniel 7:13-14: "With the clouds of heaven there came one like a son of man, and he came to the Ancient of Days and was presented before him. And to him was given dominion and glory and a kingdom, that all peoples, nations, and languages should serve him." How awesome it is to ponder such heavenly scenes involving the Father and the Son.

Revelation 5:8-10

The four living creatures and the twenty-four elders fell down before the

Lamb (5:8): Worship is the proper response of a creature to his Creator (Psalms 95:6-7; 100:3).

Each holding a harp (5:8): Harps were often used in worship settings in biblical times. David the psalmist was a gifted harpist (1 Samuel 16:18-23). The psalmist proclaimed, "On the harp I will praise You, O God, my God" (Psalm 43:4 NKJV; see also 71:22; 150:3-5). The 24 elders do the same.

And golden bowls full of incense, which are the prayers of the saints (5:8): Incense was burned on the incense altar morning and evening while the priest tended to the lamp (Exodus 37:25-26). The altar was inside the tabernacle, in front of the veil that separated the Most Holy Place from the rest of the worship area (Exodus 40:26-27). As the fumes of the incense drifted into the Most Holy Place, it metaphorically entered God's nostrils. In the Bible, incense often represents the prayers of God's people (Psalm 141:2). These facts would seem to indicate, then, that each elder (representative of the redeemed church) brought prayers before God.

They sang a new song (5:9): The new song celebrates and anticipates the final and glorious redemption that God will soon bring about and the saints will possess (Revelation 21–22).

"Worthy are you" (5:9): The Lamb of God is worthy because He shed His blood—of inestimable value—for the sins of the world (John 3:16-17). We were "ransomed...not with perishable things such as silver or gold, but with the precious blood of Christ" (1 Peter 1:18-19).

"You were slain...you ransomed people" (5:9): Christ ransomed us from sin by His substitutionary death on the cross. "Substitutionary" means He took the penalty instead of us. At the Last Supper, Jesus said, "This is my body which is given for you" (Luke 22:19). Paul exults that "God demonstrates His own love toward us, in that while we were still sinners, Christ died for us" (Romans 5:8 NKJV; see also Galatians 3:13; 1 Timothy 2:6).

"From every tribe and language and people and nation" (5:9): God's redeemed are from all the races of humanity. God loves the whole world (John 3:16) and desires all to come to repentance and be saved

(2 Peter 3:9), though obviously not all will accept Him. He desires that the message of redemption be taken to the whole world (Matthew 28:18-20).

"You have made them a kingdom and priests" (5:10): All Christians become a part of God's kingdom. They submit to Christ's rule. As priests, Christians have the privilege of entering directly into God's presence and serving Him forever (see 1 Peter 2:5-10).

"They shall reign on the earth" (5:10): Faithful believers will participate in the millennial rule of Christ—that thousand-year period in which Christ will reign on earth following the second coming (Revelation 20:6; see also 1 Corinthians 6:2-3; 2 Timothy 2:12; Revelation 3:21).

Revelation 5:11-14

I heard…the voice of many angels, numbering myriads of myriads and thousands of thousands (5:11): The word "myriad" means "vast number," "innumerable." Daniel 7:10, speaking of God, says that "ten thousand times ten thousand stood before him" (that's a hundred million). Job 25:3 understandably asks, "Is there any number to his armies?" (see also Psalm 68:17; Daniel 7:10; Luke 2:13).

"Worthy is the Lamb who was slain" (5:12): The Lamb is worthy to receive "power and wealth and wisdom and might and honor and glory and blessing!" Each of the seven qualities belong intrinsically to Christ. The word "and" is inserted between each quality to emphasize the fact that Christ possesses the fullness of each distinct quality.

I heard every creature in heaven and on earth and under the earth and in the sea (5:13): Every creature in heaven and on earth joins in praise to God. This reminds us of Psalms 148 and 150, where we behold all of creation bringing praise and worship to God.

"Amen" (5:14): This is an expression of approval and agreement.

The elders fell down and worshiped (5:14): Note that Jesus was worshiped as God many times according to the Gospel accounts, and He always accepted such worship as perfectly appropriate (Matthew 2:11; 8:2; 9:18; 15:25; 28:9,17; John 9:38; 20:28; Hebrews 1:6). Of course, only God is to be worshiped (see Exodus 34:14; Deuteronomy 6:13).

Major Themes

1. *The Lamb—a type of Christ.* A "type" is an Old Testament institution, event, person, object, or ceremony that has reality and purpose in biblical history, but which also, by divine design, foreshadows something yet to be revealed. The Passover lamb in the Old Testament (Exodus 12:21) was a type of Christ, who is the Lamb of God (John 1:29,36).

2. *The Passover.* The sacrificial lamb had to be unblemished (Exodus 12:5; Leviticus 4:3,23,32). At the time of the sacrifice, a hand would be laid on the unblemished sacrificial animal to symbolize a transfer of guilt (Leviticus 4:4,24,33). Notice that the sacrificial lamb did not thereby actually become sinful by nature; rather, sin was imputed to the animal, and the animal became a sacrificial substitute. In like manner, Christ the Lamb of God was utterly unblemished (1 Peter 1:19), but our sin was imputed to Him, and He was our sacrificial substitute on the cross of Calvary (see 2 Corinthians 5:21).

Digging Deeper with Cross-References

Strong angels—Psalm 103:20; 2 Thessalonians 1:7.

Worship and singing—Exodus 15:1-21; Judges 5:1-12; Psalms 33:3; 40:3; Isaiah 12:5-6; 27:2; 30:29; 42:10-11; 44:23; Ephesians 5:19; Colossians 3:16.

Universal worship—Psalm 22:27-28; Isaiah 45:22-23; 66:23; Romans 14:11; Philippians 2:9-11.

Life Lessons

1. *Five components of prayer.*

   - thanksgiving (Psalms 95:2; 100:4; Ephesians 5:20; Colossians 3:15)

   - praise (Psalms 34:1; 103:1-5,20-22; Hebrews 13:15)

- worship (Exodus 20:3-5; Deuteronomy 5:7; Psalm 95:6; Hebrews 12:28; Revelation 14:7)
- confession (Proverbs 28:13; 1 John 1:9)
- requests to God for specific things (Matthew 6:11; Philippians 4:6-7)

2. *Principles of answered prayer.*

   - All our prayers are subject to the sovereign will of God (1 John 5:14).
   - Prayer should be continual (1 Thessalonians 5:17).
   - Sin is a hindrance to answered prayer (Psalm 66:18).
   - Living righteously is a great benefit to prayer being answered (Proverbs 15:29).
   - We should pray in faith (Mark 11:22-24).
   - We should pray in Jesus' name (John 14:13-14).

Questions for Reflection and Discussion

1. Can you think of any recent answers to prayer or spiritual experiences with God that move you to exult, "Worthy are You, O Lord"?

2. Are you hesitant to be expressive in your worship and praise of God? Do you want to be more expressive?

3. Have you thanked Jesus lately for ransoming you from sin?

The First Four Seal Judgments

Revelation 6:1-8

Scripture Reading and Insights

Begin by reading Revelation 6:1-8 in your favorite Bible. As you read, remember that storing God's Word in your heart can help you to avoid sinning (Psalm 119:9,11).

In the previous lesson, we learned that Jesus Christ is the only one who is worthy to open the sealed scroll containing the seven seal judgments. Now let's examine the first four of those judgments. With your Bible still accessible, consider the following insights on the biblical text, verse by verse.

Revelation 6:1-2

I watched when the Lamb opened one of the seven seals (6:1): The Lord Jesus Christ, who died as the Lamb of God on the cross for the sins of humankind, is alone worthy to open the seven seals.

The book of Revelation reveals that human suffering will steadily escalate during the tribulation period. As Jesus Christ breaks each of the seven seals, a new divine judgment is unleashed on the earth.

In Jesus' Olivet Discourse (Matthew 24–25), He speaks of things that will occur during the first half of the tribulation period. More than a few Bible expositors have noticed parallels between these events and the seal judgments.

The Olivet Discourse (Matthew 24)	The Seven Seals (Revelation 6)
the rise of false Christs (verses 4-5)	the first seal: the antichrist (verses 1-2)
wars and rumors of wars (verse 6)	the second seal: the sword (verses 3-4)
famines (verse 7)	the third seal: inflation and famine (verses 5-6)
earthquakes (verse 7)	the sixth seal: an earthquake and more (verses 12-14)

I heard one of the four living creatures say with a voice like thunder, "Come!" (6:1): Each time one of the first four seals on the scroll is broken by the sovereign Lord Jesus Christ, one of the four living creatures (cherubim) summons a rider on a horse to engage in its activities on earth. These are the four horsemen of the apocalypse.

Behold, a white horse (6:2): In Scripture, horses sometimes represent God's activity on earth. They are metaphors for the forces God uses to accomplish His sovereign purposes (see Zechariah 1:7-17).

In Revelation 6, a person rides a white horse. Some have speculated that perhaps the rider is Jesus Christ because Jesus rides a white horse in Revelation 19:11. However, the contexts are entirely different. In Revelation 19 Christ returns to the earth as a conqueror at the end of the tribulation. Revelation 6 deals with a rider on a horse at the beginning of the tribulation in association with three other horses and their riders, all associated with judgments. The rider of the white horse in Revelation 6:2 is apparently the antichrist (Daniel 9:26).

Its rider had a bow, and a crown was given to him (6:2): The crown suggests that this individual is a ruler. The Greek word for "crown" (*stephanos*) is the same word used of the laurel wreaths given to winning athletes. Because the crown was given to him, some take this verse to mean that the world's inhabitants make the antichrist their leader and subsequently submit to his leadership.

The bow without an arrow may indicate that the antichrist's world government will be established without initial warfare. (Peace is not removed from the earth until the second seal is opened—verse 3.) Perhaps the antichrist will be counting on the peace covenant he will make with Israel, which begins the tribulation period (Daniel 9:24-27).

The antichrist's government apparently begins with a time of peace, but it is short-lived, for destruction will follow. This seems to be parallel to Paul's words in 1 Thessalonians 5:3: "While people are saying, 'There is peace and security,' then sudden destruction will come upon them as labor pains come upon a pregnant woman, and they will not escape."

He came out conquering, and to conquer (6:2): World dominion is the ultimate goal of the antichrist (see Revelation 13).

Revelation 6:3-4

He opened the second seal (6:3): The Lamb of God, Jesus Christ, is the only one worthy to open the seal. When He does so, one of the four living creatures summons a rider on another horse.

Out came another horse, bright red (6:4): Red represents bloodshed, killing with the sword, and war (see Matthew 24:6-7). The rider carries a large sword.

Its rider was permitted to take peace from the earth (6:4): Many world leaders will no doubt be seeking to bring about peace in the world, but such efforts will be utterly frustrated, for peace will be taken from the entire earth. As bad as this will be, however, it represents only the initial birth pangs of what is yet to come upon the earth (see Matthew 24:8; Mark 13:7-8; Luke 21:9). Of course, history tells us that war also brings economic instability and food shortages. These things will soon come on the earth.

Some Bible expositors believe that just as God permitted Satan to inflict pain and suffering on Job (see Job 1–3), so God permits the antichrist to inflict war on the earth. We must not forget that God is sovereign and remains in control on the throne in heaven even if things on earth seem tumultuous (Isaiah 46:9-11).

Revelation 6:5-6

He opened the third seal (6:5): Again, the Lamb of God, Jesus Christ, is the only one worthy to open the seal, and another one of the four living creatures summons a rider on another horse.

Behold, a black horse (6:5): Black days of famine now fall on the earth. Black is an appropriate color, for it points to the lamentation and sorrow that naturally accompany extreme deprivation. Lamentations 4:8-9 illustrates this:

> Now their face is blacker than soot; they are not recognized in the streets; their skin has shriveled on their bones; it has become as dry as wood. Happier were the victims of the sword than the victims of hunger, who wasted away, pierced by lack of the fruits of the field.

Its rider had a pair of scales in his hand (6:5): This apparently symbolizes famine (with subsequent death), as the prices for food are extravagantly high (see Lamentations 5:8-10). Such a famine would not be unexpected following global war.

This is in keeping with Jesus' words about the end times in the Olivet Discourse. He affirmed that the first three birth pangs of the end times will be false messiahs, war, and famine (Matthew 24:5-7). Much of the famine at this point in the tribulation will be due to the outbreak of war (the second horseman). Even more intense famine awaits those who refuse to take the mark of the beast (Revelation 13:18). These people will not be permitted to buy or sell, which means they will have much less food than everyone else.

I heard what seemed to be a voice (6:6): The voice in the midst of the four living creatures is not identified. It is likely that of God the Father, the ultimate source of all these judgments.

Saying, "A quart of wheat for a denarius, and three quarts of barley for a denarius, and do not harm the oil and wine" (6:6): A Roman denarius was worth about 15 cents, which was the daily wage of laborers in the first century. (Fifteen cents had a lot more buying power then than it does today!) This verse indicates that prices will be so escalated in that future day of judgment that a person will have to spend an entire day's wages just to buy either a quart of wheat or three quarts of barley.

A quart of wheat would make for one good meal. Three quarts of barley would provide three meals, but nothing would be left over for oil or wine. Foods that are considered bare necessities nowadays will become luxuries during that future day of judgment. Many people will understandably die from starvation during the tribulation period.

He opened the fourth seal (6:7): The Lamb of God, Jesus Christ, is the only one worthy to open the seal. When He does so, another of the four living creatures summons another horse.

Behold, a pale horse (6:8): This fourth horse is pale—literally, yellowish-green, the sickening color of a corpse.

Its rider's name was Death, and Hades followed him (6:8): The death symbolized here is the natural consequence of the previous three judgments. War and starvation will produce many dead bodies. This leads to an escalation in plagues and illnesses around the globe. Wild beasts feed on the dead, spreading disease even further.

Note that Hades is a biblical term for the place of the dead—a New Testament counterpart to the Old Testament Sheol. The word is fitting here because of the prevalence of death due to the judgments of God. Death and Hades are companions—death claims the body, and Hades claims the soul.

They were given authority over a fourth of the earth, to kill (6:8): The death toll will be catastrophic—a fourth of earth's population. In today's figures, about 1.7 billion people will die.

Major Themes

1. *God and judgment.* Our God of love, grace, and mercy is also a God of judgment when people will not repent of their sin. Judgment fell on the Jews for rejecting Christ (Matthew 21:43), on Ananias and Sapphira for lying to God (Acts 5), on Herod for self-exalting pride (Acts 12:21-23), and on Christians in Corinth for irreverence regarding the Lord's Supper (1 Corinthians 11:29-32; 1 John 5:16). Christians will one day stand before the judgment seat of Christ (1 Corinthians 3:12-15; 2 Corinthians 5:10). Unbelievers will be judged at the great white throne judgment (Revelation 20:11-15).

2. *Famine.* In biblical times, threats to the food supply were common even in Palestine, the land of milk and honey (Exodus 13:5). An enemy might invade and destroy all the crops. Famine almost always follows wars and extensive battle campaigns. The book of Joel speaks of a devastating swarm of locusts that ripped through Judah, resulting in famine. Joel saw in this catastrophe a foretaste of the future day of judgment coming upon the world (Joel 1:15–2:11).

Digging Deeper with Cross-References

War as a judgment from God—Leviticus 26:25,33; Deuteronomy 28:22; Isaiah 1:20; Jeremiah 5:17; 6:25; 25:9; Ezekiel 5:17; 6:3; 21:12; 32:11.

The death of the wicked—Numbers 16:30; 1 Samuel 25:38; Job 27:8; Psalms 37:9-10; 78:50; Proverbs 2:22; 10:25,27; Luke 12:20; 16:22.

Life Lessons

1. *Don't worry, trust God.* Our sovereign God remains on the throne, bringing about His eternal purposes, even when the world around us seems tumultuous. Our study this week is a bit fearful. As an antidote to fear, meditate on these Bible verses, which speak of God's absolute control of all things: Deuteronomy 10:14; 1 Chronicles 29:12; 2 Chronicles 20:6; Job 42:2; Psalms 33:8-11; 47:2; 103:19; Isaiah 46:10; Ephesians 1:20-22; John 14:1-3.

2. *Deliverance from the wrath to come.* Many prophecy scholars believe that the rapture of the church will take place before the tribulation period—before all the judgments we've examined in this chapter. It is good to remember that Jesus "delivers us from the wrath to come" (1 Thessalonians 1:10), for "God has not destined us for wrath, but to obtain salvation through our Lord Jesus Christ" (5:9).

Questions for Reflection and Discussion

1. Does the wrath that will one day come upon the unbelieving world motivate you in regard to evangelism and apologetics?

2. How can we maintain a sense of peace, knowing what will one day come upon the world? How does the sovereignty of God help us answer this question?

3. What comfort do you find in Jesus' words in John 14:1-3?

The Fifth and Sixth Seal Judgments

Revelation 6:9-17

Scripture Reading and Insights

Begin by reading Revelation 6:9-17 in your favorite Bible. As you read, remember that storing God's Word in your heart can help you avoid sin (Psalm 119:9,11).

In yesterday's reading, we examined the first four seal judgments. Now let's learn about the fifth and sixth seal judgments. With your Bible still accessible, consider the following insights on the biblical text, verse by verse.

Revelation 6:9-11

He opened the fifth seal (6:9): The Lamb of God, Jesus Christ, is the only one worthy to open the seal.

I saw under the altar the souls of those who had been slain (6:9): These believers were put to death by the forces of the antichrist for the very same reasons John had been exiled to live on Patmos: "the word of God and the testimony of Jesus" (Revelation 1:9).

The souls of these believers were in heaven while their dead bodies were yet on earth. The state of existence between physical death and the future resurrection is called the "intermediate state." It is a disembodied state. One's physical body is in the grave, but the spirit or soul is either in heaven with Christ or in a place of great suffering apart from Christ (see Luke 16:19-31; 2 Corinthians 5:8; Philippians 1:21-23).

One's destiny depends wholly upon whether one has trusted in Christ for salvation (Acts 16:31).

Human beings have both a material part and an immaterial part. The material part is the body. The immaterial part is the soul or spirit (these terms are used interchangeably in Scripture). At the moment of death, the soul or spirit departs or separates from the material body (Genesis 35:18; Ecclesiastes 12:7; Luke 23:46; Acts 7:59). This is what happened to the martyrs of Revelation 6. One day in the future, all believers will be resurrected. Their spirits will be reunited with glorious new bodies that will never die (see 1 Thessalonians 4:13-17).

They cried out with a loud voice (6:10): These martyrs had a strong sense of urgency and emotion.

"O Sovereign Lord, holy and true" (6:10): These believers recognized that God is the sovereign Ruler of the universe. He is "the blessed and only Sovereign, the King of kings and Lord of lords" (1 Timothy 6:15; see also Proverbs 21:30; Ecclesiastes 7:13; Lamentations 3:37).

In Revelation 3:7, God is called "the holy one, the true one." God is holy in that He is utterly righteous and set apart from all sin. He does not just *act* holy, He *is* holy. Likewise, God doesn't just *communicate* that which is true, He *is* true.

"How long before you will judge and avenge our blood?" (6:10): This verse raises two interesting realities to ponder—people are still conscious following the moment of death, and people still have a sense of time in the afterlife.

As for consciousness in the afterlife, Scripture reveals that following the moment of death, unbelievers are in conscious woe (see Mark 9:43-48; Luke 16:22-23; Revelation 19:20). Believers are in conscious bliss (2 Corinthians 5:8; Philippians 1:23).

Regarding a sense of time in heaven, the fact that the martyrs asked God, "How long...?" indicates that they were aware of the passing of time in heaven. Revelation provides other indications of time in heaven. God's people "serve him day and night in his temple" (7:15). The tree of life yields its fruit "each month" (22:2).

God, of course, is a timeless being. To Him, events are not a "succession of moments." Because God transcends time, because He is above time, He can see the past, present, and future as a single intuitive act. However, simply because God is beyond time does not mean that He cannot act within time. From a biblical perspective, God is eternal, but He can do temporal things.

They were each given a white robe (6:11): Each of the martyrs is given the white robe of the overcomer (Revelation 3:5). Some believe the robes are metaphorical, for how can souls wear robes? Others suggest that perhaps believers are given temporary bodies in heaven until that future day of resurrection when believers will receive their permanent, glorious resurrection bodies (Revelation 20:4).

Rest a little longer (6:11): God informs the martyrs He will deal with their murderers soon enough. He will avenge their deaths in His time (see Revelation 19:2). God elsewhere affirms, "Vengeance is mine" (Deuteronomy 32:35; Romans 12:19).

Meanwhile, these martyrs are to wait a little while longer and rest. Some expositors suggest that God is instructing them to rest from their desire for vengeance. Others suggest God desires them to simply rest in peace (see Revelation 14:13). Perhaps both senses are intended.

Until the number of their fellow servants and their brothers should be complete, who were to be killed as they themselves had been (6:11): God, in His sovereignty, has apparently predetermined a precise number of martyrs to be killed before He destroys those killing His children (see Revelation 11:7; 12:11; 14:13; 20:4-5).

Let's not forget that God is sovereign over life and death. Job 14:5 says of man, "His days are determined, and the number of his months is with you, and you have appointed his limits that he cannot pass" (see also Psalm 139:16; Acts 17:26). In view of God's sovereignty over life and death, these martyrs in Revelation 6 seem to have died by divine appointment, not by human accidents.

Revelation 6:12-14

He opened the sixth seal (6:12): The Lamb of God, Jesus Christ, is the only one worthy to open the seal.

There was a great earthquake (6:12): Scripture reveals there will be an increase in earthquakes in the end times. Jesus affirmed that "nation will rise against nation, and kingdom against kingdom, and there will be famines and earthquakes in various places" (Matthew 24:7; see also Mark 13:8; Luke 21:11). However, the earthquake associated with the sixth seal will be so severe that all the earth's faults will begin to fracture simultaneously with devastating worldwide effects.

The sun became black as sackcloth, the full moon became like blood (6:12): With the earth being shaken to its core, many volcanic eruptions will likely spew huge amounts of ash and debris into the atmosphere. This may be what causes the sun to darken and the moon to appear red (see Joel 2:31).

Others suggest the possibility that a darkened sun and reddened moon could result from nuclear explosions. Revelation 8:7 reveals that "a third of the earth was burned up, and a third of the trees were burned up, and all green grass was burned up." Revelation 16:2 says that people around the world will break out with loathsome sores—perhaps due to radiation poisoning. Some believe Jesus alluded to nuclear weaponry when He spoke of "people fainting with fear and with foreboding of what is coming on the world. For the powers of the heavens will be shaken" (Luke 21:26). If nuclear weapons are in fact detonated during the tribulation, enough dust and debris would fill the atmosphere to dim the light of the sun and moon.

The stars of the sky fell to the earth (6:13): This apparently refers to asteroids or meteor showers. There will be many cosmic disturbances during the tribulation period.

The sky vanished like a scroll that is being rolled up (6:14): The earth's atmosphere will be catastrophically affected by all these judgments (compare with Isaiah 34:4). Perhaps the terminology indicates simply that people will not be able to see the sky anymore (with all the dust and debris), thus causing great fear on the earth.

Every mountain and island was removed from its place (6:14): Another result of the global earthquake, with all the earth's faults fracturing simultaneously, will be that mountains and islands move, apparently because of the shifting of the earth's plates. The actual landscape of the earth will change.

Revelation 6:15-17

The kings of the earth (6:15): Regardless of how strong or weak one is, how rich or poor, whether one has high authority or no authority, virtually everyone on the planet will be stunned with fear as a result of these horrific judgments.

Hid themselves in the caves and among the rocks of the mountains (6:15): Some expositors take this literally, saying people will take refuge in caves and mountains. Others say that the caves and mountains are powerful metaphors for people's desperate search for escape. The mountains will have shifted, and many will be destroyed as a result of the great earthquake.

Calling to the mountains and rocks, "Fall on us" (6:16): For the first time, those who dwell on the earth recognize with sobering clarity that they are experiencing the wrath of the Lamb, the sovereign Lord Jesus. The Lamb had provided a way of escape (salvation by trusting in Him—John 3:16-17), but these unbelievers have impenitently turned their face against Him. Earth's inhabitants therefore desire to be put out of their misery.

"The great day of their wrath has come" (6:17): The wrath of God the Father (Him who is seated on the throne) and God the Son (the Lamb) is now being unleashed.

"Who can stand?" (6:17): Only those who have availed themselves of the grace of God and trusted in Jesus for salvation will be able to stand as God deals with the earth in this final period of great distress. There will be martyrs, but those who are saved are ultimately victorious.

In view of these horrific judgments, the prospect of the church being raptured prior to this time of divine wrath becomes all the more plausible and understandable (1 Thessalonians 1:10; 5:9). This gives added meaning to the rapture being described as a "blessed hope" (Titus 2:13).

Major Themes

1. *Tribulation saints*. Scripture reveals that even though the church will be raptured prior to the tribulation period (1 Thessalonians 1:10; 4:13-17; 5:9; Revelation 3:10),

many people will become believers during this time (see Matthew 25:31-46). There will be many conversions (Revelation 7:9-10), and many will become martyrs (Revelation 6:9-11).

2. *Martyrdom during the tribulation.* The tribulation martyrs will include not only those mentioned in Revelation 6:9-11 but also the great multitude mentioned in Revelation 7:9-17 and the two prophetic witnesses of Revelation 11. These two, however, will be raised from the dead after three days and then ascend into heaven (verses 8-12). In Revelation 2:13, Christ made special mention of one of His faithful martyrs—Antipas. Christian martyrs need not fear, however, for each will receive the crown of life (Revelation 2:10).

Digging Deeper with Cross-References

Cosmic disturbances in the end times—Isaiah 13:10; 24:23; Ezekiel 32:7; Joel 2:10,31; 3:15; Amos 5:20; 8:9; Zephaniah 1:15; Acts 2:20.

How long, O Lord?—Psalms 74:9-10; 79:5; 94:3-4; Habakkuk 1:2.

The wrath of God in Revelation—Revelation 11:18; 14:10; 16:19; 19:15.

Life Lessons

1. *Be aware of your mortality.* None of us know when we will die. The Old Testament patriarch Isaac once said, "Behold, I am old; I do not know the day of my death" (Genesis 27:2). Ecclesiastes 9:12 affirms, "Man does not know his time. Like fish that are taken in an evil net, and like birds that are caught in a snare, so the children of man are snared at an evil time." In Proverbs 27:1 we are urged, "Do not boast about tomorrow, for you do not know what a day may bring." The psalmist prayed, "O LORD, make me

know my end and what is the measure of my days; let me know how fleeting I am!" (Psalm 39:4).

2. *It is better to kneel in repentance than to stand in judgment.* Judgment always comes when repentance does not (see Isaiah 55:6-7; Ezekiel 18:32; Luke 13:3; Acts 3:19; 2 Peter 3:9).

Questions for Reflection and Discussion

1. If it ever came to it, would you give your life as a martyr rather than deny Jesus Christ?

2. When you are mistreated by others, do you trust God to bring about justice in His own timing, or are you tempted to return evil for evil?

3. If indeed you trust God to judge, are you able to identify any negative feelings you have toward others and release those feelings so they don't eat you up?

The 144,000 Jewish Evangelists

Revelation 7:1-8

Scripture Reading and Insights

Begin by reading Revelation 7:1-8 in your favorite Bible. As you read, remember that the Word of God teaches us, trains us, and corrects us (2 Timothy 3:15-17).

In the previous lesson, we examined the fifth and sixth seal judgments. Today we switch scenery as we focus attention on 144,000 Jewish believers who will be witnesses of Jesus Christ all over the earth. With your Bible still accessible, consider the following insights on the biblical text, verse by verse.

Revelation 7:1

After this (7:1): That is, after the events associated with the sixth seal judgment—the great earthquake, the sun becoming black as sackcloth, and the full moon becoming like blood (6:12-17).

I saw four angels standing at the four corners of the earth (7:1): Four of God's angels will be strategically positioned around the earth—north, south, east, and west.

Holding back the four winds of the earth (7:1): These four angels will temporarily nullify the earth's winds that come from the north, south, east, and west. Elsewhere in the book of Revelation, God's angels are associated with fire (14:18) and water (16:5). In the present case, nullifying the winds seems to metaphorically represent a lull before the storm of judgment resumes.

Revelation 7:2-3

I saw another angel ascending from the rising of the sun (7:2): The east often has significance in Scripture. Genesis 2:8 tells us that "the LORD God planted a garden in Eden, in the east, and there he put the man whom he had formed." Ezekiel 43:2 tells us that "the glory of the God of Israel was coming from the east." Matthew 2:1-2 tells us that "after Jesus was born in Bethlehem of Judea in the days of Herod the king, behold, wise men from the east came to Jerusalem…to worship him."

With the seal of the living God (7:2): In ancient times, a seal was a symbol of ownership (2 Corinthians 1:22) and protection (Ephesians 1:14; 4:30).

He called with a loud voice to the four angels who had been given power to harm earth and sea (7:2): The angel's loud voice indicates urgency and importance.

"Do not harm the earth or the sea or the trees, until we have sealed the servants of our God on their foreheads" (7:3): The judgments are placed on temporary hold—between the sixth seal judgment (6:12-17) and the seventh seal judgment (8:1)—until God's 144,000 Jewish witnesses become "sealed" with supernatural protection.

These Jewish believers belong to God, and by His sovereign authority He protects them during their time of service during the tribulation period (Revelation 14:1-4; see also 2 Corinthians 1:22; Ephesians 1:13; 4:30; Revelation 13:16-18).

The seal that God's Jewish servants receive seems to be a counterpart to the mark of the beast on all who follow the antichrist (see Revelation 13:17; 14:11; 16:2; 19:20).

Revelation 7:4-8

The number of the sealed, 144,000, sealed from every tribe of the sons of Israel (7:4): Some modern Christians have taken this as metaphorically referring to the church. However, the context indicates the verse is referring to 144,000 Jewish men—12,000 from each tribe—who live during the future tribulation period (see 14:4). The fact that specific tribes are mentioned along with specific numbers for those tribes removes all possibility that this is a figure of speech. Nowhere else in the Bible does a reference to the 12 tribes of Israel mean anything but the 12 tribes of Israel.

God had originally chosen the Jews to be His witnesses, to share the good news of God with all other people around the world (see Isaiah 42:6; 43:10). The Jews failed at this task, particularly when they didn't recognize Jesus as the divine Messiah. During the future tribulation, these 144,000 Jews who believe in Jesus the divine Messiah will finally fulfill this mandate from God and become His witnesses all around the world.

These 144,000 Jewish evangelists seem to emerge on the scene in the early part of the tribulation period (that is, after the rapture). They must engage in their work of evangelism early in the tribulation because some of their hearers will believe and become the martyrs of Revelation 6:9-11 in the first half of the tribulation.

These Jews probably become believers in Jesus in a way that is similar to what the apostle Paul, himself a Jew, experienced. Recall that Paul had a Damascus Road encounter with the risen Christ (see Acts 9:1-9). Interestingly, in 1 Corinthians 15:8, when the apostle Paul refers to his conversion, he describes himself as "one untimely born." Paul may have been alluding to his 144,000 Jewish tribulation brethren, who would be spiritually "born" in a way similar to him even though Paul was spiritually born far before them. These Jewish witnesses, like Paul, will be mighty witnesses of Jesus Christ.

Many believe these 144,000 have a connection to the judgment of the nations (Matthew 25:31-46), which takes place following the second coming of Christ. The nations are comprised of the sheep and the goats, representing the saved and the lost among the Gentiles. According to Matthew 25:32, they are intermingled and require separation by a special judgment.

They are judged according to their treatment of Christ's "brothers" (Matthew 25:40). Who are these brothers? They are likely the 144,000 Jews mentioned in Revelation 7, Christ's Jewish brothers who bear witness of Him during the tribulation.

These Jewish witnesses will struggle to buy food because they refused to receive the mark of the beast (Revelation 13:16-17). Only true believers in the Lord will be willing to jeopardize their lives by extending hospitality to the messengers. These "sheep" (believers) who treat the brothers (the 144,000) well will enter into Christ's millennial kingdom. The goats (unbelievers), by contrast, go into eternal punishment.

Parenthetical note on the 12 tribes. The tribes of Israel are listed in verses 5-8. Many readers wonder why the Old Testament tribes of Dan and Ephraim are omitted. Note that the Old Testament has no fewer than 20 lists of the tribes, and these lists include from 10 to 13 tribes, though the number 12 is predominant (see Genesis 49; Deuteronomy 33; Ezekiel 48). Revelation 7 and 14 maintain this number.

Most scholars today agree that Dan's tribe was omitted because it was guilty of idolatry on many occasions and, as a result, was largely obliterated (Leviticus 24:11; Judges 18:1,30; see also 1 Kings 12:28-29). To engage in unrepentant idolatry is to be cut off from God's blessing. As well, there was an early tradition that the antichrist would come from the tribe of Dan.

Ephraim's tribe was also involved in idolatry and paganized worship (Judges 17; Hosea 4:17) and was omitted from the list in Revelation 7. The readjustment of the list to include Joseph and Levi to complete the 12 thus makes good sense.

There is another reason Levi is included here. Levi is usually not included in lists of the tribes because it was the priestly tribe and therefore did not inherit land. But the priestly functions of the tribe of Levi ceased with the coming of Christ, the ultimate high priest. Indeed, the Levitical priesthood was fulfilled in the person of Christ (Hebrews 7–10). The priestly services of the tribe of Levi were no longer needed, so there was no further reason to keep this tribe distinct and separate from the others. Therefore, they were properly included in the tribal listing in the book of Revelation.

12,000 from the tribe of Judah (7:5): Judah was the fourth of Jacob's 12 sons. His mother was Leah (see Genesis 29:35; 37:26; 44:14; 49:8-10; Numbers 1:27; Judges 1:8; 2 Samuel 2:4).

12,000 from the tribe of Reuben (7:5): Reuben was the eldest son of Jacob and Leah (Genesis 29:32).

12,000 from the tribe of Gad (7:5): Gad was Jacob's seventh son. His mother was Zilpah, Leah's handmaid (Genesis 30:11-13; 46:16-18).

12,000 from the tribe of Asher (7:6): Asher was Jacob's eighth son. His mother was also Zilpah (Genesis 30:13; 35:26; 46:17; Exodus 1:4).

12,000 from the tribe of Naphtali (7:6): Naphtali was the fifth son of Jacob. His mother was Bilhah, Rachel's handmaid (Genesis 30:8).

12,000 from the tribe of Manasseh (7:6): Manasseh was Joseph's first son, who was born in Egypt (Genesis 41:51; 48:1).

12,000 from the tribe of Simeon (7:7): Simeon was Jacob's second son. His mother was Leah (Genesis 29:33).

12,000 from the tribe of Levi (7:7): Levi was the third son of Jacob by Leah (Genesis 29:34). His tribe served in the temple.

12,000 from the tribe of Issachar (7:7): Issachar was Jacob's ninth son. His mother was Leah (Genesis 30:18).

12,000 from the tribe of Zebulun (7:8): Zebulun was Jacob's tenth son, Leah's sixth (Genesis 30:20).

12,000 from the tribe of Joseph (7:8): Joseph was Jacob's eleventh son and Rachel's first. His name means "May God give increase" (Genesis 37:31-35; 39:1-6,20; 41:37-57).

12,000 from the tribe of Benjamin were sealed (7:8): Benjamin was Jacob's twelfth son and Rachel's second (Genesis 35:18).

Major Themes

1. *The remnant.* God has had His faithful remnant in all ages. For example, though the time of Elijah was characterized by great apostasy, 1 Kings 19:18 indicates that God had 7000 people who were yet faithful to Him (see also Isaiah 1:9; 4:3; 11:16; 37:4; Jeremiah 6:9; 23:3; 31:7; Ezekiel 14:22; Micah 2:12; Zephaniah 2:9; Romans 9:27; 11:5). During the tribulation period, the faithful remnant of Jews will include the 144,000 Jewish witnesses (Revelation 7) as well as God's two prophetic witnesses (Revelation 11).

2. *God protects His people.* God has a long history of protecting His people from judgment. Enoch was

transferred to heaven and Noah and his family were in the ark before the judgment of the flood. Lot was taken out of Sodom before judgment fell on the city. The firstborn among the Hebrews in Egypt were sheltered by the blood of the Paschal Lamb before judgment fell. The spies were safe and Rahab was secured before judgment fell on Jericho. Likewise, God keeps His 144,000 Jewish servants safe, but this time He does so by "sealing" them.

Digging Deeper with Cross-References

The living God—Joshua 3:10; 1 Samuel 17:26; Psalms 42:2; 84:2; Isaiah 37:17; Jeremiah 23:36; Daniel 6:26; Matthew 26:63; Acts 14:15; 1 Thessalonians 1:9; Hebrews 10:31.

Servants of God—1 Kings 18:36; 1 Chronicles 6:49; Ezra 5:11; Daniel 3:28; 6:20; Romans 1:9; 2 Timothy 1:3; James 1:1; 1 Peter 2:16.

Life Lessons

1. *God seals His people.* Just as the 144,000 Jewish believers receive God's seal, so believers today are sealed by the Holy Spirit for the day of redemption (Ephesians 1:13; 4:30). This seal guarantees that you and I will be "delivered" into eternal life on the "day of redemption." Our salvation is secure, so we can now live in joyful thanks day to day (Psalm 100:4; Philippians 4:6).

2. *We are Christ's witnesses.* Just as the 144,000 will be God's witnesses during the future tribulation period, so you and I are called to be witnesses of Jesus Christ today (see Matthew 28:19-20). Let's let our light shine (Matthew 5:14-16)!

Questions for Reflection and Discussion

1. What have you learned about the sovereignty of God in

today's passage? Does this bring comfort to you? Why or why not?

2. God is a living God. What does that mean to you personally?

3. Can you think of any opportunities you might have this month to be a witness of Christ?

The Great Multitude of Believers

Revelation 7:9-17

Scripture Reading and Insights

Begin by reading Revelation 7:9-17 in your favorite Bible. As you read, remember that the Word of God teaches us, trains us, and corrects us (2 Timothy 3:15-17).

In yesterday's reading, we focused attention on the role of the 144,000 Jewish witnesses of Jesus Christ. Now let's find out about the many people who become believers in Christ during the future time of judgment on the earth. With your Bible still accessible, consider the following insights on the biblical text, verse by verse.

Revelation 7:9-10

A great multitude that no one could number, from every nation, from all tribes and peoples and languages (7:9): Many will become believers during the tribulation period (see Matthew 25:31-46).

Many may become convinced of the truth of Christianity after witnessing millions of Christians supernaturally vanish off the planet at the rapture. (Bibles and Christian books will be left behind to explain the event.) Many will no doubt become believers as a result of the ministry of the 144,000 Jewish evangelists introduced in Revelation 7. Perhaps many become believers as a result of the miraculous ministry of the two witnesses of Revelation 11, prophets whose powers are apparently similar to those of Moses and Elijah.

Matthew 24:14 tells us that during the tribulation period, "this gospel of the kingdom will be proclaimed throughout the whole world as a testimony." Even though persecution and affliction will be widespread, and even though many will have hearts hardened against God, God in His mercy will nevertheless have His witnesses on earth who are committed to spreading His message about Jesus Christ and the coming kingdom.

In the Gospels, John the Baptist and Jesus often preached that the kingdom of God was near. God's witnesses will do the same during the tribulation period. Jesus will be presented as the divine Messiah, the King who will rule in the soon-coming millennial kingdom. The gospel of the kingdom is the good news that Christ is coming to set up His kingdom on earth and that those who receive Him by faith during the tribulation will enjoy the blessings of His millennial rule.

Standing before the throne and before the Lamb (7:9): This great multitude of believers is now pictured in heaven. They have either died or have been martyred during the tribulation. Such martyrdom is not unexpected, for in His Olivet Discourse, Jesus warned of a tribulation "such as has not been from the beginning of the world until now, no, and never will be" (Matthew 24:21). These believers' physical bodies remain buried or destroyed on earth, but their spirits or souls are with God in heaven.

The Greek word for "before" (*enopion*) in verse 9 is used a number of times in Revelation to speak of those who are in the actual physical presence of God's throne (see Revelation 5:8; 7:11; 14:3). They had previously been before the forces of antichrist, and now they are before God. How awesome!

This multitude of believers will be comprised of many different ethnic groups from around the world. God's love knows no boundaries. People from every nation will come to know the Lord in that day.

Clothed in white robes (7:9): Revelation 3:5,18 reveals that white robes are the garments of overcoming believers. These white garments point to their righteous triumph (Revelation 6:11; 7:13; 19:8,14).

With palm branches in their hands (7:9): Palm branches in Bible times were associated with celebrations (see John 12:13). Certainly this great multitude has reason to celebrate, for their suffering is over, and they now enjoy the very presence of God. Never again will they be subject to persecution or death. In the presence of God are eternal pleasures (Psalm 16:11).

Crying out with a loud voice, "Salvation belongs to our God who sits on the throne, and to the Lamb" (7:10): In this loud acclamation of praise, the theme of worship is the salvation of the saints. All recognize that this awesome salvation comes from God on the throne and the Lamb of God, Jesus Christ. Though these believers had no doubt been sorrowful during their sufferings on earth, they are now joyful in heaven, loudly singing praises to the Father and to the Lamb. Their worship is exuberant and unrestrained.

Revelation 7:11-12

And all the angels...worshiped God (7:11): All the angels—myriads upon myriads of them (Revelation 5:11)—surround God's throne and are apparently intermingled with the 24 elders and the four living creatures. The 24 elders (Revelation 4:4) represent the church, which was raptured to heaven prior to the beginning of the tribulation period. The four living creatures are apparently cherubim, for they are "full of eyes" (Ezekiel 1:18). Overcome with the majesty and glory of God, they collectively fall before God's throne and worship Him.

"Amen! Blessing and glory and wisdom and thanksgiving and honor and power and might" (7:12): This is a wondrous doxology in the book of Revelation. God surely deserves blessing, for He brings matchless blessing to others (Revelation 5:12-13). Glory is due Him because He is the God of glory, who does glorious things in rescuing His people and bringing them to heaven (Revelation 1:6; 4:11; 5:12-13; 19:1). Wisdom is ascribed to God, for He is infinitely wise in His plan of redemption (Revelation 5:12). Thanksgiving is an expression of great gratitude for what God has done for the redeemed (Revelation 4:9). Honor is certainly what God deserves, for He not only planned this great salvation but also brought it about in a way that honors His character (Revelation 4:11; 5:12-13). Power and might are ascribed to Him because He is the omnipotent One, who overcomes all lesser powers in bringing

about His plan of redemption. Satan, the antichrist, and the false prophet are no match for God (see Revelation 4:11; 5:12; 19:1).

The word "Amen" carries the idea of truthfulness, meaning that all that has just been affirmed of God is absolutely true.

Revelation 7:13-17

One of the elders addressed me, saying, "Who are these?" (7:13): One of the 24 elders asked John a question that anticipated the very question that was no doubt in John's own mind. The clarification of their identity immediately follows.

"These are the ones coming out of the great tribulation" (7:14): Why weren't these believers caught up at the rapture? The answer is simple: They had not yet become believers. Only those people who are believers prior to the tribulation are caught up in the rapture. These individuals became believers during the tribulation, and once they die, they go to be with the Lord in heaven.

"They have washed their robes and made them white in the blood of the Lamb" (7:14): This metaphoric language has in view the cleansing nature of salvation (Titus 2:11-14). The blood of the Lamb is Jesus' blood sacrifice at the cross (see Romans 3:24-25; 5:9; Revelation 1:5; 5:9).

"They are before the throne" (7:15): God's throne is a centerpiece in the book of Revelation. As we have seen, God's throne points to His absolute sovereignty over the affairs of humankind.

"Serve him day and night in his temple" (7:15): "Serve" indicates priestly activity in behalf of the Lord (Revelation 1:6; 5:10). The service is perpetual and ongoing.

"He who sits on the throne will shelter them with his presence" (7:15): God's presence among them will be intimate and unfettered. His very presence will shelter them from every form of evil and suffering. They will never again experience hunger, thirst, or scorching heat—a promise that implies that this is precisely what they had suffered while they were on earth.

"They shall hunger no more, neither thirst anymore; the sun shall not strike them" (7:16): In our present life on earth, there are times when we

go hungry and thirsty. There are times when our needs are not met. In the eternal state, however, God will abundantly meet each and every need. These verses promise that these believers will never again suffer any kind of want.

"The Lamb...will be their shepherd" (7:17): In Psalm 23 David said of his shepherd, "He leads me beside still waters." In remarkably similar language, John writes, "The Lamb in the midst of the throne will be their shepherd, and he will guide them to springs of living water." This description has led many to believe that Christ may be the shepherd who led His people beside still waters in Old Testament times.

Later in the book of Revelation, Jesus makes this declaration: "It is done! I am the Alpha and the Omega, the beginning and the end. To the thirsty I will give from the spring of the water of life without payment" (Revelation 21:6). This must have brought back memories for John, for he well remembered the words from his own Gospel about the woman at Jacob's well to whom Jesus offered the gift of living water (John 4:10). The offer John had just heard from the Alpha and Omega was the same now at the end of God's revelation in Jesus Christ as it had been at the very beginning.

"God will wipe away every tear from their eyes" (7:17): God is not only a sovereign Judge but also a compassionate and loving parent to the redeemed. He will tenderly wipe away the tears of these believers due to their sufferings (see Revelation 21:4). A truly blessed existence lies ahead for all of the redeemed.

Major Themes

1. *Christ the shepherd.* Jesus is the good shepherd, for He cares for and watches over His sheep (believers) (John 10:1-16). Jesus is the great shepherd, for He brought us peace with God through His blood (Hebrews 13:20). Jesus is the chief shepherd who will one day come again (1 Peter 5:4). Jesus is also the caring shepherd who brings His people to living water (Revelation 7:17).

2. *Living water.* John had earlier recorded Jesus' promise:

"Whoever drinks of the water that I will give him will never
be thirsty again. The water that I will give him will become
in him a spring of water welling up to eternal life" (John
4:14). Jesus also promised, "Whoever believes in me, as
the Scripture has said, 'Out of his heart will flow rivers of
living water'" (John 7:38; see also Jeremiah 2:13; 17:13).

Digging Deeper with Cross-References

> *Glory of God*—Exodus 24:17; 40:34; 1 Kings 8:11; Psalm 19:1-4;
> Isaiah 48:11; Ezekiel 10:4; Luke 2:9; Acts 7:55; 2 Corinthians
> 3:18.
>
> *Wisdom of God*—Job 12:13; Psalm 104:24; Proverbs 3:19; Romans
> 11:33; 16:27; James 3:17.

Life Lessons

1. *The Great Commission.* The book of Revelation informs
   us that God's redeemed will be from every nation, from
   all tribes and peoples and languages (Revelation 7:9).
   This will be in fulfillment of Christ's Great Commission
   (which you and I can help fulfill): "Go therefore and make
   disciples of all nations, baptizing them in the name of the
   Father and of the Son and of the Holy Spirit, teaching
   them to observe all that I have commanded you. And
   behold, I am with you always, to the end of the age"
   (Matthew 28:19-20).

2. *No more tears.* Every believer can receive comfort from
   knowing that God will one day banish all sorrow. Isaiah
   25:8 promises that God "will swallow up death forever;
   and the Lord God will wipe away tears from all faces."
   Isaiah 35:10 promises, "Sorrow and sighing shall flee away."
   Isaiah 60:20 adds, "Your days of mourning shall be ended."
   Jeremiah 31:12 promises that His people "shall languish no
   more." These verses find their ultimate fulfillment in the
   book of Revelation (7:17; 21:4). Even today, God heals our
   sorrowing hearts (Psalm 147:3).

Questions for Reflection and Discussion

1. The redeemed will come from every nation on the earth. What does that tell you about the heart of God?

2. Do you ever fall on your knees before God in worship, praise, or prayer (Revelation 7:11)?

3. Does pondering the afterlife affect your outlook? How?

The Seventh Seal Judgment

Revelation 8:1-6

Scripture Reading and Insights

Begin by reading Revelation 8:1-6 in your favorite Bible. As you read, never forget that you can trust everything that is recorded in the Word of God (Matthew 5:18; John 10:35).

In yesterday's reading, we focused attention on the great company of people who become believers in Christ during the tribulation period. Today we shift attention back to the seventh seal judgment. This last seal judgment actually constitutes a whole new series of judgments to be unleashed on the earth. With your Bible still accessible, consider the following insights on the biblical text, verse by verse.

Revelation 8:1-2

The Lamb opened (8:1): The Lamb of God—the Lord Jesus Christ, who died on the cross for the sins of humankind (see 2 Corinthians 5:19-21)—He alone is worthy to open the seventh seal.

The seventh seal (8:1): Once the Lamb of God breaks the seventh seal, the seven trumpet judgments are unleashed on the earth. In other words, the seventh seal judgment actually constitutes a whole new series of judgments—the trumpet judgments. Later we will see that the seven bowl judgments proceed out of the seventh trumpet judgment.

Silence in heaven (8:1): After the seal is opened, heaven is silent for about half an hour. Scholars offer various opinions about this. Many believe (myself included) that all of heaven becomes soberly aware of what now lies ahead for the earth and its inhabitants. All of heaven becomes awestruck at what they learn. One might consider this time of silence to be the lull before a very bad storm.

The seal judgments were bad enough, but now the trumpet judgments are about to be unleashed. All in heaven recognize that the first four trumpet judgments will bring about a destruction of earth's ecology (Revelation 8:6-12). The last three will devastate earth's inhabitants (chapter 9). Therefore a sobering silence falls on the halls of heaven. Charles Swindoll offers this sobering observation:

> Until this moment in John's visions, there have been sounds of enormous volume—all creatures in antiphonal worship, angelic hosts belting out hallelujahs, a cacophony of earthly calamities, and a reverberating celebration of praise among the redeemed. Yet when Christ broke the seventh and final seal and a distinct group of seven unidentified angels were handed seven trumpets, all that explosion of noise turned to silence…When God prepares to intensify His wrath, every creature is reduced to open-mouthed silence.[1]

My friend Skip Heitzig puts it this way:

> All of the exaltation stops, all of the alleluias cease; all the music is put on pause. No one says a word. This is a silence of awe, a stillness of solemn anticipation as the citizens of heaven gaze upon the opened scroll and see the calamities to come upon the earth. They know what is about to happen.[2]

A look through Scripture reveals that silent moments before the Lord are common, especially when judgment is about to fall. "From the heavens you uttered judgment; the earth feared and was still" (Psalm 76:8). "Be silent before the Lord God! For the day of the Lord is near" (Zephaniah 1:7). "Be silent, all flesh, before the Lord, for he has roused himself from his holy dwelling" (Zechariah 2:13). "The Lord is in his holy temple; let all the earth keep silence before him" (Habakkuk 2:20).

Other scholars take a different approach to the silence in heaven.

They believe it may relate to the respectful silence of those who witness temple ceremonies. Ed Hindson explains it this way:

> The imagery that follows, including the half hour of silence, follows the liturgy of the Jewish temple services. After the sacrificial lamb was slain, the altar of incense was prepared. Two of the priests would go into the holy place and take the burnt coals and ashes from the golden altar and relight the lamps of the golden lampstand. One priest filled the golden censer with incense while the other placed burning coals from the altar into a golden bowl. Deep silence fell over the temple during this solemn ceremony.[3]

Either way, the silence is short-lived—about a half hour.

I saw the seven angels...and seven trumpets (8:2): God Himself is likely the One who gives the seven angels the seven trumpets during this 30 minutes of silence. After all, we often find angels around the throne of God (see Revelation 1:4; 3:1; 8:6; 15:1).

Trumpets in Bible times were sometimes used to sound an alarm or a call to arms, much like bugles were still used on battlefields centuries later. Here, the trumpets let people know that serious things are about to happen.

It is not precisely clear who the seven angels are. Some identify them with the pastors of the seven churches mentioned in Revelation 2–3. But human pastors have no power to inflict judgment, so this view seems unlikely.

Others relate the seven angels to the seven archangels of Jewish tradition—Uriel, Raphael, Raguel, Michael, Sarakiel, Gabriel, and Phanuel (these angels are named in the Jewish Book of Jubilees, Tobit, and 1 Enoch). Scripture, however, only delineates one archangel, and he is named Michael (1 Thessalonians 4:16; Jude 9).

It seems best to conclude that these are simply seven other angels who have great authority. We know they have great authority because they stand before God (Revelation 8:2).

This brings to mind the angel who told Zechariah and Elizabeth they would have a son, John the Baptist. Zechariah responded in disbelief: "How shall I know this? For I am an old man, and my wife is advanced in years" (Luke 1:18). The angel appealed to his commission: "I am Gabriel, who stands in the presence of God, and I was sent to speak to you and to bring you this good news" (verse 19).

The angels of the seven trumpet judgments also stand before God. Some theologians conclude that these angels must be preeminent, perhaps in the same league as Gabriel.

Revelation 8:3-4

Another angel came and stood at the altar with a golden censer (8:3): Another angel appears on the scene and engages in priest-like activities. A censer is a golden pan suspended by a chain. Priests used censers to transport fiery coals from the brazen altar to the altar of incense.

In our text, the angel stands before the golden incense altar in heaven. He receives more incense to add to the prayers of the saints already there. Some expositors interpret this to mean that the prayers of those who become believers during the tribulation period are now joined with the prayers of the rest of God's people. They collectively beseech God to bring about justice on earth, put an end to evildoers, and inaugurate God's glorious kingdom.

The smoke of the incense, with the prayers of the saints, rose before God (8:4): The angel offered the incense on the coals of the golden incense altar. As incense is thrown on the altar, the smoke represents the prayers of God's people mingling together and rising into God's holy presence. Scholars have been careful to point out that even though an angel is engaged in this activity, only Jesus Christ is the true mediator between God and man (1 Timothy 2:5).

Revelation 8:5-6

The angel took the censer and filled it with fire...and threw it on the earth (8:5): After the angel took the censer and filled it with fire, he threw this fire (representing judgment) on the earth. The result was massive thunder, lightning, and an earthquake. These are mere foreshocks of the seven trumpet judgments to come. These judgments appear to be thrown on the earth in response to the prayers of God's people.

Note that God's judgment of evildoers in answer to the prayers of His people is not unique to the book of Revelation. Exodus 3:7-10 shows that God brought judgment against the Egyptians in direct response to the prayers of His people: "I have surely seen the affliction of my people in Egypt and have heard their cry…Come, I will send you [Moses] to Pharaoh that you may bring my people, the children of Israel, out of Egypt."

The seven angels who had the seven trumpets prepared to blow them (8:6): In response to the prayers of God's people, the seven trumpet judgments are about to be unleashed on the earth. The judgments escalate in horror and intensity throughout the tribulation period.

Scripture reveals that God is a God of patience. He says, "I have no pleasure in the death of anyone" (Ezekiel 18:32). He urges, "I have no pleasure in the death of the wicked, but that the wicked turn from his way and live" (Ezekiel 33:11). The wicked of the tribulation period, however, harden themselves against God. Judgment in this case is inevitable.

Major Themes

1. *Angels execute judgments.* Angels not only announce God's impending judgments but also execute them. In Acts 12, an angel of God put Herod to death because Herod was a pretender to the divine throne and chose not to give God glory (Acts 12:22-23). Likewise, in Revelation 8, the angels of God unleash the seven trumpet judgments that are poured out on humankind (see also Revelation 16:1).

2. *Similarities to the Exodus judgments.* Some Bible expositors have noted the similarity of the trumpet judgments to the Exodus judgments. For example, the trumpet judgments include hail and fire falling on the earth, the sea turning to blood, and a variety of cosmic disturbances—all of which God inflicted upon the Egyptians. Moreover, the general

attitude of people during the tribulation will be much like that of Pharaoh, who pridefully and defiantly asked, "Who is the LORD, that I should obey his voice?" (Exodus 5:2).

3. *Trumpets.* In the Old Testament, trumpets gathered the Lord's people (Numbers 10:7-8), assembled the Lord's army (Numbers 10:9), and announced a new king (1 Kings 1:34-39). Trumpets also play a major role in Bible prophecy. John was summoned up into heaven by a trumpet (Revelation 4:1). The rapture of the church will be accompanied by a trumpet blast (1 Corinthians 15:52; 1 Thessalonians 4:16). Now, in Revelation 8–9, we encounter the trumpet judgments.

Digging Deeper with Cross-References

"Another angel" in Revelation—Revelation 7:2; 8:3; 10:1; 14:6,8-9,15-18; 18:1.

Earthquakes in Revelation—Revelation 6:12; 8:5; 11:13,19; 16:18.

God answers prayer—Psalms 50:15; 91:15; 99:6; 118:5; 138:3; Isaiah 30:19; 58:9; 65:24; Jeremiah 29:12; Daniel 9:21-23; 10:12; Matthew 7:7.

Fire and God's judgment—Exodus 9:23-24; Leviticus 10:1-2; Numbers 11:1; 16:35; 2 Kings 1:10; Psalm 97:3; Isaiah 47:14; 66:16.

Life Lessons

1. *Silence before God.* Sometimes it is good to be silent before God. In Psalm 62:1 the psalmist says, "For God alone my soul waits in silence; from him comes my salvation." Later he exhorts himself, "For God alone, O my soul, wait in silence, for my hope is from him" (verse 5; see also Psalm 37:34). In Lamentations 3:26 we are told, "It is good that one should wait quietly for the salvation of the LORD."

2. *Angels.* In this portion of the book of Revelation, the angels do scary things related to judgment, but let's keep

all this in perspective. Remember the good things angels do on our behalf. Angels are celestial guardians of God's people (2 Kings 6:17; Psalm 91:9-11). God sometimes uses angels to answer the prayers of God's people (Acts 12:5-10), escort believers into heaven following the moment of death (Luke 16:22), and minister to us in a variety of ways (Hebrews 1:14).

Questions for Reflection and Discussion

1. Your prayers are always heard directly by God in heaven. How does knowing that make you feel?

2. Do you ever feel moved to silence as you contemplate the things of God?

3. Are you thankful for the ministry of angels in your life even though you may never perceive their actual presence or activities? Do you think you've ever been rescued by an angel?

The First Four Trumpet Judgments

Revelation 8:7-13

Scripture Reading and Insights

Begin by reading Revelation 8:7-13 in your favorite Bible. As you read, never forget that you can trust everything that is recorded in the Word of God (Matthew 5:18; John 10:35).

In the previous lesson, we witnessed an announcement of the seventh seal judgment, which actually constitutes seven new trumpet judgments. Now let's find out the details of the first four trumpet judgments. With your Bible still accessible, consider the following insights on the biblical text, verse by verse.

Revelation 8:7

The first angel blew his trumpet, and there followed hail and fire, mixed with blood (8:7): The seal judgments were bad, but the trumpet judgments are even worse. They are so bad that when heaven's inhabitants become aware of them, they are silent for 30 minutes.

In the first trumpet judgment, hail and fire, mixed with blood, fall upon the earth. This reminds us of God's plague on the Egyptians at the hand of Moses (Exodus 9:18-26).

It is not clear how hail and fire could be mixed with blood. But remember that this will be a supernatural judgment, so it is entirely possible. Joel 2:30 prophesied a judgment of "blood and fire and columns of smoke" in the end times.

This judgment sounds very much like catastrophic volcanic activity—something that could result from the powerful earthquake mentioned just earlier (Revelation 8:5). Volcanic lava spewing into the atmosphere could look like hail and fire falling on the earth. It could mix with other dust and debris (and perhaps even birds) in the atmosphere, producing blood or a blood-like residue.

A third of the earth was burned up…(8:7): A third of the earth and trees will be incinerated, as will all of the grass. This would seem to imply that much of the earth's crops will also be destroyed, depleting food supplies on an already starving planet.

Volcanoes erupting around the world could account for a third of the trees burning up. We have seen that as a result of God's judgments, the earth's plates will shift and some mountains will be flattened. Massive global volcanic activity will likely result.

Some modern prophecy scholars suggest the possibility that nuclear detonations could play a role in this judgment. This could easily explain how a third of the earth could be burned in a short time. Other Scripture verses might substantiate this, such as Revelation 16:2, which tells us that people around the world will break out with loathsome and malignant sores. Could this be a result of radiation poisoning following the detonation of nuclear weapons? As well, some believe Jesus Himself may have alluded to nuclear weaponry: "There will be…people fainting with fear and with foreboding of what is coming on the world. For the powers of the heavens will be shaken" (Luke 21:25-26). At any rate, the technology now exists for a third of the earth to be burned up, causing mass casualties.

Revelation 8:8-9

The second angel blew his trumpet, and something like a great mountain, burning with fire, was thrown into the sea (8:8): As a result of this, a third of the sea turns bloody. Some suggest this might be a massive island volcano that explodes, hurling what appears to be a fiery mountain into the sea. Others see this fiery mountain as something that falls from the heavens onto the earth—an asteroid. Still others suggest this refers to a large fiery nuclear missile plunging into the sea and detonating.

The waters could turn bloody because of the blood of dead sea creatures. Or this could refer to a "red tide," in which billions of dead microorganisms contaminate the water and make it appear red. Or this could be much like an extension of the first plague in Egypt, where God supernaturally turned the waters of the Nile River into blood (Exodus 7:17-21).

A third of the living creatures in the sea died (8:9): This not only fouls (and possibly bloodies) the waters but also further cuts into the food supply. The effect on the world economy will be devastating.

A third of the ships were destroyed (8:9): A giant asteroid striking the ocean would create such a gigantic tidal wave that a third of the earth's ships could easily be destroyed. At present, tens of thousands of ships transport industrial goods across the seas. The shipping industry will be in chaos once this judgment strikes, for a third of the ships will no longer be available for service. This too will have a catastrophic effect on the world economy.

Revelation 8:10-11

The third angel blew his trumpet, and a great star fell...on a third of the rivers (8:10): Many prophecy scholars believe this will be a "deep impact" of a massive meteor or asteroid. It looks like a star because it bursts into flames in the earth's atmosphere.

It turns a third of the waters bitter, and many people die. It may contaminate this large volume of water by the residue that results from the meteor disintegrating as it races through earth's atmosphere. Or the debris may plummet into the headwaters of some of the world's major rivers and underground water sources, thereby spreading the poisonous water to many people on earth.

The name of the star is Wormwood (8:11): Wormwood is a woody herb common to Palestine that has a strong, bitter taste (see Deuteronomy 29:18; Proverbs 5:4; Jeremiah 9:15; Lamentations 3:15). The plant is used in the book of Revelation as a symbol of bitterness. This wormwood-like asteroid will render a third of the earth's waters unfit for human consumption.

Today's top scientists are saying that the question is not *if* such a celestial body will strike the earth, but *when*. The mathematical probabilities render this an eventual certainty. And when it happens, it will likely involve a significant celestial body striking the earth at a minimum of 130,000 miles per hour. The sad reality is that this event will in fact happen during the tribulation period, and the result will be truly catastrophic. Many will die.

Revelation 8:12

The fourth angel blew his trumpet, and a third of the sun was struck (8:12): The severe cosmic disturbances continue. The diminishing of sunlight, moonlight, and starlight may be due to thousands of tons of dust from the large meteor or asteroid strike associated with the third trumpet judgment. Volcanoes will also be spewing debris into the atmosphere.

Of course, our text does not demand such natural explanations for the diminishing of light from these stellar bodies. God Himself could supernaturally cause the heavenly bodies to dim.

Whatever the case, all of this will lower the global temperature, and with a third of the trees already having been destroyed, there will be much less firewood to keep people warm. Moreover, plant life will suffer, thereby further reducing the food supply. And things will continue to go from bad to worse.

Revelation 8:13

I heard an eagle crying... "Woe, woe, woe" (8:13): This may be the eagle-like angelic creature mentioned in Revelation 4:7-8. Three trumpet judgments remain, so the angel proclaims, "Woe, woe, woe." The first four trumpet judgments have been bad enough, but the last three will be unimaginably worse.

Major Themes

1. *Earth: a center of divine activity.* The first four trumpet judgments assault the earth's environment—a tragedy in view of the important role the earth has in the Bible. Relatively speaking, the earth is but an astronomical atom among the whirling constellations, only a tiny speck of dust among the ocean of stars and planets in the universe. But the earth is nevertheless the center of God's work of salvation in the universe. Here God created man and appeared to people throughout biblical times. Here Jesus became incarnate and died for the sins of man, and to the earth the Lord Jesus will come again. He will then create the new heavens and new earth (Revelation 21:1-2; 22:3).

2. *Woe.* The word "woe" in the book of Revelation should be understood against its Old Testament backdrop. Old Testament prophets used the Hebrew word for "woe" to point to impending doom, grief, and sorrow. It warns of a dire threat in the face of present or coming danger. Isaiah uses the word "woe" 22 times—more than any other book of the Bible. Jesus pronounced severe woes on the scribes and Pharisees (see Luke 11:42-44). Revelation uses the word to describe God's judgments during the tribulation period.

3. *Those who dwell on the earth.* The book of Revelation often refers to "those who dwell on the earth" (see 3:10; 6:10; 8:13; 11:10; 13:14). This term communicates not only geographical location but also personal character. In other words, their character is earthly instead of heavenly. They are worldlings who reject the things of God.

Digging Deeper with Cross-References

> *Eagles*—Exodus 19:4; Proverbs 23:5; 30:19; Isaiah 40:31; Lam-
> entations 4:19; Ezekiel 1:10; Revelation 4:7; 12:14.
>
> *A loud voice*—Deuteronomy 5:22; 1 Samuel 28:12; 2 Samuel
> 19:4; 2 Chronicles 15:14; Matthew 27:46,50; Luke 19:37;
> Revelation 1:10; 5:2,12; 6:10; 7:2,10; 8:13; 10:3; 11:12; 12:10;
> 14:2,7,9,15,18; 16:1,17; 19:1,17; 21:3.
>
> *Hail*—Exodus 9:23; Joshua 10:11; Psalm 18:13; Isaiah 28:2; Eze-
> kiel 13:11; Revelation 8:7.

Life Lessons

1. *Repent early.* God often intensifies judgment and discipline
   in order to move people to repentance. Some people
   become hardened against God to the point of no return, as
   seems to be the case with many on earth during the future
   tribulation. But others respond by turning to God. Even
   in the case of Christians, God may escalate His discipline
   to move us to repent. David took almost a full year to
   repent of his sin with Bathsheba. God had to discipline
   him severely. When he finally did repent, he beseeched
   God, "Let the bones that you have broken rejoice" (Psalm
   51:8; see also Psalm 32:3-4; Hebrews 12:5-11). The lesson:
   Repenting promptly is always in our best interest.

2. *Avoid worldliness.* Christians should not have a worldly
   character, focused only on the things of this earth like
   "those who dwell on the earth" in the book of Revelation.
   One of the best ways for us to avoid worldliness is to
   regularly feed on the Word of God and allow it to do its
   transforming work in our lives. As the apostle Paul put it,
   "Do not be conformed to this world, but be transformed
   by the renewal of your mind" (Romans 12:2).

Questions for Reflection and Discussion

1. Do you ever struggle with worldliness? Do you ever feel that you have been contaminated by the things of this world?

2. Consider the influences on your life. Do you ever feel contaminated by the books you read? By the TV shows you watch? By the movies you go to? By the music you listen to?

The Fifth and Sixth Trumpet Judgments

Revelation 9

Scripture Reading and Insights

Begin by reading Revelation 9 in your favorite Bible. As you read, trust God to open your eyes so you can discover wondrous things from His Word (Psalm 119:18).

In yesterday's reading, we learned about the first four trumpet judgments. Now let's examine the details of the fifth and sixth trumpet judgments. With your Bible still accessible, consider the following insights on the biblical text, verse by verse.

Revelation 9:1-12

The fifth angel blew his trumpet (9:1): The fifth trumpet judgment—the worst so far—is now unleashed.

I saw a star fallen from heaven to earth (9:1): Angels are sometimes associated with the stars in Scripture (see Job 38:7; Psalm 148:1-3; Revelation 12:3-4,7-9). Many Bible expositors believe the star (or angel) in verse 1 is "the angel of the bottomless pit" mentioned in verse 11. We know that the "star" is not a literal star, for it is called "he" in verses 1-2.

Some suggest that this verse may refer to Satan (compare with Isaiah 14:12-15). Jesus once commented to His disciples, "I saw Satan fall like lightning from heaven" (Luke 10:18).

He was given the key to the shaft of the bottomless pit (9:1): The bottomless pit is the abyss, or the abode of imprisoned demons and disobedient spirits. It is the place to which Jesus sent demons when He expelled them from people, a place they clearly dreaded (Luke 8:31). The term is translated seven times as "the bottomless pit" (Revelation 9:1-2,11; 11:7; 17:8; 20:1,3) and two times as "the abyss" (Luke 8:31; Romans 10:7). The angel, whatever his identity, was given the keys to the abyss.

He opened the shaft…from the shaft rose smoke…the sun and the air were darkened (9:2): Hideous demons are released from the bottomless pit. Smoke is a graphic visual description of a huge locust swarm. The "smoke" arises out of the abyss, so the swarm is undoubtedly demonic. This metaphor points to an unimaginably large company of fallen angels exiting the bottomless pit.

From the smoke came locusts on the earth (9:3): A devastating swarm of locusts can rip through the land like a black cloud, devouring crops almost instantly. Locusts are therefore an apt metaphor for the desolation the demonic spirits will inflict on the world.

They were given power like the power of scorpions (9:3): Scorpion bites can be agonizing and cause people to foam at the mouth and grind their teeth in pain. These demonic spirits will inflict torturous wounds that could be physical, spiritual, or both.

They were told not to harm the grass of the earth or any green plant or any tree (9:4): Satan and demonic spirits are "on a leash." They cannot go beyond what God will allow them (as Job 1–2 demonstrates). The demonic spirits are not permitted to harm the grass, green plants, or trees.

Only those people who do not have the seal of God (9:4): The 144,000 Jewish evangelists will be kept safe from the torment of these spirits. The converts of the 144,000 will also likely be exempt. It seems likely that all who have trusted the Lord for salvation will be sealed in some special way and protected from torment.

They were allowed to torment them for five months (9:5): The life cycle of locusts is typically from May to September—five months. The hideous locust-like demonic spirits will relentlessly torment people during this time, but they will not be permitted to kill them.

People will seek death (9:6): People will long for death rather than repent before a holy God. We are not told how their death wishes are frustrated, but God is sovereign over life and death, so no one can die before God's appointed time (Job 14:5; Acts 17:26; Psalms 31:15; 139:16).

The locusts were like horses prepared for battle (9:7): To describe these evil spirits, John is forced to use the term "like" nine times.

On their heads were what looked like crowns of gold (9:7): These demonic spirits evidently have a higher rank or level of authority than other demonic spirits.

Their faces were like human faces (9:7): The locusts have some humanlike characteristics—perhaps rationality and intelligence.

Their hair like women's hair, and their teeth like lions' teeth (9:8): Locusts are elsewhere described as having bristles like hair (see Jeremiah 51:27). Insects also often have long antennae for navigation. Like lions, these evil spirits will be fierce predators. Just as an unarmed human is no match for a lion, so people will not be able to escape the torment of these demonic spirits.

They had breastplates (9:9): Iron breastplates are designed to protect one's organs. The metaphor indicates that these fallen angels are invulnerable.

The noise of their wings (9:9): People jolt out of the way at the sound of a locust (a fear reflex). But when people sense the presence of these tormenting spirits, they won't be able to escape.

They have tails and stings like scorpions (9:10): Scorpions carry an agonizing sting, but they aren't generally lethal. These demonic spirits will cause similar agony for five months.

They have as king over them the angel of the bottomless pit...Abaddon... Apollyon (9:11): Abaddon and Apollyon both mean "destruction." This angel-king is characterized by destruction.

Scripture reveals that there are ranks among fallen angels (Ephesians 6:12). Their ranks include principalities, powers, rulers of the darkness of this world, and spiritual wickedness in high places. All fallen angels, regardless of their individual ranks, follow their malevolent commander in chief—Satan. Many expositors believe that Apollyon may be among Satan's most notable subordinate commanders.

Others suggest that Satan himself is the angel of the bottomless pit and is therefore the destroying angel. Jesus, speaking of Satan, once said, "The thief comes only to steal and kill and destroy" (John 10:10). Satan's natural tendency is to destroy.

The first woe has passed (9:12): The "first woe" is the first of the last three trumpet judgments. Two more remain—the sixth (9:13-21; 11:14) and seventh trumpets (11:15-19).

Revelation 9:13-21

The sixth angel blew his trumpet (9:13): The sixth trumpet judgment is now unleashed. The horror increases.

I heard a voice from the four horns of the golden altar (9:13): Each corner of the golden altar had small protrusions, or horns (Exodus 30:2). In Old Testament times, people went to the golden altar to obtain mercy. Here, a metaphorical voice calls out for vengeance. Perhaps the voice is that of the Lamb, Jesus Christ.

"Release the four angels who are bound at the great river Euphrates" (9:14): The Euphrates was one of four rivers that flowed through the Garden of Eden (see Genesis 2:14). It is the longest river of Western Asia (almost 1800 miles), and many ancient cities, including Ur and Babylon, were located on it. This region has given birth to many pagan and idolatrous religions.

In the sixth trumpet judgment, fallen angels bound at the Euphrates are released. We know that these four angels are fallen, for no holy angel of God is ever bound as these angels are.

The four angels…were released to kill a third of mankind (9:15): Adding this to the one-fourth who were killed as a result of the fourth seal judgment, about half of the earth's population is killed.

The number of mounted troops was twice ten thousand times ten thousand (9:16): This is 200 million—an incalculably large army.

The horses…and those who rode them (9:17): Through the years, many people have assumed this must refer to the army of China, which has long claimed to be able to mount an army of 200 million. Contextually, however, this does not seem to make sense. We have seen that these 200 million are led by four fallen angels. Besides, the description of these "mounted troops" on strange horses appears to be anything but human in verse 17. Note also that the horses themselves and their killing power seem to be the primary focus of attention in these verses, not the riders. Apparently, these are demonic spirits led by four fallen angels, and they murder millions of people (verses 15,18).

By these three plagues a third of mankind was killed (9:18): A biblical plague is a disease or epidemic that God causes or allows for the purpose of judgment. The end times will bring a massive outbreak of plagues (see Revelation 6:8; 9:20; 11:6; 15:1,6,8; 16:9,21; 18:4,8; 21:9; 22:18). The three plagues mentioned in Revelation 9:18—fire, smoke, and sulfur—will kill a third of humankind.

The power of the horses (9:19): These are apparently not natural horses, but fallen angels who are instruments of divine judgment. They supernaturally wound people of the earth.

The rest of mankind...did not repent (9:20): Amazingly, the rest of humankind who are still alive refuse to repent of their evil acts. The hearts of these people are hardened against God. This reminds us of Pharaoh, who refused to repent despite the plagues brought by Moses (see Exodus 7:22; 9:7).

These hardened humans refuse to cease their worship of demons and their idolatry. The rapture of the church will have taken place prior to the tribulation period, so false religion, spirit worship, and idolatry will rapidly escalate. Satan, of course, has always wanted to be worshiped (Isaiah 14:12-15; Matthew 4:8-10).

Nor did they repent of their murders or their sorceries or their sexual immorality or their thefts (9:21): One would think that after witnessing such unbelievable horror and suffering, any person would be moved to repentance. But these tribulation rebels refuse, falling ever deeper into sin and occultism, thereby justifying God's judgments.

Major Themes

1. *Violation of some of God's Ten Commandments.* During the tribulation, people will break a number of God's Ten Commandments. By making and then worshiping pagan idols, they will break God's first and second

commandments. In murdering other people, they will violate God's sixth commandment. In engaging in theft, they will break the eighth commandment. By their sexual immorality, they will break God's seventh commandment. These will be evil times.

2. *Some angels are confined.* There are two broad classes of demons. One group is free and actively opposing God and His people (Ephesians 2:1-3). The other is confined (see Luke 8:31; 2 Peter 2:4; Jude 6; Revelation 9:1-3,11). The confined fallen angels are apparently being punished for some sin other than the original rebellion against God (Isaiah 14:12-17; Ezekiel 28:11-19). Some theologians believe these angels are guilty of the heinous unnatural sin mentioned in Genesis 6:2-4.

Digging Deeper with Cross-References

Murder—Genesis 9:5-6; Exodus 20:13; Numbers 35:16,30-31; Deuteronomy 5:17; Psalm 5:6; Matthew 15:19; 1 John 3:15.

Sexual immorality—Acts 15:20; 1 Corinthians 5:9-10; 10:8; Galatians 5:19; Colossians 3:5; 1 Thessalonians 4:3; 2 Peter 2:14; Jude 7.

Suicide—1 Samuel 31:4-6; 2 Samuel 17:23; Matthew 27:3-10; Acts 1:18-19; John 8:22.

Life Lessons

1. *Avoid idolatry.* Idolatry involves worshiping other things in place of God. It can take many forms: the desire to be rich, materialism, the pursuit of fame, sexual immorality, and more. The New Testament consistently urges Christians to beware of idolatry (1 Corinthians 5:11; 10:7,14; 2 Corinthians 6:16; Galatians 5:20; Colossians 3:5; 1 John 5:21).

2. *Avoid occultism.* Some Christians today flirt with whitewashed occultism. Though God condemns mediums

and psychics (Leviticus 20:27; Deuteronomy 18:11), today
there are so-called Christian psychics. God condemns
witchcraft (1 Samuel 15:23), but we see so-called Christian
witches. Moreover, many Christians read astrology
columns (see Isaiah 47:13; Jeremiah 10:2; Daniel 4:7).
Christian beware: Avoid all occultism.

Questions for Reflection and Discussion

1. What is your attitude toward the Ten Commandments?
   How do you relate the Ten Commandments to the New
   Testament teaching that we live under grace and not the
   law (Ephesians 2:15)?

2. Do you enjoy watching television shows featuring
   psychics? Do you read the astrology columns in
   newspapers?

3. Do you prioritize anything in your life higher than God?

The Message of the Little Scroll

Revelation 10

Scripture Reading and Insights

Begin by reading Revelation 10 in your favorite Bible. As you read, trust God to open your eyes so you can discover wondrous things from His Word (Psalm 119:18).

In the previous lesson, we examined the fifth and sixth trumpet judgments. Now, in a brief interlude, we read of a little scroll that is both sweet and sour to John—sweet because it contains God's Word but sour because of the promises of judgment. With your Bible still accessible, consider the following insights on the biblical text, verse by verse.

Revelation 10:1-4

I saw another mighty angel (10:1): We now have an interlude between the sixth and seventh trumpet judgments. During the interlude, God's people are assured that God is absolutely sovereign over the affairs of earth and that victory is soon coming.

This angel is characterized as a mighty angel. This reminds us of the "mighty angel" mentioned in Revelation 5:2. Scripture reveals that all angels excel in strength (Psalm 103:20), but apparently some angels are more powerful than others (Daniel 10:12-14).

This mighty angel is apparently a high-ranking angel character-ized by splendor, brightness, and strength (compare with Revelation

5:2; 8:3; 18:1). God's angels can appear so glorious that people may be tempted to worship them (Revelation 22:8-9).

Wrapped in a cloud (10:1): Clouds are often biblical metaphors for the glory of God (Exodus 13:21; 40:28-34; Job 37:15-16; Matthew 26:64; Revelation 14:14). Perhaps this angel is often in the presence of the God of glory and continues to emanate God's glory as he engages in his assigned duties. Recall that after Moses had been with God on the mountain, "the skin of his face shone because he had been talking with God" (Exodus 34:29).

With a rainbow over his head (10:1): In the Noahic covenant, the rainbow was a sign that God would never again destroy the entire world with a flood. The rainbow is thus a potent reminder that even in the midst of woe and judgment, God is also a God of mercy (Habakkuk 3:2).

His face was like the sun, and his legs like pillars of fire (10:1): When an angel appeared to shepherds in a field to announce the birth of Jesus, "the glory of the Lord shone around them, and they were filled with great fear" (Luke 2:9). Angels are often so glorious that humans are terrified when they show up. When Daniel saw an angel he was left without strength (Daniel 10:8). Zechariah was gripped with fear when an angel appeared to him (Luke 1:12). The Roman soldiers trembled with fear and became as dead men when an angel appeared and rolled back the stone blocking Jesus' tomb (Matthew 28:2-4).

Some Bible interpreters believe this angel might be an appearance of the Lord Jesus Christ. After all, in an earlier vision, Jesus' face shines like the sun, and his feet are like burnished bronze (Revelation 1:15-16). However, Christ is never called an angel anywhere in the New Testament. Further, the angel is introduced as "another angel," indicating that this angel is in the same class as other angels in Revelation. Further, this angel is mighty but not Almighty, which God (Jesus) is throughout Scripture (for example, see Revelation 19:6). In the book of Revelation, Jesus is not a mighty angel but is rather the King of kings and Lord of lords (Revelation 19). Scripture consistently reveals that the next time Christ comes to the earth will be at the second coming and not before.

Moreover, Jesus was physically resurrected from the dead, and even today in heaven, Jesus retains His permanent glorified (human) resurrection body. When Christ comes again at the second coming, He will come as the Son of Man (Matthew 26:64; see also Acts 1:11).

All things considered, it seems best to interpret the angel's glory as a reflection of God's glory, much as the moon brightly reflects the light of the sun at night.

He had a little scroll (10:2): We aren't told what is written on the scroll, but it probably represents the Word of God. Another possibility is that it contains the angel's written orders for the mission he was about to fulfill.

He set his right foot on the sea, and his left foot on the land (10:2): Standing with one foot on the sea and the other on the land conveys the image of taking possession. The angel is God's representative, so his action represents God's absolute sovereignty over this planet. This is a direct challenge to Satan, who has long engaged in the role of "god of this world" (2 Corinthians 4:4; see also John 12:31).

When he called out, the seven thunders sounded (10:3): The seven thunders indicate that more powerful storms of judgment are impending. God's voice is often compared to or associated with thunder (Job 26:14; 37:5; Psalm 29; John 12:28-29).

I heard a voice…"Seal up what the seven thunders have said" (10:4): We do not know what the seven thunders uttered, because a heavenly voice—perhaps that of Jesus Himself—commanded John to seal up what he had heard (compare with Daniel 12:4,9). The message is to remain concealed until God's appointed time (Revelation 22:10; Daniel 8:26-27).

Revelation 10:5-7

The angel…raised his right hand to heaven (10:5): A person raises a hand when taking an oath or a solemn vow. The angel is portrayed as taking an oath with his hand raised toward God. The oath apparently affirms the solemnity and certainty of the words.

Swore…there would be no more delay (10:6): Only by the authority of the sovereign and mighty eternal Creator can the angel make the declaration about how and when "the mystery of God" will be fulfilled and finished (verse 7).

The phrase "no more delay" indicates that when the seventh angel sounds the seventh trumpet (11:15), the seven bowl judgments will begin (chapter 16). Following this, the tribulation period will rapidly come to a close, and the Lord Jesus will gloriously return again to set up His kingdom (chapters 19–20).

That "there would be no more delay" would be good news for the tribulation martyrs who asked the Lord when they would be vindicated (Revelation 6:10-11). These words also indicate that the question long ago asked of Christ by the disciples on the Mount of Olives is now being answered: "Tell us, when will these things be, and what will be the sign of your coming and of the end of the age?" (Matthew 24:3). The age would soon close. The prayer of all Christians, "Your kingdom come" (Matthew 6:10), is about to be answered.

In the past God delayed judgments so that human beings would have sufficient time to repent and turn to Him for salvation. "The Lord is not slow to fulfill his promise as some count slowness, but is patient toward you, not wishing that any should perish, but that all should reach repentance" (2 Peter 3:9). Now, however, time is running out. God's final judgments are about to fall.

The mystery of God would be fulfilled (10:7): Prophecy expositors have many opinions on the "mystery of God." Some relate it to past prophetic announcements of the glorious return of the Son of God and the establishment of His righteous kingdom. Others suggest it has to do with God's plan to punish evildoers. Still others suggest it involves prophecy relating to the middle and second half of the tribulation period. Still others say it relates more generally to the final consummation of all things. Still others interpret it as relating to why God allows bad things to happen on the earth. In view of such diversity of opinion, it is unwise to be dogmatic on this mystery. It's a mystery!

Revelation 10:8-11

The voice...spoke..."Go, take the scroll" (10:8): The command comes from either God or the Lord Jesus Christ. John obeys without hesitation.

He said to me, "Take and eat it" (10:9): The Bible often uses the language of ingesting in a figurative sense. We are urged, "Oh, taste and see that the LORD is good" (Psalm 34:8). Jeremiah affirmed of God's Word, "Your words were found, and I ate them, and your words became to me a joy and the delight of my heart" (Jeremiah 15:16). The apostle Peter instructed young believers, "Like newborn infants, long for the pure spiritual milk" (1 Peter 2:2). The writer of Hebrews speaks of "solid food" for mature Christians (5:14). The apostle Paul informed the immature Corinthian Christians, "I fed you with milk, not solid food" (1 Corinthians 3:1-2).

John obeyed the angel's instruction to eat the scroll, and it was sweet as honey in his mouth. The symbolism indicates that God's Word was sweet to John, for it abounds with the glorious promises of God. The Word of God speaks of victory in the end for God's people. For this reason, God's Word is more to be desired "than gold, even much fine gold; sweeter also than honey and drippings of the honeycomb" (Psalm 19:9-10).

However, the scroll quickly soured in John's stomach. The Word of God is bitter to unbelievers because it promises woe and judgment. Scripture promises doom, not victory, for those who reject God. So this passage of the Word of God is both sweet and bitter.

I took the little scroll...and ate it (10:10): As instructed by the angel, John took the scroll and ate it. Just as promised, it was both delightful and bothersome.

I was told, "You must again prophesy" (10:11): John's work was not yet complete. He was called to sound a warning about the approaching bitter judgment in the seventh trumpet, which constitutes the seven bowl judgments.

Major Themes

1. *Mystery (Revelation 10:7)*. A biblical mystery is a truth that cannot be discerned simply by human investigation, but requires special revelation from God. Generally, this word refers to a truth that was unknown to people living in Old Testament times but was revealed to humankind by God in the New Testament (Matthew 13:17; Colossians 1:26).

2. *God's servants the prophets (Revelation 10:7)*. The Hebrew word for prophet, *nabi*, refers to people who are taken over by the power of God and who speak God's words to the people. Often their words were directed at specific situations or problems that needed to be dealt with. In other cases, they spoke of the future. They typically prefaced their words with "Thus saith the Lord," thereby indicating that their words were not their own but came from God. These prophets were called into service directly by God, some even before birth (Jeremiah 1:5; Luke 1:13-16).

Digging Deeper with Cross-References

Seal up—Isaiah 8:16; Daniel 8:26; 12:4; Revelation 10:4; 22:10.
Him who lives forever—Revelation 4:9-10; 10:6; 15:7.
God the Creator—Genesis 1; Exodus 20:11; Psalm 33:6,9; Isaiah 44:24; Jeremiah 32:17; John 1:3; 1 Corinthians 8:6; Colossians 1:16; Hebrews 1:2; 11:3.

Life Lessons

1. *A burden for the lost*. Our passage speaks of the bitter circumstances of unbelievers during the tribulation period. This reality ought to give you and me a burden for the lost. The more people we can reach for Christ prior to the tribulation, the more people will participate in the rapture and thereby escape this approaching bitterness. Christ's Great Commission thus takes on new significance: "Go therefore and make disciples of all nations" (Matthew 28:19-20).

2. *A sense of urgency*. Our passage refers to God having "no more delay" as His prophetic plan moves toward its culmination. You and I ought not delay in our commitment to God, for life is all too short. James 4:14 tells us that we are like "a mist that appears for a little

time and then vanishes." The psalmist expresses a similar sentiment: "Behold, you have made my days a few handbreadths, and my lifetime is as nothing before you. Surely all mankind stands as a mere breath!" (Psalm 39:5). It is wise for each of us to give our time to God while there is yet time to give.

Questions for Reflection and Discussion

1. Do you have a burden for the lost? If yes, what are you doing about it?

2. Do you yearn for God to have "no more delay" in bringing history to its close so we can dwell with Jesus face to face in the new heavens and new earth?

The Ministry of the Two Prophetic Witnesses

Revelation 11:1-6

Scripture Reading and Insights

Begin by reading Revelation 11:1-6 in your favorite Bible. As you read, allow the Word of God to bring revival to your soul (Psalm 119:25,93,107).

In yesterday's reading, we briefly focused attention on the little scroll that was both sweet and sour to John—sweet because it contained God's Word but sour because of promises of judgment. Now we zero in on God's two prophetic witnesses who emerge during the tribulation period. With your Bible still accessible, consider the following insights on the biblical text, verse by verse.

Revelation 11:1-2

I was given a measuring rod..."Measure the temple of God..." (11:1): In Bible times, the measuring rod was a bamboo-like reed that was light and rigid (see Ezekiel 40:3,5).

Bible expositors offer several interpretations of what the measuring symbolizes. Some say the act of measuring the temple indicates that God is making a claim for it—that He owns it (compare with Revelation 21:15). Despite how the Gentiles (the evil forces of the antichrist) are oppressing the city, God says, "It's all mine!"

Other expositors suggest that the temple and worshipers are measured to ascertain their character. In this view, the temple and the Jews have been measured and found to be apostate, in need of revival and restoration. Eventually, the Jews will be restored to their Messiah when they call out for deliverance from the antichrist at Armageddon. (More on this later in the book.)

"Do not measure the court outside the temple" (11:2): Gentiles were prohibited from entering the inner court of the temple (a prohibition enforced by the death penalty), but they were permitted access to the outer court. God's instruction that John was not to bother measuring the outer court (with its Gentiles) symbolizes God's rejection of the unbelieving Gentiles for their oppression of the Jews, God's covenant people, for 42 months (three and a half years).

"It is given over to the nations" (11:2): The holy city had been oppressed by Assyria, Babylon, Medo-Persia, Greece, and Rome. During the tribulation period, the holy city will be oppressed by the antichrist and his forces. The antichrist will proclaim himself to be God and set up an image of himself in the Jewish temple, thereby defiling it (2 Thessalonians 2:4).

As the holy city is being trampled by Gentile forces—apparently during the last three and a half years of the tribulation period—God shelters the Jews in the wilderness from these evil forces. These Jews will exit Jerusalem right at the midpoint of the tribulation period, when the antichrist exalts himself as God (see Matthew 24:20-22).

Revelation 11:3-6

"I will grant authority to my two witnesses" (11:3): During the tribulation period, God will raise up two mighty witnesses who will testify to the true God, His judgment, and His salvation with astounding power. In the Old Testament two witnesses were required to confirm testimony (Deuteronomy 17:6). These two witnesses will confirm God's truth to those living in tribulation times.

The time frame of these two witnesses—1260 days—equals three and a half years. This period is elsewhere defined as 42 months (Revelation 11:2) and "a time, and times, and half a time" (12:14). A "time" is one year, "times" is two years, and "half a time" is a half a year.

It is not clear from Revelation 11 whether this is the first or last three and a half years of the tribulation. It may be best to conclude that the two witnesses do their miraculous work during the first three and a half years, for the antichrist's execution of them seems to fit best with other events that will transpire at the midpoint of the tribulation, such as the antichrist's exaltation of himself to godhood. Moreover, the resurrection of the two witnesses—after being dead for three days—would make a bigger impact on the world at the midpoint of the tribulation than at the end, just prior to the glorious second coming of Christ.

Clothed in sackcloth (11:3): These witnesses will wear clothing made of goat or camel hair, garments that symbolically express mourning (see Genesis 37:34). The mourning is over the wretched spiritual condition and lack of repentance in the world.

These are the two olive trees and the two lampstands (11:4): The imagery here is taken from Zechariah 3–4. Bible expositors offer several interpretations. One understanding is that lamps in biblical days were typically fueled by olive oil. The reference to olive trees and lampstands is believed to symbolize the light of spiritual revival. The preaching of the two witnesses will bring this light of revival during the dark days of the tribulation.

Other Bible expositors relate this imagery to the Holy Spirit. Zechariah 4:2-14 focuses on Joshua the high priest and Zerubbabel the governor. Both these individuals were empowered by the Holy Spirit, something symbolized by the olive oil. It is thus inferred that the two witnesses of Revelation 11 will likewise be empowered by the Holy Spirit during their ministry and will shine as lights, just like a lamp.

If anyone would harm them, fire pours from their mouth and consumes their foes (11:5): Prior to their execution by the antichrist, the two witnesses are sustained by the supernatural protection of God. Similarly, Jesus was providentially protected during His ministry. Once Jesus' ministry was over, He was put to death on the cross. Until that time, Jesus continually affirmed that His time had not yet come (see, for example, John 7:6-8). Likewise, only when the ministry of these two witnesses is complete will they finally be executed by the forces of the antichrist. And, like Jesus, they will be resurrected and ascend into heaven.

Anyone who tries to harm either of the two prophetic witnesses will come to a fiery end. Their ministry is unstoppable for three and a half years, until "they have finished their testimony" (Revelation 11:7).

In the Bible, fire can point to the wrath of God. Scripture tells us that God's "wrath is poured out like fire" (Nahum 1:6). God said, "My wrath [will] go forth like fire, and burn with none to quench it, because of the evil of your deeds" (Jeremiah 4:4). Those who stand against God's two prophets will come face to face with God's wrath.

They have the power to shut the sky...they have power over the waters... and to strike the earth with every kind of plague (11:6): In both testaments, God uses miracles to authenticate His messengers (Acts 2:43; Romans 15:18-19; 2 Corinthians 12:12). In the tribulation period, when the world is overrun by supernatural demonic activity, false religion, murder, sexual perversion, and unrestrained wickedness, these two witnesses will perform supernatural signs that will mark them as true prophets of God.

Some expositors believe the two witnesses will actually be Moses and Elijah. These are some of their reasons:

1. In the tribulation period, God deals with the Jews, just as He did in the first 69 weeks of Daniel. Moses and Elijah are two of the most influential figures in Jewish history. Their appearance during the tribulation period would thus make good sense.

2. Both Old Testament and Jewish tradition expected Moses (Deuteronomy 18:15,18) and Elijah (Malachi 4:5) to return in the future.

3. Moses and Elijah appeared on the mount of transfiguration with Jesus. This shows their centrality. Therefore, we might expect them to appear during the tribulation.

4. The miracles portrayed in Revelation 11 are similar to those performed by Moses and Elijah (see Exodus 7–11; 1 Kings 17; Malachi 4:5).

5. Both Moses and Elijah left the earth in unusual ways.
   Elijah never died, but rather was transported to heaven in a
   fiery chariot (2 Kings 2:11-12). God supernaturally buried
   Moses' body in an unknown location (Deuteronomy 34:5-
   6; Jude 9).

These are some of the reasons why some Bible expositors suggest
that in the tribulation period, God will send two of His mightiest servants: Moses, the great deliverer and spiritual legislator of Israel, and
Elijah, a prince among Old Testament prophets. These individuals rescued Israel from bondage and idolatry before, and they may appear
again during the tribulation period to warn Israel against succumbing
to the false religion of the antichrist and the false prophet.

Other Bible expositors have suggested that perhaps the two witnesses will be Enoch and Elijah. After all, Enoch and Elijah were both
upright men who were raptured to heaven. Neither one of them experienced death. Both of them were prophets—Enoch a Gentile and
Elijah an Israelite. The church fathers unanimously held to this view
during the first three hundred years of church history. God may ordain
Elijah to speak to the Jews and Enoch to speak to the Gentiles during
the tribulation.

Still other expositors say that these two witnesses will not be biblical personalities of the past. They reason that the text would surely
identify famous Old Testament personalities if they were indeed coming back. They conclude the two witnesses will likely be new prophets that God specially raises up for ministry during the tribulation (see
Matthew 11:14).

Major Themes

1. *Previous Jewish temples.* The first Jewish temple was built
   by Solomon, son of David, in Jerusalem in about 960 BC
   (1 Kings 6–7; 2 Chronicles 3–4). It was the heart and
   center of Jewish worship for the kingdom of Judah. It was
   destroyed by Nebuchadnezzar and the Babylonians in
   587 BC. The second temple was a smaller, leaner temple

built after the Babylonian exile, completed in 515 BC, and
not nearly as magnificent as Solomon's temple (see Ezra
3:12). It lasted some 500 years. The third temple was built
by King Herod the Great, who believed this would endear
the Jews (his subjects) to him. It was completed in AD 64
but destroyed in AD 70 along with the rest of Jerusalem by
Titus and his Roman army.

2. *Authority.* God gave His two witnesses authority
   (Revelation 11:3). The term "authority" surfaces often in
   Revelation.

   - Jesus received authority from the Father (2:27; 12:10).

   - Jesus will give authority to overcomers in the millennial
     kingdom (2:26).

   - Death and Hades will be given authority over a fourth
     of the earth (6:8).

   - Satan, the dragon, gives authority to the antichrist (Rev-
     elation 13:2,4).

   - The antichrist exercises authority for three and a half
     years (13:5).

   - He is given authority over "every tribe and people and
     language and nation" (13:7).

   - The false prophet is also given authority (13:12).

   - Angels have authority during the tribulation period
     (14:18; 18:1).

   - Kings of the earth have authority for a short time
     (17:12).

Digging Deeper with Cross-References

Gentile oppression of the Jews—2 Kings 25:8-10; Psalm 79:1; Isaiah 63:18; Lamentations 1:10.

Two witnesses—Deuteronomy 17:6; 19:15; Matthew 18:16; John
8:17; Hebrews 10:28.

Sackcloth—Genesis 37:34; 2 Samuel 3:31; 2 Kings 6:30; 19:1; Esther 4:1; Isaiah 22:12; Jeremiah 6:26; Matthew 11:21.

Life Lessons

1. *Spiritual drought.* Just as a physical drought can ravage the land, a spiritual drought can parch people's souls. In Psalm 63:1, the psalmist affirms, "My soul thirsts for you...in a dry and weary land where there is no water." Psalm 68:6 affirms that "the rebellious dwell in a parched land." Isaiah 1:30 indicates that those who are disobedient to God are "like a garden without water." Returning to the Lord in repentance is the only solution to spiritual drought (Isaiah 41:17).

2. *God's Word can seem both bitter and sweet.* God's Word can seem bitter when we disobey its teachings. "Oh, that my ways were steadfast in obeying your decrees! Then I would not be put to shame when I consider all your commands" (Psalm 119:5-6 NIV). The good news is that Scripture is also especially sweet because it can revive our souls and fill us with joy (see Psalm 119:11,28; Romans 12:12; Ephesians 4:22-23; Colossians 3:16; 2 Timothy 3:15-17).

Questions for Reflection and Discussion

1. Do you ever feel as if you are suffering a spiritual drought? What steps can you take today to help satisfy your spiritual thirst?

2. Self-examination is healthy. Ask yourself, "Am I in complete submission to the authority of God in all areas of my life? Am I holding anything back?"

3. Are you in need of revival from God's Word? I recommend Psalm 119.

The Death, Resurrection, and Ascension of the Two Witnesses

Revelation 11:7-14

Scripture Reading and Insights

Begin by reading Revelation 11:7-14 in your favorite Bible. As you read, allow the Word of God to bring revival to your soul (Psalm 119:25,93,107).

In the previous lesson, we were introduced to God's two mighty prophetic witnesses. In today's reading, we find out about their death, resurrection, and ascension into heaven. With your Bible still accessible, consider the following insights on the biblical text, verse by verse.

Revelation 11:7-10

When they have finished their testimony (11:7): We have seen that during the tribulation period, God will raise up two mighty witnesses who will testify to Him with astounding power. The miracles they perform are reminiscent of Moses (Exodus 7–11) and Elijah (1 Kings 17; Malachi 4:5). These prophetic witnesses apparently emerge on the scene at the beginning of the tribulation period. They continue to minister for 1260 days, or three and a half years.

Only when "they have finished their testimony" are they permitted to be killed. God's obedient servants are immortal until their work is done. Once they are finished, they are executed by the antichrist.

The word "finished" in this verse is the same word used by Jesus on the cross when He said, "It is finished" (John 19:30). Christ died in Jerusalem after He had finished His work of redemption. The two witnesses die in Jerusalem after they complete their work of redemptive ministry.

The beast that rises from the bottomless pit will make war on them (11:7): The fact that the beast, or antichrist, ascends out of the bottomless pit (the habitation of demons) may point to the antichrist's apparent death and resurrection (Revelation 13:3-4). Some suggest that while the antichrist's wounded body appears dead, his spirit visits the bottomless pit and later ascends out of the bottomless pit to rejoin his "resurrected" body. (More on this hypothesis later.)

Once the two witnesses complete their ministry, God will withdraw His providential protection from them. At this point, the antichrist will kill them, something that many had already lost their lives attempting to do. The witnesses will not die prematurely. All goes according to God's divine timing.

Their dead bodies will lie in the street of the great city (11:8): The bodies of the witnesses lie lifeless in Jerusalem. Jerusalem is referred to as "the great city," something true only from a human perspective. God looks not at externals but at spiritual realities. From a spiritual perspective, Jerusalem is anything but great at this time.

Sodom and Egypt (11:8): Jerusalem is figuratively called "Sodom and Egypt" because of the people's apostasy and rejection of God. Sodom was brimming with perverted sex, and Egypt was known for its persecution of God's people. Both cities were rebellious against God. The description of Jerusalem as no better than Sodom and Egypt indicates that this once holy city is now in the same league as those known for their hatred of the true God and His Word.

For three and a half days...gaze at their dead bodies (11:9): It is apparently by television and the Internet that "the peoples and tribes and languages and nations" will gaze at the dead witnesses for three and a half days. Our modern technology has set the stage for the things we read about in the tribulation period and may indicate that we are living in the end times.

Refusing to bury a corpse was a way of showing contempt (see Acts 14:19). The Old Testament prohibits this practice (Deuteronomy 21:22-23). By leaving the dead bodies in the street, the people of the world render the greatest possible insult to God's spokesmen. This was considered among the greatest indignities that could be perpetrated on someone (see Psalm 79:2-3). It is equivalent to people spitting on the corpses.

Even though our text does not say so, the antichrist will no doubt receive glory from people around the globe for putting the witnesses to death. He will be their hero, their deliverer.

Those who dwell on the earth will rejoice (11:10): In the book of Revelation, "those who dwell on the earth" refers to unbelievers. The phrase carries the idea of earth dwellers or worldlings—those characterized by the anti-God world system.

These worldlings will essentially have a satanic Christmas celebration when the witnesses are put to death. They exchange presents, apparently because they do not have to listen to these convicting messages from God any longer. Biblical history seems to indicate that the only prophets people love are dead ones. This is the only instance of rejoicing during the tribulation period recorded in the book of Revelation.

Revelation 11:11-14

A breath of life from God entered them (11:11): The Christmas celebration quickly gives way to fear as people witness a mighty act of God. The lifeless corpses suddenly stand up in full view of television and Internet feeds. Clips of this event will no doubt be replayed over and over on various media and go viral on the Internet. The resurrection and ascension of God's two witnesses will be huge exclamation points to their prophetic words throughout their three-and-a-half-year ministry.

The term "breath" recalls the ancient prophecy of the dry bones, in which God promised, "I will cause breath to enter you, and you shall live" (Ezekiel 37:5). This refers to the rebirth of the nation of Israel, which was fulfilled in 1948. Likewise, in terms of the two witnesses, "a breath of life from God entered them," and they are resurrected from the dead. God is a master of bringing new life!

Then they heard a loud voice from heaven saying to them, "Come up here!" (11:12): The loud voice is authoritative. "Come up here" is a sovereign directive to ascend into heaven, which the two witnesses promptly do. The apostle John was commanded, "Come up here" in Revelation 4:1 so he could receive God's great prophetic revelation of the future.

The witnesses go up to heaven in a cloud, perhaps a cloud of God's glory. This recalls how Christ Himself, following His resurrection, ascended into the clouds (Acts 1:9). This is also similar to the rapture, in which the dead in Christ rise first, and then living believers on earth "will be caught up together with them in the clouds to meet the Lord in the air" (1 Thessalonians 4:17).

The enemies of the two witnesses will see it all and will likely hate them all the more as a result of their victorious resurrection and ascension. As well, the whole world will surmise that the antichrist's murderous activities have been overruled by heaven.

There was a great earthquake (11:13): Following this ascension, the city of Jerusalem—where the murder takes place and the bodies are publicly displayed—will receive a sudden judgment. Jerusalem will suffer an immense earthquake that will destroy one-tenth of the city and kill 7000 inhabitants.

The rest were terrified and gave glory to the God of heaven (11:13): After witnessing this, many will give glory to God. This does not mean that all these people will become believers, but at the very least many will acknowledge God's hand in these events. Apparently, many (but not all) will just be giving lip service to God. Soon enough many of these same people will be cursing Him. "People gnawed their tongues in anguish and cursed the God of heaven for their pain and sores. They did not repent of their deeds" (Revelation 16:10-11).

Some scholars suggest that God's resurrection of the two prophetic witnesses and the verbal witness of God's 144,000 Jewish evangelists will expose millions of souls to the truth about God. How wonderful to contemplate that despite the horrific efforts of the antichrist and the false prophet to promote false religion, God will give a powerful testimony of Himself during the tribulation.

Let's never forget that God has no pleasure in the death of the wicked (Ezekiel 18:32; 33:11) but rather desires that all people be saved (see 2 Peter 3:9). Despite the hardness of heart of many people during those days, many others will nevertheless turn to the Lord and be saved. We know this to be true, for by the time the Lord comes again at the second coming, Christ will invite all believers who have survived the woes of the tribulation period into His millennial kingdom (see Matthew 25:31-46).

The second woe has passed (11:14): But things are about to get even worse!

Major Themes

1. *Jerusalem.* Jerusalem has often been referred to as the holy city. It is famous for being the scene of Jesus' arrest, trial, crucifixion, and resurrection. The city itself rests in the Judean hills at about 2640 feet above sea level. During Jesus' time, the city was probably home to about a quarter of a million people. The Jews believed no city could possibly compare with Jerusalem. It was the geographical heart of the Jewish religion. Jesus Himself made a number of visits there (Luke 2:22-51; 10:38-42; 13:34). How sad to see Jerusalem so morally and spiritually degraded in the end times.

2. *Burial customs.* Funerals in biblical times were performed quickly because the hot climate rapidly caused decay and odor. When people died, they were immediately bathed and then wrapped in strips of linen. Sometimes a gummy combination of spices was applied to the wrappings of the body. It was then carried by stretcher to the place of burial, whether in the ground or in a cave. In some cases, entire families might be buried in a large cave. Eventually,

because some areas lacked space in caves, bones would later be removed from a cave and stored in a wooden or stone chest.

Digging Deeper with Cross-References

Testimony—1 Chronicles 16:8-9; Psalms 9:11; 26:7; 119:172; 145:12; Isaiah 12:4; Jeremiah 51:10; Matthew 5:15; 10:32; John 15:27; Acts 1:8; Romans 10:9; 2 Timothy 1:8; Hebrews 2:12; 1 Peter 3:15.

War on the saints—Daniel 7:25; Revelation 6:9-11; 7:9-14; 13:7,10; 20:4-5.

Bottomless pit—Revelation 9:1-2,11; 11:7; 17:8; 20:1.

Life Lessons

1. *Giving a testimony.* Like the two witnesses, we ought always to be willing to give our testimony to others. We should never hesitate to speak about how Jesus has changed our lives forever (see 1 John 1:3). Giving your personal testimony of what the Lord Jesus has done in your life is a very important component of any witnessing encounter (see 1 Chronicles 16:8-9; Matthew 10:32; Mark 5:19-20; John 4:28-30,39; 2 Timothy 1:8; 1 Peter 3:15). Talk about the full assurance you have that your sins are forgiven and the joyful expectation of spending all eternity with Jesus. Remember, you may not be an expert on every verse in the Bible, but you are an expert on what Jesus has done in your life!

2. *Standing strong in the face of persecution.* We may not die for our faith, as will the two witnesses, but we will all likely encounter persecution for our faith. The wicked despise the godly (Proverbs 29:27), and the godly will suffer persecution (2 Timothy 3:12). We should not be surprised if the world hates us (1 John 3:13). However, as Jesus indicated, those who are persecuted for righteousness are

blessed (Matthew 5:10-11). We ought to rejoice in being counted worthy to suffer (Acts 5:41). We ought also to pray for those who persecute us (Matthew 5:44).

Questions for Reflection and Discussion

1. Are you comfortable or uncomfortable in giving your testimony to others? If you need some help becoming a stronger witness for Jesus, I recommend my friends at EvanTell (www.evantell.org).

2. Can you think of a time when someone mocked you or spoke condescendingly of you for being a Christian? How did you respond? Do you have a thick skin or a thin skin when it comes to standing for Jesus?

The Seventh Trumpet Judgment

Revelation 11:15-19

Scripture Reading and Insights

Begin by reading Revelation 11:15-19 in your favorite Bible. As you read, never forget that God urges you to quickly obey His Word in all things (Psalm 119:60).

In yesterday's reading, we focused on the death, resurrection, and ascension of God's two prophetic witnesses. Now we shift attention back to the seventh trumpet judgment. This last trumpet judgment actually constitutes a whole new series of judgments to be unleashed on the earth. With your Bible still accessible, consider the following insights on the biblical text, verse by verse.

Revelation 11:15

The seventh angel blew his trumpet, and there were loud voices in heaven (11:15): We often read of a loud voice in heaven (Revelation 1:10; 5:2,12; 6:10; 7:2,10; 8:13; 10:3; 11:12; 12:10; 14:7,9,15,18; 16:1,17; 19:1,17; 21:3.). On this occasion, however, we read of loud voices (plural). They likely belong to the whole host of heaven.

The seventh trumpet includes the seven bowl judgments, which are God's final judgments to be unleashed on the earth. They include all the events that lead up to Christ's second coming (chapter 19) and the establishment of His kingdom on earth (chapter 20). Things are rushing toward a culmination at this point.

"The kingdom of the world has become the kingdom of our Lord" (11:15): The loud voices proclaim that the long-awaited kingdom of Jesus Christ will soon commence (see Revelation 20:1-10; see also Psalm 2:2; Isaiah 9:6-7; Ezekiel 21:26-27; Daniel 2:35,44; 4:3; 6:26; 7:14,26-27; Zechariah 14:9). This will take place after the judgments associated with the seventh trumpet have run their course.

The term "Lord" refers to the Father, the first person of the Trinity. The phrase "and of his Christ" refers to Jesus, the second person of the Trinity.

This verse points forward to Jesus' establishment of the millennial kingdom, over which He will rule for a thousand years. Following His second coming, Christ will set up this kingdom and will assume the throne of David, as promised in the Davidic covenant (2 Samuel 7:12-14).

The world has long been a part of Satan's kingdom. He is portrayed as "the ruler of this world" (John 12:31; 14:30; 16:11) and "god of this world" (2 Corinthians 4:4). As well, ungodly human governments have long been under Satan's relentless influence (Psalm 2:2; Acts 4:26). Such evil governments will soon come to an end. Christ will set up the long-promised messianic kingdom (Isaiah 2:2-3; Daniel 2:44; 7:13-14,18,22,27; Luke 1:31-33).

Revelation 11:16-18

The twenty-four elders...fell on their faces and worshiped God (11:16): To review, the 24 elders are glorified, crowned, and enthroned—traits that seem to indicate that they are redeemed human beings. Scripture elsewhere reveals that believers will be judged (1 Corinthians 3:1-10; 2 Corinthians 5:10) and then rewarded with crowns (for example, 2 Timothy 4:8; James 1:12; 1 Peter 5:4; Revelation 2:10). Apparently then, the 24 elders symbolize the church in heaven.

When they hear the announcement of the soon establishment of Christ's kingdom, the elders—representing the church—fall prostrate before God and worship Him. What a contrast this is to the rebellious defiance of God on earth.

"We give thanks to you, Lord God Almighty" (11:17): The elders express

thanks to God for this wonderful reign. God is addressed in majestic terms. "Lord" points to His sovereignty; "Almighty," His omnipotence.

God is also called the One "who is and who was," referring to God's eternal nature. As Psalm 90:2 put it, "Before the mountains were brought forth, or ever you had formed the earth and the world, from everlasting to everlasting you are God." God's endless existence points to His endless rule over all things. That rule is now about to be enforced *in toto*. Until now, God has permitted hostile rulers, culminating with the antichrist. But soon all evil rule will be put to an end, and Christ will rule over all.

The 24 elders address God: "You have taken your great power and begun to reign." Does this mean that Christ's reign begins at this very moment? Some expositors think so, but their affirmation is more likely an anticipation of Christ's nearing millennial rule. The event is viewed as so absolutely certain that it is spoken of as having already begun. Christ does not claim His royal rights until He returns at the second coming, but the actual victory has already been won.

We might call this a "past tense of certainty," indicating that this rule is as good as done. We find this literary device elsewhere in Scripture. In Romans 8:30, believers are said to be justified and glorified. Our future glorification is so certain that it is spoken of as having already happened.

"The nations raged, but your wrath came" (11:18): The elders speak of the raging response of unbelieving Gentiles on earth (compare with Psalm 2:1,5,12). God has given them plenty of opportunities to repent and turn to Him, but they continue to harden their hearts against Him. God in His righteousness and justice pours out His wrath against such rebellion (Romans 2:5,8).

The demonic rage of these Gentiles culminates when they attempt to fight against Christ at the second coming. Revelation 16:14 tells us that demonic spirits will "go abroad to the kings of the whole world, to assemble them for battle on the great day of God the Almighty." Revelation 19:19 informs us, "I saw the beast and the kings of the earth with their armies gathered to make war against him who was sitting on the horse and against his army." Of course, this action is utterly futile, for Christ will slay them in an instant. (More on this later.)

"And the time for the dead to be judged, and for rewarding your servants, the prophets and saints" (11:18): The elders again speak as if future events are already present realities. The dead are as good as judged, and the saints are as good as rewarded. This is anticipatory language. These events have not yet occurred but will surely occur soon.

Notice that two groups of believers are mentioned—the prophets and saints. More specifically, the verse refers to both Old and New Testament prophets as well as saints, a term that embraces all other believers.

"Those who fear your name, both small and great" (11:18): "Fear" means reverence for God. "Both small and great" recognizes that not all saints are the same: Some are fervent and completely committed to Christ while others may be more timid in their faith. But all are saved and will be rewarded.

"Destroying the destroyers of the earth" (11:18): The elders also recognize God's judgment against those who, because of their rank and unrepentant rebellion, experience judgments that destroy the earth itself. These destroyers include Babylon, the antichrist, the false prophet, the forces of the antichrist, and Satan.

Revelation 11:19

God's temple in heaven was opened (11:19): Recall that at the beginning of Revelation 11, John witnesses the temple of God on earth being measured. Now we find the temple in heaven being opened to John. Some believe that this opening of the temple symbolizes believers in heaven enjoying intimate fellowship with God.

The ark of his covenant was seen within his temple (11:19): Many Bible expositors see the ark to be an emblem of God's atonement, His faithfulness, and His presence among the Israelites. We last saw God's ark of the covenant in 2 Chronicles 35:3, when it was put in Solomon's temple. The ark's present whereabouts is currently unknown, though many Christian archaeologists continue to look for it. Multiple theories have emerged as to what has happened to it, including these three:

- It was destroyed when Nebuchadnezzar burned the temple in 586 BC.

- It was destroyed during the Babylonian captivity (see 1 Kings 14:26; 2 Kings 25:9; 2 Chronicles 33:7; Jeremiah 3:16).

- Jeremiah hid it in a cave at Mount Sinai (see 2 Maccabees 2:4-8).

All this is probably a moot point, however, for many Bible expositors believe that Revelation 11 refers to a heavenly counterpart to the earthly ark of the covenant. Hebrews 9:24 tells us, "For Christ has entered, not into holy places made with hands, which are copies of the true things, but into heaven itself, now to appear in the presence of God on our behalf" (see also Hebrews 10:20).

In any event, the fact that the ark is mentioned here indicates that God will soon faithfully fulfill His covenant promises to Israel (represented by the ark). A remnant of Israel will soon come to faith in Jesus and will come into full possession of the ancient land promises in the millennial kingdom.

There were flashes of lightning, rumblings, peals of thunder, an earthquake, and heavy hail (11:19): Notice that this verse addresses both heaven and earth. Lightning, rumblings, and peals of thunder emanate from God's throne in heaven, and an earthquake and heavy hail inflict further damage on earth. As John witnesses glory in heaven, he witnesses destruction on earth.

Major Themes

1. *Jesus the King.* Genesis 49:10 includes a prophecy that the Messiah would come from the tribe of Judah and reign as King. The Davidic covenant in 2 Samuel 7:16 promised a Messiah who would reign on an eternal throne. Daniel 7:13-14 tells us that the Messiah-King will have an

everlasting dominion. In the New Testament, an angel appeared to Mary and informed her she would give birth to a son who would "reign over the house of Jacob forever, and of his kingdom there will be no end" (Luke 1:32-33). At the second coming, Jesus will be revealed as the King of kings and Lord of lords (Revelation 19:16).

2. *The ark of the covenant.* Scripture indicates that the ark symbolized God's presence (1 Samuel 4:3-22). It was kept in the Most Holy Place, the innermost shrine of the tabernacle and the temple (Exodus 26:33). The lid of the ark held great significance. It was known as the mercy seat or atonement cover. On the annual Day of Atonement, the high priest sprinkled the blood of a sacrificial animal on it to symbolize the nation's repentance for the sins committed the previous year. Israel's guilt was transferred to the animal (Leviticus 23:27; Numbers 29:7).

Digging Deeper with Cross-References

God rewards Old Testament saints—Daniel 12:1-3; see also 1 Corinthians 3:8; 4:5; Revelation 22:12.

God rewards church-age saints—Romans 14:10-13; 1 Corinthians 15:51-52; 2 Corinthians 5:9-11; 1 Thessalonians 4:13-18.

God rewards tribulation saintsj—Revelation 20:4.

Life Lessons

1. *The fear of God.* Christians are called to live in reverent fear of God (1 Samuel 12:14,24; 2 Chronicles 19:9; Acts 10:35; 1 Peter 1:17; 2:17). Fear of the Lord motivates one to be obedient to God (Deuteronomy 5:29; Ecclesiastes 12:13), to serve Him (Deuteronomy 6:13), and to avoid evil (Proverbs 3:7; 8:13; 16:6). Fear of the Lord is true wisdom (Job 28:28; Psalm 111:10) and the beginning of knowledge (Proverbs 1:7). God blesses those who fear Him (Psalm 115:13). Fear of the Lord leads to riches, honor, and

long life (Proverbs 22:4). God shows mercy to those who fear Him (Luke 1:50).

2. *Forfeiting rewards.* Spend a few minutes meditating on the following Bible passages: Romans 14:10-13; 1 Corinthians 15:51-52; 2 Corinthians 5:9-11; 1 Thessalonians 4:13-18. Did you know Scripture reveals that some Christians will actually forfeit rewards because of unrepentant sin or a failure to obey God? Some Christians will even experience a sense of shame at the judgment (see 2 John 8). We ought to follow the resolution of Jonathan Edwards (1703–58): "Resolved, never to do anything, which I should be afraid to do, if it were the last hour of my life."

Questions for Reflection and Discussion

1. Does your lifestyle at home and at work or school consistently show that you revere the Lord?

2. Does the possibility of losing a reward at the judgment seat of Christ motivate you or scare you?

3. Would you like to make any resolutions?

Day 20

The Outbreak of War

Revelation 12

Scripture Reading and Insights

Begin by reading Revelation 12 in your favorite Bible. As you read, never forget that God urges you to quickly obey His Word in all things (Psalm 119:60).

In yesterday's reading, we were introduced to the seventh trumpet judgment, which actually constitutes seven new bowl judgments. These judgments will be unleashed on the earth just a bit later in Revelation. In today's reading, we focus attention on a preliminary event: Satan's ousting from heaven and his great persecution of Israel. With your Bible still accessible, consider the following insights on the biblical text, verse by verse.

Revelation 12:1-2

A great sign appeared in heaven: A woman (12:1): The woman represents Israel, the wife of God (Isaiah 54:5-6; Jeremiah 3:6-8; 31:32; Ezekiel 16:32; Hosea 2:16). The moon alludes to God's covenant relationship with Israel. New moons are associated with covenant worship (1 Chronicles 23:31; 2 Chronicles 2:4; 8:13). The 12 stars represent the 12 tribes of Israel.

She was pregnant and was crying out in birth pains (12:2): This likely refers to the harsh experience of the Jewish nation throughout the centuries as it awaits the eventual "birth" (or appearance) of its Messiah.

Revelation 12:3-6

Behold, a great red dragon (12:3): This is Satan. Red may imply bloodshed, for Satan has always been a murderer (John 8:44).

Seven heads and ten horns, and on his heads seven diadems (12:3): From similar descriptions in Daniel 7:7-8,24 and Revelation 13:1, we infer that this points to Satan's control over world empires during the tribulation period, apparently through the antichrist.

The ten horns apparently represent the ten kings of Daniel 7:7 and Revelation 13:1, over whom the antichrist—empowered by Satan—will gain authority. The ten countries headed by the ten kings will form the nucleus of the world empire that the antichrist (and thus Satan) will control. The seven heads and seven crowns apparently refer to the principal rulers of the empire.

Satan, the dragon, is also called a serpent (Genesis 3:1; Revelation 12:9). The serpent is characterized by treachery, deceitfulness, venom, and murder.

His tail swept down a third of the stars of heaven (12:4): The first five verses of Revelation 12 appear to contain a minihistory of Satan. Verse 4 refers to the fall of the angels who followed Satan. (The word "stars" is sometimes used of angels in the Bible—Job 38:7.) Lucifer apparently convinced a third of the angelic realm to join him in his rebellion against God.

So that...he might devour it (12:4): Satan desired to kill the promised Messiah at birth. Under the providence of God, Satan was unsuccessful. Some expositors believe the mention of the dragon seeking to devour the child alludes to Herod's massacre of male children—an attempt to kill Jesus Christ as a child (Matthew 2:13-18). The image of Satan devouring people reminds us of 1 Peter 5:8.

She gave birth to a male child (12:5): The male child is Jesus, born as a Jew (Matthew 1:1; 2 Timothy 2:8; see also Romans 1:3; 9:4-5).

Caught up to God and to his throne (12:5): Jesus ascended to heaven following His resurrection (Acts 1:9; 2:33; Hebrews 1:1-3; 12:2).

The woman fled into the wilderness (12:6): In the middle of the tribulation, the antichrist will break his covenant with Israel and exalt himself as deity, even putting an image of himself in the Jewish temple (2 Thessalonians 2:4). Christ, in His Olivet Discourse, warns of how quickly the Jews will have to flee for their lives (Matthew 24:16-31). Many will apparently flee to the deserts and mountains, perhaps in the area of Bozrah or Petra, about 80 miles south of Jerusalem. Others suggest Moab, Ammon, and Edom to the east.

The Lord will take care of this remnant of Jews in the wilderness for 1260 days, or three and a half years. This is the last half of the tribulation period.

Revelation 12:7-9

War arose in heaven (12:7): War now erupts in heaven between God's holy angels and the evil angels. Michael the archangel leads God's angels, and Satan leads the fallen angels.

Michael the archangel is called a chief prince (Daniel 10:13) and "the great prince" (Daniel 12:1). He appears to be specially related to Israel as its guardian. His name means "Who is like God?" It speaks of his unwavering devotedness to God, in stark contrast to Satan, who wanted to take God's place (see Isaiah 14:14).

He was defeated, and there was no longer any place for them in heaven (12:8): Satan and his fallen angels are no match for God's heavenly hosts, under the leadership of the archangel Michael. Though Satan previously had access to heaven (as in the book of Job), that access now permanently ends.

The great dragon was thrown down (12:9): The great dragon is "that ancient serpent" that tempted Adam and Eve in the Garden of Eden (Genesis 3:1). He is called the devil (Matthew 4:1), a title meaning "adversary" or "slanderer." The name Satan also carries the idea of "adversary."

Satan is "the deceiver of the whole world." He is the "father of lies" (John 8:44) and blinds people to the truth (2 Corinthians 4:4). He spreads deception through false prophets (Matthew 24:11) and especially through the antichrist (2 Thessalonians 2:9-11).

Revelation 12:10-12

I heard a loud voice in heaven (12:10): The loud voice may be a burst of praise from all the tribulation martyrs in heaven. They exult in God's salvation and His exercise of authority in overcoming Satan.

"The accuser of our brothers has been thrown down, who accuses them day and night" (12:10): Accusing God's people is Satan's continuous, ongoing work. He does this in two ways. First, he accuses believers before the throne of God (Job 1:6; 2:1; Zechariah 3:1; Romans 8:33). Second, he accuses believers to their own consciences, causing excessive guilt in order to bring depression and defeat.

"They have conquered him by the blood of the Lamb" (12:11): No accusation of Satan against believers in Jesus can stand. Their sins have been forgiven because of the shed blood of the Lamb (Romans 8:33-39).

"The word of their testimony" (12:11): These individuals openly witnessed about Jesus during the tribulation period. They did not back down from witnessing in the face of death threats. They would rather give up their lives than deny Jesus.

"Therefore, rejoice, O heavens...But woe to you, O earth" (12:12): Notice the contrast between the rejoicing and the woe in this verse. Satan's access to heaven is removed, and he will no longer be able to stand before the throne of God and accuse Christians. For this there is rejoicing in heaven. On earth, however, Satan is filled with fury because he knows his time is short. Only half of the tribulation period is now left, so Satan knows his time is limited to a mere 1260 days, the last three and a half years of the tribulation period. This brings woe to the earth.

Revelation 12:13-17

The dragon...pursued the woman (12:13): Once Satan is ousted from heaven and is thrown down to the earth, he seeks to persecute the Jews, from whose lineage the Messiah was born. Part of this persecution will no doubt be carried out through the antichrist (Daniel 9:27; Matthew 24:15; 2 Thessalonians 2:4).

Scripture reveals that Jesus will not return until the Jewish people are endangered at Armageddon and the Jewish leaders cry out for deliverance from Him, their divine Messiah (see Zechariah 12:10). In his perverted thinking, Satan may reason that if he can destroy the Jews, he can prevent the second coming of Christ and save himself from defeat.

The woman was given the two wings of the great eagle (12:14): Wings often represent protection and deliverance in the Bible (see Psalm 91:4; Isaiah 40:31). For example, after God delivered the Jews from Egyptian bondage, He affirmed, "You yourselves have seen what I did to the Egyptians, and how I bore you on eagles' wings and brought you to myself" (Exodus 19:4). Therefore, the "two wings" in this verse point to God's supernatural delivering power (see Matthew 24:16; Mark 13:14; Luke 21:21).

God will preserve a remnant of Jews through this persecution, but this should not be taken to mean that all Jews will survive. Zechariah prophesies, "In the whole land, declares the LORD, two thirds shall be cut off and perish, and one third shall be left alive" (13:8). Many will die, but a remnant will survive the onslaught.

She is to be nourished for a time, and times, and half a time (12:14): God preserves the Jews throughout the last three and a half years of the tribulation period (see Daniel 7:25; 12:7).

The serpent poured water like a river out of his mouth (12:15): Some Bible expositors take this to mean that Satan will cause a flood in an attempt to dislodge and destroy the Jews. Others take the flood metaphorically, suggesting that a satanically driven army will rapidly advance against the Jews like a flood. It may also refer more broadly to an outpouring of hatred and anti-Semitism.

The earth came to the help of the woman (12:16): Whichever of the above interpretations is correct, the earth comes to the aid of the Jews, under God's providence. If the flood is literal water, perhaps God causes the earth to open up and swallow the water. If the flood is a rapidly advancing army (or militant anti-Semitics), perhaps such people will be destroyed by an earthquake that causes the ground to open up (see Matthew 24:7; Revelation 6:12; 8:5; 11:13,19; 16:18).

Recall that God promised the Jews in Isaiah 54:17, "No weapon that is fashioned against you shall succeed." Not even water, literal or metaphorical.

The dragon became furious with the woman and went off to make war on the rest of her offspring (12:17): In view of his failure to destroy the Jews, an infuriated Satan now resorts to war against a related group—believers in Jesus Christ. These are the spiritual offspring of the woman, or Israel (see Galatians 3:29). Satan wars against the saints.

Major Themes

1. *Symbolic women in the book of Revelation.* The woman in our passage symbolizes Israel. Other symbolic women include the great prostitute, or apostate religion (Revelation 17:3-6); Jezebel, or paganism (2:20); and the bride of the Lamb, or the church (19:7).

2. *Horn.* Animals used horns as weapons (Genesis 22:13; Psalm 69:31), so horns eventually came to be seen as symbols of power and might. They became emblems of dominion, representing kingdoms and kings (Daniel 7–8; Revelation 12:13; 13:1,11; 17:3-16).

Digging Deeper with Cross-References

Israel as a mother giving birth—Isaiah 26:17-18; 54:1; 66:7-12; Hosea 13:13; Micah 4:10; 5:2-3; Matthew 24:8.

Christ's ascension—Mark 16:19; Luke 24:51; John 6:62; 20:17; Acts 1:9; Ephesians 4:8; Hebrews 4:14; 9:24; 1 Peter 3:22.

The blood of the Lamb—Matthew 26:28; Mark 14:24; John 6:53; Acts 20:28; Romans 5:9; 1 Corinthians 11:25; 1 John 1:7; Revelation 1:5; 5:9.

Life Lessons

1. *Christ our advocate.* Satan is our accuser, but Jesus is our advocate: "We have an advocate with the Father, Jesus Christ the righteous" (1 John 2:1). The word "advocate" means defense attorney. When Satan accuses us before the divine Judge (the Father), Jesus, our defense attorney, steps up to the Father and reveals that our slate has been wiped

clean by His blood sacrifice. We are therefore innocent of
the crimes we have committed.

2. *Faithful unto death.* Revelation 12:11 speaks of believers
   who were so bold in their faith that they "loved not their
   lives even unto death." Recall the Lord's instructions to the
   Christians at Smyrna: "Do not fear what you are about to
   suffer. Behold, the devil is about to throw some of you into
   prison, that you may be tested…Be faithful unto death,
   and I will give you the crown of life" (Revelation 2:10).
   Never fear—eternal life awaits all Christians.

Questions for Reflection and Discussion

1. Has Satan ever neutralized your spiritual life by inflicting
   relentless guilt on your conscience for your perceived
   weaknesses and failures?

2. Do you live every day with the confidence that Christ is
   your advocate and defender?

The Rise of the Antichrist

Revelation 13:1-4

Scripture Reading and Insights

Begin by reading Revelation 13:1-4 in your favorite Bible. As you read, ask God to help you understand His Word (Psalm 119:73).

In the previous lesson, we focused on Satan's ousting from heaven and his subsequent persecution of the Jews. In today's reading, we witness the rise of the antichrist, who will come into great power during the tribulation period. With your Bible still accessible, consider the following insights on the biblical text, verse by verse.

Revelation 13:1

I saw a beast rising out of the sea (13:1): Revelation pictures the antichrist as a beast 32 times. The image points to the brutal, bloody, uncontrolled, and wild character of this diabolical dictator. It also contrasts the antichrist with Christ, who is most commonly called the Lamb. The Lamb saves sinners, but the beast persecutes and executes the saints. The Lamb is gentle, whereas the beast is ferocious. The Lamb is loving, but the beast is heartless and cruel.

This beast rises out of the sea. The sea refers to the Gentile nations (17:15), indicating that the antichrist will be a Gentile. "Anti" can mean "instead of" or "against" or "opposed to." So "antichrist" can mean "instead of Christ," "against Christ," or "opposed to Christ." The antichrist is the "man of lawlessness," the "son of destruction," who will lead the world into rebellion against God (2 Thessalonians 2:3,8-10; Revelation 11:7) and deceive multitudes (Revelation 19:20).

With ten horns and seven heads (13:1): We have seen that because animals use horns as weapons (Genesis 22:13; Psalm 69:31), horns eventually became symbols of power and then of dominion, representing kingdoms and kings. Comparing this text with Daniel 7:16-24, we conclude that the antichrist will rise up from ten kingdoms that will constitute a revived Roman Empire, the final form of Gentile world power before Christ returns.

Some Bible expositors say the seven heads are the principal rulers of the antichrist's revived Roman Empire. Others suggest that the seven heads may be successive world empires—Egypt, Assyria, Babylon, Medo-Persia, Greece, Rome, and the antichrist's revived Roman Empire. Still others say the seven heads represent seven mountains (Revelation 17:9). A mountain can symbolize a kingdom (see Daniel 2:34-35,44-45). This may be a veiled reference to Rome, which was built on seven hills (Revelation 17:18). All these views support the idea that antichrist's kingdom will be a revived Roman Empire.

With ten diadems on its horns (13:1): The ten diadems, or crowns, point to the dominion of the antichrist's kingdom, which will eventually embrace the entire globe.

And blasphemous names on its heads (13:1): These point to the antichrist's character—he will have a mouth full of blasphemy (verses 5-6) and will exalt himself above all that is called God or that is worshiped (2 Thessalonians 2:4).

Revelation 13:2

The beast that I saw was like a leopard (13:2): Much of the imagery in this verse is from Daniel 7. The leopard was known for swiftness, cunning, and agility (see Daniel 7:6). This imagery in Daniel represents Greece under Alexander the Great, which had a swift, cunning, and agile army. Such will be the case with the antichrist as he comes into world dominion.

Its feet were like a bear's (13:2): The bear in Daniel's account refers to Medo-Persia (Daniel 7:5), well known for its strength and fierceness in battle (Isaiah 13:17-18). Such strength and fierceness will certainly characterize the antichrist and his forces.

Its mouth was like a lion's (13:2): The lion in Daniel's account refers to Babylon (Daniel 7:4), with lion-like qualities of power and strength. Babylon was known for its ability to move quickly (like a lion). Such qualities will characterize the antichrist.

A comparison of Revelation 13:2 with Daniel 7 reveals that the final world empire of the antichrist—a revived Roman Empire—will be rooted in all the previous empires. It will unite in a single kingdom the evil and power that characterized all the previous kingdoms.

To it the dragon gave his power and his throne and great authority (13:2): The ultimate source of the antichrist's power is Satan.

Revelation 13:3

Seemed to have a mortal wound (13:3): Some Bible expositors believe this mortal wound refers to the pagan Roman Empire, which died in the past but will be revived in the end times. Others say a historical character of the past, such as Nero, Judas Iscariot, Mussolini, Hitler, or Stalin, will come back to life and fulfill the role of the antichrist in the end times.

Others say the antichrist will actually be killed and then resurrected. Still others say that perhaps the antichrist will be severely wounded, and Satan will supernaturally heal this wound. Perhaps he will simply appear to be killed, though he really is not, and through satanic trickery will appear to be resurrected.

The revived Roman Empire view seems unfeasible because verse 12 specifically refers to "the first beast, whose mortal wound was healed." The "first beast" is the antichrist. Then, in verse 14, we find a parallel reference to "the beast that was wounded by the sword and yet lived." This verse is interpreted most naturally as referring to a person—not a reincarnation of a past person, but a unique anti-God person of the future.

It is unlikely that the antichrist will actually be resurrected, but he may give the appearance of having been resurrected. Satan has supernatural abilities (John 12:31; 2 Corinthians 4:4; Ephesians 2:2), but he is not powerful enough to resurrect people from the dead. Only God can create life (Genesis 1:1,21; Deuteronomy 32:39); the devil cannot (see Exodus 8:19).

The devil has great power to deceive people (Revelation 12:9). He is a master magician and a superscientist. With his vast knowledge of God, man, and the universe, he is able to perform counterfeit miracles (2 Thessalonians 2:9).

Some theologians believe Satan may be able to perform limited "grade-B" miracles. But only God can perform "grade-A" miracles. Only God can fully control and supersede the natural laws He Himself created.

Satan will likely engage in a grade-B miracle in healing the wounded (but not dead) antichrist, or engage in some kind of masterful deception, or perhaps a combination of both. In any event, the antichrist will appear to be resurrected from the dead. Second Corinthians 4:4 informs us that Satan can blind people's minds. If Satan pulls off some kind of counterfeit resurrection, he may blind people's minds so that they accept this as an indication of the antichrist's power and deity and subsequently worship him.

If the antichrist only appears to be dead but is not genuinely dead, a scenario suggested by Bible scholar Walter Price becomes viable:

> The apostle Paul was stoned in Lystra, and the citizens "dragged him out of the city, supposing that he was dead" (Acts 14:19). While in an unconscious state, Paul "was caught up into Paradise, and heard unspeakable words, which it is not lawful for a man to utter" (2 Cor. 12:4)... At the same time he was thought to be dead, his spirit was caught up into the third heaven and there received a profound revelation from God. This same thing, in reverse, will happen to the Antichrist. The Antichrist...will be no more dead than was the apostle Paul. But just as the citizens of Lystra thought Paul was dead, so the Antichrist will be thought dead.[1]

Just as Paul's spirit departed from his body and was taken to heaven, where he received further revelations, so the antichrist's spirit may depart from his body and be taken into the abyss, where Satan will offer the world's kingdoms to him.

The antichrist's spirit will then return from the abyss (Revelation 11:7), reenter what appears to be a dead body, and thereby give the appearance of a resurrection from the dead. Mark Hitchcock suggests that while his spirit is in the abyss, the "Antichrist probably receives his orders and strategy from Satan, literally selling his soul to the devil, and then comes back to earth with hellish ferocity to establish his world domination over a completely awestruck earth."[2]

The whole earth marveled as they followed the beast (13:3): This event will no doubt make headlines around the world. Internet videos of the event will go viral. Television reports of the event will be shown around the clock.

Revelation 13:4

They worshiped the dragon (13:4): During Christ's three-year ministry, Satan tried to persuade Him to fall down and worship him (Matthew 4:9). Before that, Lucifer (Satan's original name) sought to put himself in the place of God (see Isaiah 14:12-17; Ezekiel 28:11-19). Satan will finally have what he has yearned for—worship.

They worshiped the beast… "Who is like the beast?" (13:4): This contrasts with believers, who say to God, "Who is like you, O LORD?" (Exodus 15:11).

Major Themes

1. *The genius of the antichrist.* Scripture reveals that the antichrist will be a genius in intellect (Daniel 8:23), commerce (Daniel 11:43; Revelation 13:16-17), war (Revelation 6:2; 13:2), speech (Daniel 11:36), and politics (Revelation 17:11-12).

2. *The antichrist mimics Christ.* Christ is God (John 1:1-2; 10:36), and the antichrist will claim to be God (2 Thessalonians 2:4). Christ did miracles (Matthew 9:32-33; Mark 6:2); the antichrist will mimic such miracles (Matthew 24:24; 2 Thessalonians 2:9). Christ is crowned

with many crowns (Revelation 19:12); the antichrist is crowned with ten crowns (Revelation 13:1). Christ rides a white horse (Revelation 19:11) as does the antichrist (Revelation 6:2). Christ was resurrected (Matthew 28:6); the antichrist will appear to be resurrected (Revelation 13:3,14). Christ is a member of the holy Trinity—Father, Son, and Holy Spirit (2 Corinthians 13:14), but the antichrist is a member of an unholy trinity—Satan, the antichrist, and the false prophet (Revelation 13).

Digging Deeper with Cross-References

Blasphemy—Exodus 20:7; Leviticus 19:12; 22:32; Deuteronomy 5:11; Matthew 12:31-32; 2 Thessalonians 2:4.

Satanic power—Job 1:12; Luke 4:6; Acts 26:18; Ephesians 6:12; 2 Thessalonians 2:9.

The worship of evil spirits (such as Satan)—Leviticus 17:7; Deuteronomy 32:17; 2 Chronicles 11:15; Psalm 106:37; 1 Corinthians 10:20; Revelation 9:20.

Life Lessons

1. *Who is like the Lord?* People will worship both the devil and the antichrist, saying, "Who is like the beast?" (Revelation 13:4). We, however, proclaim with the Scriptures, "Who is like you, O LORD?" (Exodus 15:11). The Lord declares, "There is none who can deliver from my hand" (Isaiah 43:13). The true God is incomparably great.

2. *Test all things.* We ought to consistently test all doctrines and religious ideas against Scripture. Even today, the spirit of antichrist is at work promoting heretical doctrine (see 1 John 4:1-3; 2 John 7). Scripture often warns against being deceived by false doctrine (Matthew 7:15-16; 24:4,11; Acts 20:28-30; 2 Corinthians 11:2-3; 2 Timothy 4:3-4). We protect ourselves by testing all teachings against Scripture (Acts 17:11; 1 Thessalonians 5:21).

Questions for Reflection and Discussion

1. Have you ever been awestruck at how the Lord came through for you, such that you were moved to ask, "Who is like you, O Lord" (Exodus 15:11)?

2. Do you think you could ever be deceived by false doctrine? Why or why not? (See Acts 17:11; 1 Thessalonians 5:21.)

Day 22

The Blasphemy of the Antichrist

Revelation 13:5-10

Scripture Reading and Insights

Begin by reading Revelation 13:5-10 in your favorite Bible. As you read, ask God to help you understand His Word (Psalm 119:73).

In yesterday's reading, we were introduced to the person of the antichrist. Now let's find out more about his blasphemous, self-exalting nature. With your Bible still accessible, consider the following insights on the biblical text, verse by verse.

Revelation 13:5-6

The beast was given a mouth uttering haughty and blasphemous words (13:5): The root meaning of the Greek word for blasphemy can range from showing a lack of reverence for God to a more extreme attitude of contempt for either God or something considered sacred (see Leviticus 24:16; Matthew 26:65; Mark 2:7). It can involve speaking evil against God (Psalm 74:18; Isaiah 52:5; Romans 2:24; Revelation 13:1,6; 16:9,11,21) or showing contempt for the true God by making claims of divinity for oneself (see Mark 14:64; John 10:33). The antichrist will engage in all these aspects of blasphemy.

When the antichrist first comes into power, he will appear to be a dynamic, charismatic leader who can solve the problems of the world. At the midpoint of the tribulation period, however, he will deify himself. He will set up an image of himself in the Jewish temple, thereby committing the "abomination of desolation" (Matthew 24:15).

In the book of Daniel, the phrase "the abomination that makes desolate" (11:31; 12:11; see also 9:27) conveys a sense of outrage or horror at the witnessing of a barbaric act of idolatry in God's holy temple. Such acts utterly profane and desecrate the temple.

Daniel 11:36 confirms that the antichrist "shall exalt himself and magnify himself above every god." We also read in 2 Thessalonians 2:4 that the antichrist ultimately "opposes and exalts himself against every so-called god or object of worship, so that he takes his seat in the temple of God, proclaiming himself to be God." There is no greater blasphemy than this. The antichrist truly is anti-Christ, putting himself in Christ's place.

The antichrist—the world dictator—will then demand that the world worship and pay idolatrous homage to him. Any who refuse will be persecuted, and many will be martyred. The false prophet, who is the antichrist's first lieutenant, will see to this.

It was allowed to exercise authority for forty-two months (13:5): Just as Satan is on a leash (Job 1–2), answerable to our sovereign God, so the antichrist is on a leash as well. God has set well-defined parameters regarding what the antichrist will be permitted to do and say. God will grant authority to the antichrist to act as he desires during the great tribulation, the last three and a half years of the tribulation.

It opened its mouth to utter blasphemies against God (13:6): The blasphemous words of the antichrist are in keeping with his blasphemous nature (2 Thessalonians 2:3-4). Recall that in the Old Testament, Satan himself blasphemed God: "I will set my throne on high...I will make myself like the Most High" (Isaiah 14:13-14). The antichrist, energized by Satan, now utters blasphemies, claiming to be God and demanding to be worshiped.

Notice the specific objects of the antichrist's blasphemy in Revelation 13:6. First is God's name. In biblical times, a person's name represented everything that person was. It pointed to his or her very nature. It included the very attributes of a person. For the antichrist to blaspheme God's name means that he is blaspheming God's very identity and His nature.

The antichrist also blasphemes God's dwelling, or heaven (see Hebrews 9:23-24).

"Those who dwell in heaven" includes both the holy angels and the glorified saints (believers who were caught up in the rapture and then taken to heaven prior to the tribulation period). This will be the antichrist's way of saying to God, "I disdain everything about You."

Revelation 13:7-8

It was allowed to make war on the saints (13:7): The antichrist will be permitted to persecute God's people during the tribulation period. Recall that in Revelation 6:11, martyrs in heaven are informed that there will be still more martyrs: "They were each given a white robe and told to rest a little longer, until the number of their fellow servants and their brothers should be complete, who were to be killed as they themselves had been." Revelation 13:5-7 appears to refer to some of these new martyrs.

On the one hand, Israel—which gave birth to the divine Messiah, Jesus Christ—will come under heavy persecution by the antichrist. This will take place in the middle of the tribulation when the antichrist moves into Jerusalem and sets up an image of himself in the Jewish temple, proclaiming himself to be God (see Daniel 9:27; see also Matthew 24:16-22).

On the other hand, Christians will also be persecuted. Daniel 7:25 prophetically affirms that the antichrist "shall wear out the saints of the Most High…and they shall be given into his hand for a time, times, and half a time." The phrase "time, times, and half a time" refers to the last three and a half years of the seven-year period of antichrist's power. This is the same as the "42 months" mentioned in Revelation 13:5.

Authority was given it over every tribe and people and language and nation (13:7): The antichrist now exercises global dominion. He is not only a political leader but also the central religious object of worship (2 Thessalonians 2:4). He thus exercises both political and religious authority—an all-encompassing global authority over all peoples.

Even today, we witness a movement toward globalism in many

different areas, including economics, banking, commerce and trade, business, management, manufacturing, environmentalism, population control, education, religion, agriculture, information technologies, the entertainment industry, the publishing industry, science and medicine, and even government. Revelation 13 tells us that the antichrist will ultimately lead a global anti-God union. It will be a political union, an economic union, and a religious union.

When one considers the multiple cascading problems now facing humanity—including the Middle East conflict, terrorism, overpopulation, starvation, pollution, national and international crime, cyber warfare, and economic instability—it is entirely feasible that increasing numbers of people will come to believe that ultimately such problems can be solved only on a global level. They may think that the only hope for human survival is a strong and effective world government.

The technology that makes possible a world government—including instant global media through television and radio, cyberspace, and supercomputers—is now in place. Technology has "greased the skids" for the emergence of globalism in our day. Without such technology, a true globalism would be impossible.

All who dwell on earth will worship it (13:8): Just as all in heaven worship Him who sits on the throne and the Lamb (Revelation 4–5), so all who are on earth will worship the antichrist, empowered by the devil.

Everyone whose name has not been written before the foundation of the world (13:8): The names of the redeemed were written in the book of life in eternity past, before the world even began. As Ephesians 1:4 puts it, "He chose us in him before the foundation of the world."

In the book of life (13:8): Paul speaks of believers as those "whose names are in the book of life" (Philippians 4:3). Revelation mentions the book of life six times (3:5; 13:8; 17:8; 20:12,15; 21:27). It contains the names of all those belonging to God.

Of the Lamb who was slain (13:8): The book of life belongs specifically to the Lamb of God, Jesus Christ (Revelation 21:27). Those not recorded in the Lamb's book of life will worship the antichrist.

Revelation 13:9-10

If anyone has an ear, let him hear (13:9): This phrase is similar to the instruction given to the seven churches in Revelation 2–3. However, it is shorter, for the churches were told, "Let him hear what the Spirit says to the churches." Perhaps reference to the churches is omitted here because the church was raptured prior to the tribulation period (see Revelation 3:10).

If anyone is to be taken captive, to captivity he goes (13:10): This passage speaks of God's perfect justice. Those who are sovereignly destined for captivity (such as the antichrist, the false prophet, and the forces of antichrist) will indeed one day end up as captive forever in the lake of fire. Perfect justice will be rendered.

Here is a call for the endurance and faith of the saints (13:10): The assurance that God will punish evildoers helps to sustain the faith of those who are persecuted during these difficult days (see 1 Peter 2:19-24). As the saints patiently endure, they can rest assured that vengeance is God's (Romans 12:19).

Major Themes

1. *God's sovereign allowance.* We often witness God's sovereign allowance of prophetic events, as in Revelation 13:5. Revelation 6:4 tells us that the rider of the red horse "was permitted to take peace from the earth," and in verse 8, the rider of the pale horse was "given authority over a fourth of the earth, to kill with sword and with famine." Revelation 7:2 refers to "four angels who had been given power to harm earth and sea." Revelation 9:5 tells us that demonic spirits "were allowed to torment" earth dwellers for five months.

2. *Satan, the antichrist, and godhood.* The antichrist takes on the character of the one who energizes him (Satan). Just as Lucifer (Satan) aspired to make himself like God in Isaiah 14:13-14, so the antichrist proclaims himself to be God

(2 Thessalonians 2:4). Just as Lucifer was judged for his pretense to godhood (Ezekiel 28:17), so will the antichrist (Revelation 19:20).

3. *Satan, the antichrist, and murder.* Jesus speaks of the devil's character in John 8:44: "He was a murderer from the beginning." The devil empowers the antichrist, who shares his murderous nature (see Revelation 13:7).

Digging Deeper with Cross-References

War on the saints—Daniel 7:23-25; 8:25; Matthew 24:15-22; Revelation 6:9-11; 11:7; 17:14.

The book of life—Revelation 3:5; 17:8; 20:12,15; 21:27.

Christ the Lamb—Isaiah 53:7; John 1:29; 1 Corinthians 5:7; 1 Peter 1:19; Revelation 7:9.

Life Lessons

1. *Obey God.* In every age, God appeals to all who will "hear"—that is, those who receive His message and act on it (see Matthew 11:15; 13:9,43; Mark 4:9,23; Luke 8:8; 14:35). As James put it, "Be doers of the word, and not hearers only, deceiving yourselves" (James 1:22). Obedience to God's Word is nonnegotiable.

2. *Satan's attack against Christians.* Satan will attack God's people during the tribulation period, and he spiritually attacks Christians today. God gives us instructions on overcoming this diabolical enemy. He provides spiritual armor for our defense (Ephesians 6:11-18). We are told, "Resist the devil, and he will flee from you" (James 4:7). We are to "stand firm" against the devil (Ephesians 6:13-14). We should be aware of Satan's strategies (2 Corinthians 2:11; 1 Peter 5:8). We should depend on the Holy Spirit, all the while remembering John's comforting words: "He who is in you is greater than he who is in the world" (1 John 4:4). As well, God has assigned His angels to watch over us (Psalm 91:9-11).

Questions for Reflection and Discussion

1. Your name was written in God's book of life before the world was even created. How does this make you feel? Does it give you a sense of security in your salvation?

2. Are you suffering any guilt or shame in your life? Did you know there is a close connection between these emotions and a failure to obey God's Word? Faithfulness to God's Word is a key to emotional stability.

The Rise of the False Prophet

Revelation 13:11-14

Scripture Reading and Insights

Begin by reading Revelation 13:11-14 in your favorite Bible. As you read, remember that God's Word is the true source of hope (Psalm 119:81).

In the previous two readings, we learned much about the antichrist. Now let's find out about his first lieutenant—the false prophet. With your Bible still accessible, consider the following insights on the biblical text, verse by verse.

Revelation 13:11

I saw another beast rising out of the earth (13:11): Many false prophets will emerge on the religious landscape in the end times (Matthew 24:4-5,24). Such prophets are mouthpieces of Satan, spreading doctrines of demons (1 Timothy 4:1). We are about to see that during the tribulation period, one supreme false prophet will emerge who will be the antichrist's "right-hand man."

The antichrist will primarily be a military and political leader, and the false prophet will primarily be a religious leader. In fact, we might say that a diabolic trinity will emerge during the tribulation period— the antichrist (the first beast), the false prophet (the second beast), and Satan (the dragon), each with a distinctive role.

Today's passage in Revelation reveals that the false prophet will control religious affairs on earth and will be motivated by Satan (verse 11). He will promote the worship of the antichrist (verse 12) and will execute those who refuse (verse 15). He will control commerce to enforce worship of the antichrist (verse 17). He will perform apparent signs and miracles (verse 13) and will promote deception and false doctrine (verse 14).

Verse 11 describes the false prophet as "another beast." The Greek word for "another" is *allos*, meaning "another of the same kind." Together, this beastly duo will wreak havoc on the earth for seven years.

The second beast rising "out of the earth" is a subject of much discussion. Some expositors suggest that the antichrist will be a Gentile who emerges out of the "sea" of nations (verse 1), but the false prophet will be a Jew. My friend David Reagan explains.

> Just as the sea is used symbolically in prophecy to refer to the Gentile nations, the land (or earth) is used to refer to Israel. This does not mean the False Prophet will be an Orthodox Jew. It only means that he will be of Jewish heritage. Religiously, he will be an apostate Jew who will head up the One World Religion of the Antichrist."[1]

Other Bible expositors, including my former mentor John F. Walvoord, say this is reading too much into the word "earth."

> While the first beast was a Gentile, since he came from the entire human race as symbolized by "the sea" (v. 1), the second beast was a creature of the earth. Some have taken this as a specific reference to the Promised Land and have argued that he was therefore a Jew. There is no support for this in the context as the word for "earth" is the general word referring to the entire world…Actually his nationality and geographic origin are not indicated.[2]

Still other Bible expositors believe that the phrase "rising out of the earth" could relate to rising out of the abyss that lies below the earth. The abyss is the bottomless pit, the abode of demons. It is suggested that perhaps the false prophet will be energized by a powerful demon from below.

In view of the diversity of opinions, it is wise to not be overly dogmatic on the issue.

It had two horns like a lamb (13:11): The antichrist will have ten horns (Revelation 13:1). Horns indicate dominion, so we can infer that the false prophet will have less authority than the antichrist. He will be like a lamb in the sense that he will be more meek and gentle in his dealings with others. Notice that this is the only verse in Revelation where the term "lamb" does not refer to Jesus Christ.

It spoke like a dragon (13:11): True prophets are inspired by the Holy Spirit, but the false prophet is inspired by the *un*holy spirit—the dragon, or Satan.

We can infer from Scripture that the false prophet will be a gifted communicator—particularly adept at inspiring commitment to the false world religion and to the antichrist. John Phillips explains:

> The role of the False Prophet will be to make the new religion appealing and palatable to men…The dynamic appeal of the False Prophet will lie in his skill in combining political expediency with religious passion, self-interest with benevolent philanthropy, lofty sentiment with blatant sophistry, moral platitude with unbridled self-indulgence. His arguments will be subtle, convincing, and appealing. His oratory will be hypnotic, for he will be able to move the masses to tears or whip them into a frenzy. He will control the communication media of the world and will skillfully organize mass publicity to promote his ends. He will be the master of every promotional device and public-relations gimmick. He will manage the truth with guile beyond words, bending it, twisting it, and distorting it. Public opinion will be his to command. He will mold world thought and shape human opinion like so much potter's clay. His deadly appeal will lie in the fact that what he says will sound so right, so sensible, so exactly what unregenerate men have always wanted to hear.[3]

Revelation 13:12

It exercises all the authority of the first beast in its presence (13:12): The source of authority for both the false prophet and the antichrist is Satan. Both are empowered by this diabolical spirit. And the authority of the false prophet is a delegated authority—that is, he speaks on behalf of the antichrist.

Makes the earth and its inhabitants worship the first beast (13:12): This is the goal of the false prophet. In his efforts to move the entire world to worship the antichrist, this second beast will be the epitome of a false prophet because he will point to a god other than the Creator.

People will worship the antichrist because they will believe he was raised from the dead, just as Jesus Christ was. We have seen that Satan will engage in a limited grade-B miracle in healing a wounded (but not dead) antichrist, or he will engage in some kind of masterful deception or perhaps a combination of both. The antichrist will appear to have been resurrected, and people therefore worship him.

Revelation 13:13-14

It performs great signs (13:13): We have seen that Satan, the energizer of the antichrist and the false prophet, cannot perform grade-A miracles the way God does. He can only perform grade-B miracles, but those are nonetheless impressive. He empowers the false prophet to perform these kinds of miracles (see Exodus 7:11; 2 Timothy 3:8). People will be mesmerized into worshiping Satan's substitute for Christ, the antichrist (see Daniel 9:27; 11:31; 12:11; Matthew 24:15).

The word "performs" is a present tense in the Greek. This indicates the false prophet will engage in one miraculous sign after another. People will be impressed.

The miracles are "great." The Greek word indicates that which is outstanding, significant, important, or prominent. The signs performed by the false prophet will seem similar to those of prophets like Elijah (1 Kings 18:38; 2 Kings 1:10-15) and God's two prophetic witnesses (Revelation 11:5).

By the signs…it deceives those who dwell on earth (13:14): These miraculous signs are designed to deceive people. The Greek word for "deceive" (*planaw*) literally means "to lead astray, cause to wander, mislead." The word is often used in the Bible in connection with false teachers who lead people into false forms of worship (2 Thessalonians 2:9-12).

Of course, Satan is a master deceiver. His deception is rooted in his character. John 8:44 affirms, "When he lies, he speaks out of his own character, for he is a liar and the father of lies." The word "father" is used here metaphorically of the originator of a family or company of persons animated by a deceitful character. Satan was the first and greatest liar. All who follow his lead—including the false prophet—are deceivers as well.

Telling them to make an image for the beast that was wounded by the sword and yet lived (13:14): The deception will be so enormous that humans willingly make an image for the beast. This image of the antichrist will be placed in the Jewish temple at the midpoint of the tribulation period (see Matthew 24:15).

The apostle Paul earlier revealed that the antichrist himself will sit in God's temple (see 2 Thessalonians 2:4) and receive worship that properly belongs only to God. Some suggest that when the antichrist is not present in the temple, an image of him will be placed there to provide an object of worship in his absence (see Revelation 14:9,11; 16:2; 19:20; 20:4).

Major Themes

1. *The significance of signs.* The Greek word translated "sign," *semeion*, carries the idea of "a miracle with a message." A sign is a miracle that attests to something. Jesus' signs (miracles) attested that He was who He claimed to be (John 2:11; 4:54; 6:2; 12:18). The apostles' signs (miracles) attested that they were genuine messengers of God (Hebrews 2:3-4). The unspoken assumption is this: Where miracles are, there God is. The false prophet's signs are deceptive. They seem to support the antichrist's claim

to deity. However, these are "false signs and wonders" (2 Thessalonians 2:9).

2. *Satan, the arch-deceiver of humanity.* Satan has long sought to bring about the ruin of humankind through deception. He does this in many ways. He distorts the Scriptures (Genesis 3:4-5; Matthew 4:6). He schemes to outwit humans (2 Corinthians 2:11). He masks himself by appearing as an angel of light (2 Corinthians 11:14). He is a master "deceiver of the whole world" (Revelation 12:9).

Digging Deeper with Cross-References

Fire from heaven—Genesis 19:24-25; Exodus 9:23-24; 2 Kings 1:9-12; Luke 9:51-55; Revelation 8:1-9; 11:5.

Earth and its inhabitants—Psalm 33:14; Isaiah 26:9,21; 40:22; Jeremiah 25:29-30; 46:8; Lamentations 4:12; Daniel 4:35; Zephaniah 1:18; Micah 7:13.

Life Lessons

1. *Submission to the lordship of Christ.* During the tribulation period, most of the world will submit to the authority of the antichrist and the false prophet (Revelation 13:12). You and I are always to submit to the authority and lordship of Jesus Christ. Jesus has complete authority in heaven and earth (Matthew 28:18; John 3:35). He is the Creator and Sustainer of the universe (Colossians 1:16-17) and is thus sovereign over it (Hebrews 1:3). He calls you and me to always obey Him (John 10:27; 14:15; 15:14).

2. *Christians can be deceived.* Revelation 13:14 says that those who dwell on the earth will be deceived. Did you know that God's people can be deceived as well? Ezekiel 34:1-7 affirms that God's sheep can be led astray by wicked shepherds. Jesus warned His followers to beware of false prophets who may appear to be good on the outside but on the inside are dangerous (Matthew 7:15-16).

Why would Jesus warn His followers to beware if they could not possibly be deceived? (See also Acts 20:28-30; 2 Corinthians 11:2-3; Ephesians 4:14; 2 Timothy 4:3-4.) Christians who are not grounded in biblical truth are especially vulnerable.

Questions for Reflection and Discussion

1. Why is consistent submission to the authority and lordship of Christ so critically important?

2. How much time do you spend each week reading and meditating on the Word of God? How does that compare with other activities, such as watching TV?

The False Prophet's Exaltation of the Antichrist

Revelation 13:15-18

Scripture Reading and Insights

Begin by reading Revelation 13:15-18 in your favorite Bible. As you read, remember that God's Word is the true source of hope (Psalm 119:81).

In yesterday's reading, we were introduced to the false prophet. Now let's find out about his global mission to exalt the antichrist. With your Bible still accessible, consider the following insights on the biblical text, verse by verse.

Revelation 13:15

It was allowed to give breath to the image of the beast (13:15): Some Bible expositors believe the antichrist's image will breathe and speak mechanically, like some robots today. Others say that some kind of hologram may be employed. Satan certainly has great intelligence and could likely accomplish this sort of thing. Still others see something more supernatural going on here. J. Hampton Keathley offers this explanation:

> We are told that the false prophet is able to give breath to the image. This gives it the appearance of life. However, it isn't *real* life but only breath. Since breath or breathing is one of the signs of life, men think the image lives, but

John is careful not to say that he gives life to the image. Only God can do that. It is something miraculous, but also deceptive and false…Then we are told the image of the beast, through this imparted breath, speaks. This is to be a further confirmation of the miraculous nature of the beast's image. Some might see this as the result of some product of our modern electronic robot-type of technology. But such would hardly convince people of anything spectacular. Evidently it will go far beyond that.[1]

Christian scholars may differ on the specifics, but the apparent animation of the image sets it apart from typical Old Testament idols. "The idols of the nations are silver and gold, the work of human hands. They have mouths, but do not speak; they have eyes, but do not see" (Psalm 135:15-16). "Woe to him who says to a wooden thing, Awake; to a silent stone, Arise! Can this teach? Behold, it is overlaid with gold and silver, and there is no breath at all in it" (Habakkuk 2:19).

That the image of the beast might even speak and cause those who would not worship the image of the beast to be slain (13:15): The ultimate goal of the false prophet's supernatural acts is to induce people around the world to worship the antichrist. Because the antichrist puts himself in the place of Christ, the antichrist seeks worship, just as Jesus was worshiped many times during His three-year ministry on earth (Matthew 2:11; 28:9,17; John 9:38; 20:28).

Exodus 34:14 instructs us, "You shall worship no other god, for the LORD, whose name is Jealous, is a jealous God." When the antichrist demands worship, he places himself in the position of deity. Those who refuse to worship him are slain.

Revelation 13:16-17

It causes all…to be marked on the right hand or the forehead (13:16): Followers of both the antichrist and Christ will have identifying marks during the tribulation period. Christ's 144,000 Jewish witnesses will be supernaturally marked on their foreheads (Revelation 14:1). It would seem that the antichrist's "mark of the beast" is a parody of God's sealing of these 144,000 witnesses.

Receiving the mark of the beast is a serious business, for Revelation 14:9-11 affirms that those who do so will be on the receiving end of God's wrath and will be tormented with fire forever and ever. Even before they die, however, they also suffer painful sores (Revelation 16:2). Such words are sobering. Any who express loyalty to the antichrist and his cause will suffer the wrath of our holy and just God (see Psalm 75:8; Isaiah 51:17; Jeremiah 25:15-16).

By contrast, Revelation 20:4 reveals that believers in the Lord Jesus will choose death instead of receiving the mark of the beast. They will be rewarded for their loyalty.

No one can buy or sell unless he has the mark (13:17): This mark will be a commerce passport during the second half of the tribulation period. It will indicate that one is religiously orthodox—as defined by the antichrist and the false prophet. The mark will identify the submissive followers of the beast and worshipers of his image. Those without the mark are labeled as traitors.

A cashless economic system seems to be the means by which the antichrist will control who can buy or sell. After all, if the world economy were still cash-based, people anywhere who possessed cash could still buy and sell. Only in a cashless world with a centralized electronic transaction system would such control be possible.

Someone once said that prophetic events cast their shadows before them. Today the technology is now in place—with supercomputers, the Internet, online banking, and the like—to make possible the economic control of the world. The stage has thus been set for the future dominion of the antichrist.

Even today, certain aspects of our society are already cashless. For example, airlines sell sandwiches during flights, but you can't use cash to buy them. Toll roads use smart technologies to automatically charge credit cards or bank accounts to avoid time-consuming transactions at tollbooths. Paychecks are deposited electronically.

Economists tell us that the amount of real cash in circulation today is about half that used in the 1970s. Why so? Because more and more people are using cashless options, such as credit cards and debit cards. That is the wave of the future. Even checks today are often read by check scanners that instantly transfer money from the payer's bank account to the payee's account.

Presently, more than 70 percent of all consumer payments are electronic, and the writing of checks continues to plummet. More than 2 billion credit cards are used in the United States alone. The nature of how we pay for things is changing drastically. Some financial experts are saying that in the next few years, we may have to pay a surcharge to pay for items with cash.

Technology makes a cashless society convenient and quick. Small chips could soon be injected or implanted beneath the surface of the skin—in the fatty part of one's palm, for example—so that wherever a person goes, the information stored in that chip is accessible. Financial data stored on such a chip would make it easy to just wave one's hand to pay for a bus fare, a toll fare, or a product in a store. Such chips are now being tested at the university level in England.

So, for example, bank transactions and purchases could be electronically enabled for people who submit to receiving the mark of the beast—and disallowed for those who don't.

It is important to differentiate between this technology and the mark of the beast, for the technology itself is not the mark. The mark itself will identify allegiance to the antichrist, but that is separate and distinct from the technology that enables him to enforce his economic system. This mark will be *on* people, not *in* them (like some kind of microchip). It will be on the right hand or forehead and will be clearly visible (perhaps like a tattoo), not hidden beneath the skin. But a microchip might indeed be inserted beneath people's skin as a means of enforcing the mark.

Revelation 13:18

This calls for wisdom (13:18): John says wisdom is required to figure out the number of the beast (Revelation 17:9; see also Daniel 9:22; 12:10). Those in the tribulation period who are able to figure out the beast's number will be able to recognize him for who he really is.

His number is 666 (13:18): Bible interpreters have offered many suggestions as to the meaning of 666. Some believe that inasmuch as seven is the number of perfection, and 777 reflects the Trinity, perhaps 666 points to a being who aspires to perfect deity (like the Trinity) but never attains it. (In reality, the antichrist is just a man, though influenced and possibly indwelt by Satan.)

Others suggest that perhaps the number refers to a specific man—such as the Roman emperor Nero. It is suggested that if Nero's name is translated into the Hebrew language, the numerical value of its letters is 666. Some suggest that the antichrist will be a man similar to Nero of old. Of course, all this is highly speculative. Scripture does not clearly define what is meant by 666. Interpreting this verse therefore involves some guesswork.

One thing is certain. In some way that is presently unknown to us, this number will be a crucial part of the antichrist's identification. Receiving the mark of the beast is apparently an unpardonable sin (Revelation 14:9-10). The decision to receive the mark is an irreversible decision. Once made, there is no turning back.

Receiving the mark signifies approval of the antichrist as a leader and agreement with his purpose. No one accidentally takes this mark. One must volitionally choose to do so with all the facts on the table. It will be a deliberate choice with eternal consequences. Those who choose to receive the mark will do so with the full knowledge of what they have done.

Major Themes

1. *Marks of preservation.* Ezekiel 9:4 speaks of putting a mark on the foreheads of people who are dismayed by abominations. This mark on the forehead was one of preservation, just as blood on the doorposts spared the Israelites from death during the tenth plague in Egypt (see Exodus 12:21-29). In the case of the antichrist, the mark of the beast will be a mark of preservation in the sense that those who receive it will be preserved from famine and martyrdom.

2. *Marks of ownership.* In biblical times, soldiers, slaves, and even temple devotees were commonly branded. Such devotees would have a tattoo indicating ownership by a certain god (compare with Isaiah 44:5). The antichrist's brand, which will be visible on the hand or forehead, will mark people as possessions of the antichrist.

Digging Deeper with Cross-References

Breath—Genesis 2:7; Psalm 135:17; Jeremiah 10:14; 51:17; Habakkuk 2:19.

Mark—Revelation 14:9-11; 15:2; 19:20; 20:4.

Life Lessons

1. *Trust God for provision.* Those living during the future tribulation period will not be able to obtain daily needs without submitting to the antichrist and receiving his mark. Today, you and I as Christians trust our sovereign God for daily provisions (Psalms 33:19; 34:10; Proverbs 30:8; Matthew 6:11; John 6:31).

2. *Pursue wisdom.* Those living during the tribulation period will need wisdom to figure out the number of the beast (Revelation 13:18). Actually, God desires that we all have wisdom on all matters. The Hebrew word for wisdom (*hokmah*) was commonly used for the skill of craftsmen, sailors, singers, administrators, and counselors. *Hokmah* points to the experience and efficiency of these various workers in using their skills. Similarly, a person who possesses *hokmah* in his spiritual life is one who is both knowledgeable and experienced in following God's way. Biblical wisdom involves skill in the art of godly living. Want wisdom? Read the book of Proverbs.

Questions for Reflection and Discussion

1. Have you expressed thanks to God lately for providing for

your food and shelter? Thanksgiving should be a regular component of all our prayers (Psalm 100:4; Ephesians 5:20; Colossians 3:15).

2. Do you possess the kind of wisdom described in the Bible? Have you considered reading through the book of Proverbs three or four times a year (in addition to your other Scripture reading)?

Announcements from Heaven

Revelation 14

Scripture Reading and Insights

Begin by reading Revelation 14 in your favorite Bible. As you read, remember that great spiritual wisdom comes from studying God's Word (Psalm 119:98-104).

In the previous lesson, we saw that the false prophet will exalt the antichrist around the world. In today's reading, we pause for a glimpse of a glorious scene that will take place following the second coming of Christ. With your Bible still accessible, consider the following insights on the biblical text, verse by verse.

Revelation 14:1-5

On Mount Zion stood the Lamb, and with him 144,000 (14:1): These introductory verses provide a preview of what will take place following the second coming. Christ's second coming does not actually occur until chapter 19. However, in his panoramic vision, John sees it here as if it were taking place now. The description of an event as if it were already happening is a Hebrew literary device that indicates assurance that it will happen.

John here witnesses Jesus, the Lamb of God, standing on Mount Zion with the 144,000 Jewish witnesses who evangelized the earth. This is apparently the literal Mount Zion in earthly Jerusalem. Mount

Zion typically refers to the hill in Jerusalem where the Jewish temple was built.

These Jewish witnesses will have had the protective seal of God on them throughout the tribulation (Revelation 7:3-4) so they could not be killed. This means they will still be alive on earth at the end of the tribulation. Following the second coming, they are invited directly into Christ's earthly millennial kingdom (compare with Matthew 25:34).

I heard a voice from heaven (14:2): The identity of the voice is not clear. Some suggest it could be that of Christ (see Revelation 1:15). Others suggest it could be the tribulation martyrs (Revelation 6; 7:9-10). Still others suggest it could be either one angel (Revelation 6:1) or many angels (Revelation 5:11-12; 7:11-12; 19:6). All things considered, I opt for the tribulation martyrs, for verse 3 indicates that they sing a redemptive song, which is quite fitting for redeemed humans.

They were singing a new song (14:3): The new song celebrates God's mercies and victories. It anticipates God's final and glorious redemption, which the saints will soon fully possess (Revelation 21–22).

No one could learn that song except the 144,000 (14:3): Perhaps this is because they alone went through half of the tribulation. They could fully appreciate what the song expressed. That they learn the song implies that someone teaches it to them. Perhaps the martyrs who sing the song in heaven end up teaching it to the 144,000 on earth. (They will all be together soon enough.)

These who have not defiled themselves with women...who follow the Lamb (14:4): As celibates, these men were able to focus their full attention on serving Christ (see Matthew 19:12; 1 Corinthians 7:26-38).

Firstfruits for God and the Lamb (14:4): These 144,000 may be the first of many who will enter directly into Christ's millennial kingdom in their mortal bodies (not yet resurrected). Or perhaps they are like "firstfruit sacrifices" to God, blameless and perfect—the cream of the crop.

In their mouth no lie was found (14:5): These witnesses had told the truth in a tribulation environment filled with deception (Revelation 12:9; 13:14; 19:20).

Revelation 14:6-13

Then I saw another angel directly overhead with an eternal gospel to proclaim (14:6): John shifts to a new scene in his panoramic vision. He sees an angel that flies "directly overhead" so that all people everywhere can hear him. The gospel is eternal in that it has eternal consequences, and it is gospel because it is good news.

"Fear God…worship him" (14:7): The message reveals that God's final series of catastrophic judgments are ready to fall on humankind. The angel calls on its hearers to fear God—to show reverence to Him (see Ecclesiastes 12:13; Luke 12:5). Those who truly fear God seek to obey God and honor Him in the way they live. Fearing God and worshiping Him is the proper response of a creature before his Creator (Nehemiah 9:6; Psalms 33:6-9; 146:6).

Another angel… "Fallen, fallen is Babylon the great" (14:8): The prophetic message from this angel anticipates the fall of Babylon that will be fully described in Revelation 17–18. The repetition of "fallen" points to the certainty and completeness of the coming judgment.

Many have taken the term "Babylon" to metaphorically refer to various cities—from Rome to New York—but it is best to take this as a literal Babylon on the Euphrates River. This is in keeping with the way other geographical references in Revelation refer to real places (Revelation 1:9; 2:1,8,12,18; 3:1,7,14).

Though Babylon is a literal city, it is also a symbol for ungodliness and immorality. Babylon was a literal city that represented anti-God values. In the end times, the rebuilt city will represent the entire worldwide political, economic, and religious kingdom of the antichrist. Our present verse personifies Babylon as a temptress who seduces people to partake of her sin and fornication.

Another angel… "If anyone worships the beast and its image and receives a mark on his forehead or on his hand, he also will drink the wine of God's wrath" (14:9-10): This angel pronounces doom and torment on those who receive the mark of the beast, and he urges believers to remain faithful and not give in to receiving the mark (see Matthew 10:28).

The Greek word for "torment" in this verse is *basanizo*, meaning "to vex with grievous pain," or torture. The same word is used to describe the pains of childbirth (Revelation 12:2), palsy (Matthew 8:6), and suffering in Hades (Luke 16:23,28).

The smoke of their torment goes up forever (14:11): The torment is never ending. The endless smoke points to endless suffering. The punishment in the lake of fire will be eternal (Matthew 25:46; Romans 2:3-9; 2 Thessalonians 1:6-9). The words translated "forever and ever" literally mean "to the ages of the ages." The plural forms reinforce the idea of never-ending duration. This same emphatic construction is used of the eternality of God in Revelation 4:10 and 10:6. The physical torment of the wicked is endless.

Here is a call for the endurance of the saints (14:12): Those who are loyal to the antichrist will be on the receiving end of endless torment, so true believers are called to patiently endure and not give in to the antichrist. Submitting to the antichrist for temporal relief will ultimately end in eternal suffering. It's not an even trade.

I heard a voice from heaven… "Blessed are the dead who die in the Lord from now on" (14:13): The voice John heard is likely that of Jesus Christ (see Revelation 1:10-11; 10:4,8; 11:12; 14:2; 18:4; 21:3). The primary message is that great blessing awaits all martyrs.

Though the Lord Jesus likely speaks the initial words of blessing here, the Holy Spirit also speaks. He affirms that those who die in the Lord will enjoy serene rest (see Hebrews 4:10). This is in noted contrast to the lack of rest of unbelievers, who are tormented forever.

Revelation 14:14-16

A white cloud, and seated on the cloud one like a son of man (14:14): The white cloud John sees is likely a cloud of glory (Daniel 7:13-14; Matthew 24:30; 26:64; Acts 1:9-11). The one like a son of man is the Lord Jesus Christ. "Son of Man" is a common messianic title of Christ (Daniel 7:13-14; Matthew 8:20; 24:30; 26:64; John 5:27).

With a golden crown on his head, and a sharp sickle in his hand (14:14): The crown signifies that Christ will be victorious over the antichrist and his forces. The sickle represents swift and devastating judgment.

Another angel…calling… "Put in your sickle, and reap" (14:15): Christ is not in submission to an angel. After all, Christ Himself created the angels (Colossians 1:16), and they worship Him (Hebrews 1:6). Recognizing that the earth had yielded a large crop of unbelievers, the angel merely affirmed that this crop was now ready to be "harvested" (punished).

He who sat on the cloud swung his sickle (14:16): Just as a sickle easily cuts wheat, so Jesus' sickle easily cuts down the enemies of God.

Revelation 14:17-20

The angel swung his sickle across the earth and gathered the grape harvest (14:19): The judgment spoken of here will apparently take place at the end of the tribulation period. Like some of the preceding verses, this verse is a proleptic description of the coming judgment. That is, it represents something as existing before it actually does.

The winepress was trodden…blood flowed (14:20): In biblical days, grapes were squeezed to get the grape juice out, which was then used for wine. This squeezing took place by putting the grapes into small vats with special floors that were angled toward container jars. Hired workers would literally stomp on the grapes with their bare feet, causing the juice to flow into the jars. This treading upon grapes became a common metaphor for judgment. Instead of grape juice flowing, however, the blood of unbelievers would flow.

Scripture reveals that a final battle in the campaign of Armageddon will take place near Jerusalem, in the Valley of Jehoshaphat. In this final battle, the carnage will be so horrific that the blood will rise up to the height of the horses' bridles (about four and a half feet). The distance (1600 stadia) is about 160 miles.

Major Themes

1. *Harvest and judgment.* The term "harvest" is sometimes used in the Old Testament to point to divine judgment. "Put in the sickle, for the harvest is ripe. Go in, tread, for the winepress is full. The vats overflow, for their evil is

great" (Joel 3:13). Jesus referred to grain harvests in the same way (Matthew 13:30,39).

2. *Believers will endure.* Revelation 14:12 speaks of the endurance of the saints. Other verses speak of the endurance of Christians today. For example, "If God is for us, who can be against us?…In all these things we are more than conquerors through him who loved us" (Romans 8:31,37). "I give them eternal life, and they will never perish" (John 10:28). "Everyone who has been born of God overcomes the world. And this is the victory that has overcome the world—our faith" (1 John 5:4).

Digging Deeper with Cross-References

Mount Zion—2 Samuel 5:7; Psalm 48:1-2; Isaiah 2:3; 24:23; Joel 2:32; Obadiah 17,21; Micah 4:1-2,7.

Singing a new song—Psalms 33:3; 40:3; 96:1; 98:1; 144:9; 149:1; Isaiah 42:10.

Eternal torment in the lake of fire—Matthew 25:41; 2 Thessalonians 1:8-9; Revelation 19:20; 20:10; 21:8.

Life Lessons

1. *Following Jesus.* Like the 144,000, you and I are called to follow the Lamb, regardless of the cost. "If anyone would come after me, let him deny himself and take up his cross and follow me" (Matthew 16:24). Jesus affirmed, "My sheep hear my voice, and I know them, and they follow me" (John 10:27). He stated, "If anyone serves me, he must follow me" (John 12:26). Jesus calls for a life of no compromise.

2. *No deceit.* The 144,000 Jewish evangelists were said to have no deceit. God desires that you and I avoid deceit as well. The Lord detests deceivers (Psalm 5:6). We should keep our lips from telling lies (1 Peter 3:10). God desires truth

(Psalm 51:6), so we ought to always speak the truth (Psalm 120:2; Proverbs 12:17; 14:25; Zechariah 8:16).

Questions for Reflection and Discussion

1. If you were ever accused of being a Christian, would there be enough evidence to convict you?

2. Why do you think God puts such a high priority (in both testaments) on living without deceit?

Day 26

Prelude to the Bowl Judgments

Revelation 15

Scripture Reading and Insights

Begin by reading Revelation 15 in your favorite Bible. As you read, remember that great spiritual wisdom comes from studying God's Word (Psalm 119:98-104).

On day 19, we were introduced to the seventh trumpet judgment, which constitutes the seven bowl judgments. In today's reading, we read of the prelude to the unleashing of these judgments—tribulation martyrs in heaven worshiping and praising God. With your Bible still accessible, consider the following insights on the biblical text, verse by verse.

Revelation 15:1-4

I saw another sign in heaven, great and amazing (15:1): This signifies that God's final series of judgments are about to be unleashed. These "great and amazing" judgments represent the climax of God's holy wrath poured out on God-rejecting humankind, the antichrist, and the false prophet.

Seven angels with seven plagues (15:1): God used angels in the unleashing of the seal and trumpet judgments, and now He does so again in the unleashing of the bowl judgments. The angels are doing the bidding of God (see Psalm 103:20). Bible expositors have noticed similarities between the bowl judgments and the plagues that God inflicted on the Egyptians at the hand of Moses. Just as God severely judged the ancient Egyptians, so God now severely judges the God-rejecting inhabitants of the earth.

The last, for with them the wrath of God is finished (15:1): The last judgments are the worst of all. These bowl judgments are apparently unleashed at the end of the seven-year tribulation period. They unfold rapidly, with each new judgment worse than the former.

I saw what appeared to be a sea of glass mingled with fire (15:2): We saw in Revelation 4:6 that "before the throne there was as it were a sea of glass, like crystal." When Moses and the elders of Israel saw the Lord, "there was under his feet as it were a pavement of sapphire stone, like the very heaven for clearness" (Exodus 24:10).

The fire may indicate that judgment is about to be unleashed on the earth from the throne room of heaven. It could also refer to the fire of God's holiness, which calls for wrath against sin.

Those who had conquered the beast and its image and the number of its name, standing beside the sea of glass (15:2): These are the ones who conquered the antichrist and its image in the Jewish temple and its mark. These are tribulation martyrs who refused to go along with the antichrist and his diabolical agenda. They have "loved not their lives even unto death" (Revelation 12:11).

Harps of God in their hands (15:2): Harps are used in worship. Because of God's awesome deliverance for these martyrs, their response is worshipful (compare with Revelation 5:8).

They sing the song of Moses (15:3): Moses' song of victory seems particularly appropriate for these tribulation martyrs.

> I will sing to the LORD, for he has triumphed gloriously...
> The LORD is my strength and my song, and he has become
> my salvation; this is my God, and I will praise him...I will
> exalt him...In the greatness of your majesty you overthrow
> your adversaries...Who is like you, O LORD, among the
> gods? Who is like you, majestic in holiness, awesome in
> glorious deeds, doing wonders? (Exodus 15:1-11).

Moses brought deliverance to God's people in Old Testament times, and Jesus brings a much greater deliverance to God's people during the tribulation period.

The song of the Lamb (15:3): The song of the Lamb is not recorded elsewhere in Scripture. The song's lyrics seem to be recorded in verses 3-4: "Great and amazing are your deeds, O Lord God the Almighty! Just and true are your ways, O King of the nations!" Notice that the absolute deity of Jesus Christ is affirmed in this song. He is the Almighty, as He amply demonstrates in overcoming the antichrist and his forces on earth.

"Who will not fear, O Lord, and glorify your name?" (15:4): The tribulation martyrs continue to sing. This brings to mind the incomparability of Yahweh in the Old Testament. In the midst of various polytheistic nations and their many gods, Yahweh was often shown to be incomparably great. One of the ways the Old Testament demonstrates this is with a rhetorical question, such as the one we just saw in Exodus 15:11: "Who is like you, O Lord, among the gods? Who is like you, majestic in holiness, awesome in glorious deeds, doing wonders?"

"You alone are holy" (15:4): The tribulation martyrs sing of the holiness of Christ. Jesus is the holy (Luke 1:35) and righteous One (Acts 3:14). He had no sin (2 Corinthians 5:21; Hebrews 4:15) and was holy and blameless (Hebrews 7:26-28) and utterly unblemished (Hebrews 9:14; 1 Peter 1:18-19).

"All nations will come and worship you" (15:4): This will ultimately be fulfilled in Christ's millennial kingdom, which follows the second coming. Christ will physically rule on the throne of David in Jerusalem, and all the nations will come and worship Him.

Revelation 15:5-8

After this I looked, and the sanctuary of the tent of witness in heaven was opened, and out of the sanctuary came the seven angels with the seven plagues (15:5-6): This sanctuary of the tent of witness is apparently the Most Holy Place, in which the ark of the covenant was kept. Once the sanctuary was open, the angels who initiate the horrific bowl judgments, under God's directive, were permitted to exit.

Clothed in pure, bright linen (15:6): This points to holiness and righteousness. Scripture consistently reveals that God's angels are holy. Angels are sometimes called "holy ones" (Job 5:1; 15:15; Psalm 89:7; Daniel 4:13,17,23; 8:13; Jude 14). The word "holy" literally means "set apart." The title "holy ones" is appropriate because God's angels are set apart from sin to God's service. Their service here involves judgment against an unbelieving, unrepentant world.

With golden sashes around their chests (15:6): Scholars have different views as to what this may symbolize. Some suggest it may point to the majesty and glory of these angels. Some relate it to purity. Others relate it to the punitive nature of the angels' mission. In any event, the angels are about to engage in their task.

One of the four living creatures gave to the seven angels seven golden bowls full of the wrath of God (15:7): The four living creatures are apparently cherubim (Revelation 4:6), for they are full of eyes (Ezekiel 1:18). Many believe the word "cherubim" came from a word meaning "to guard." Certainly this meaning fits well with their function of guarding the entrance of Eden (Genesis 3:24). It also fits with the cherubim embroidered on the temple veil that barred entrance into the Most Holy Place (Exodus 26:31; 2 Chronicles 3:14).

Here, as a guardian of God's holiness, one cherub gives the seven bowls to the seven angels who will unleash judgments on an unholy world. These bowl judgments are full of the wrath of our eternal God, appropriate for a God-rejecting and unrepentant world.

The sanctuary was filled with smoke (15:8): Smoke often appears when God is present. For example, Exodus 19:18 tells us that "Mount Sinai was wrapped in smoke because the LORD had descended on it in fire." Some expositors relate this smoke to the cloud of glory that often surrounds God. Exodus 40:34 tells us that "the cloud covered the tent of meeting, and the glory of the LORD filled the tabernacle." First Kings 8:10 reveals that "when the priests came out of the Holy Place, a cloud filled the house of the LORD." Second Chronicles 5:13-14 tells us that the house of the Lord "was filled with a cloud, so that the priests could not stand to minister because of the cloud, for the glory of the LORD filled the house of God" (see also Isaiah 6:4; Ezekiel 11:23; 44:4).

No one could enter the sanctuary until the seven plagues of the seven angels were finished (15:8): This is not said of the earlier seal and trumpet judgments, so we can assume that this display of God's awesome glory within the sanctuary points to the climactic nature of the bowl judgments.

Major Themes

1. *God's eternality.* The eternal nature of God is a common theme in Scripture ("who lives forever and ever"—Revelation 15:7). God is from everlasting to everlasting (Psalm 90:2). He is the Alpha and the Omega (Revelation 1:8) and the "King of the ages, immortal" (1 Timothy 1:17), who abides forever (Psalm 102:27; Isaiah 57:15).

2. *Yahweh's incomparability.* Moses often expressed God's incomparability by negation: "There is no one like the LORD our God" (Exodus 8:10). He also used rhetorical questions: "Who is like you, O LORD, among the gods?" (Exodus 15:11). The implied answer is, no one in all the universe. This was particularly significant in view of Moses' experience with Egypt, which was brimming with false gods. In the tribulation period, God's incomparability will be shown in contrast to the false god of the antichrist (Revelation 15:3-4).

Digging Deeper with Cross-References

"I saw," "I looked"—Revelation 13:1,11; 14:1,6,14; 15:2,5.
Tribulation martyrs—Revelation 6:9-11; 7:9-17; 12:11; 14:1-5,13.
Universal worship of Jesus during the millennial kingdom—Psalms 2:8-9; 24:1-10; 66:1-4; 72:8-11; 86:9; Isaiah 2:2-4; 9:6-7; 66:18-23; Jeremiah 10:7; Daniel 7:14; Zephaniah 2:11; Zechariah 14:9.

Life Lessons

1. *Deliverance from wrath.* We have focused heavily on the wrath of God in this section of Revelation. But remember that God's church—that's you, me, and all believers in

Jesus—are not appointed to this wrath. First Thessalonians 1:10 instructs us to "wait for his [God the Father's] Son from heaven…Jesus who delivers us from the wrath to come." In 1 Thessalonians 5:9 we read, "For God has not destined us for wrath, but to obtain salvation through our Lord Jesus Christ." These verses point to the rapture of the church.

2. *Music and worship.* In our passage we read of harps and singing (Revelation 15:2-3). Musical instruments have long played a pivotal role in the worship of God. Many of the psalms were originally designed for musical accompaniment. Psalm 4 was to be accompanied with stringed instruments. Psalm 5 was to be accompanied with flutes. The psalmist proclaims, "I will praise you with the lyre, O God, my God" (Psalm 43:4). He exults: "I will also praise you with the harp for your faithfulness, O my God; I will sing praises to you with the lyre, O Holy One of Israel" (Psalm 71:22). Indeed, "Praise him with trumpet sound; praise him with lute and harp! Praise him with tambourine and dance; praise him with strings and pipe! Praise him with sounding cymbals; praise him with loud clashing cymbals!" (Psalm 150:3-5). We ought to rejoice at the variety of musical instruments now available for worship.

Questions for Reflection and Discussion

1. Are you living in joyful anticipation as you await the rapture of the church, which could take place at any time? Do you feel you are morally and spiritually prepared?

2. Do you prefer traditional hymns or contemporary Christian music? Do you appreciate both? What do you think are the strengths and weaknesses of each?

The First Four Bowl Judgments

Revelation 16:1-9

Scripture Reading and Insights

Begin by reading Revelation 16:1-9 in your favorite Bible. As you read, remember that reading Scripture can strengthen your faith in God (Romans 10:17).

In yesterday's reading, we focused on a prelude to the seven bowl judgments in which the tribulation martyrs in heaven worship and praise God. Now let's find out what happens on earth when the first four bowl judgments are unleashed. With your Bible still accessible, consider the following insights on the biblical text, verse by verse.

Revelation 16:1-2

I heard a loud voice…"Go and pour out on the earth the seven bowls" (16:1): To review, human suffering will steadily escalate throughout the tribulation period. First are the seal judgments, involving bloodshed, famine, death, economic upheaval, a great earthquake, and cosmic disturbances (Revelation 6). Then come the trumpet judgments, involving hail and fire mixed with blood, the sea turning to blood, water turning bitter, further cosmic disturbances, affliction by demonic scorpions, and the death of a third of humankind (Revelation 8:6–9:21). Then come the increasingly worse bowl judgments, which are introduced in Revelation 16.

We have seen that the seven bowl judgments constitute the seventh trumpet judgment, just as the trumpet judgments constitute the seventh seal judgment. The bowl judgments are the last and most severe of God's judgments to be unleashed on the earth.

The first four bowl judgments target people and lead to increasing misery. The last three judgments are international and lead to the war campaign of Armageddon.

The "loud voice from the temple" was apparently that of God Himself. Recall that in Revelation 15:8, God is in the heavenly temple, and no other heavenly being is permitted to enter it "until the seven plagues of the seven angels were finished." That the voice is loud indicates that the revelation to follow was both important and urgent.

Notice that God instructs the seven angels at the same time. This would seem to indicate that the judgments will fall upon the earth rapidly.

The first angel went and poured out his bowl (16:2): The first angel's bowl brings harmful and painful sores on people loyal to the antichrist. The Greek word for "sores" carries the idea of skin ulcers on the surface of the body. Some expositors wonder whether this could come about as a result of some kind of germ warfare or even radiation poisoning from nuclear weapons. (We have seen that in Revelation 8:7 we are told that "a third of the earth was burned up, and a third of the trees were burned up, and all green grass was burned up.")

Revelation 16:3

The second angel poured out his bowl (16:3): When the second angel poured out his bowl, the sea became like blood, leading to the death and extinction of sea creatures. One will recall that in the second trumpet judgment, the waters were turned into blood, but only one-third of the sea creatures died (Revelation 8:8-9). In the present judgment, all life in the sea is destroyed.

Some Bible commentators view this verse symbolically, referring to the "sea of humanity" dying. However, nothing in the context of this passage indicates that it is symbolic. It would appear that the real sea will become "like the blood of a corpse." This, of course, brings to mind God's first judgment against the Egyptians (Exodus 7:17-21).

Revelation 16:4-7

The third angel poured out his bowl (16:4): Now the rivers and springs of water became blood, just like the sea. This is particularly devastating because there will be no remaining fresh water sources. When God turned the Nile into blood, the people "could not drink the water of the Nile" (Exodus 7:24). Psalm 78:44 puts it this way: "He turned their rivers to blood, so that they could not drink of their streams." People can live for a time without food, but they can't live long without water. This will greatly increase people's suffering during the tribulation.

I heard the angel…"Just are you, O Holy One…you brought these judgments" (16:5): An angel now proclaims the justice of God in the light of these judgments against a Christ-rejecting world. This particular angel is called "the angel in charge of the waters." Scripture sometimes relates angels to various elements of nature. For example, "He makes his messengers winds, his ministers a flaming fire" (Psalm 104:4; see Hebrews 1:7). Revelation 7:1 tells us that four of God's angels hold back the four winds of the earth. Revelation 14:18 mentions an angel who has authority over fire. So it is not surprising to read of an angel of the waters, who apparently has authority over the sea and bodies of fresh water.

The theme of God's justice runs like a thread through the pages of Scripture. Justice is a foundation of God's throne (Psalm 89:14). God always deals with the earth justly (Genesis 18:25). He always judges with righteousness (Psalm 98:9). He stands against injustice (see Deuteronomy 32:4; Job 34:12). This means that as bad as these bowl judgments are, they are just judgments against an unbelieving world. The earth's inhabitants are ripe for such judgment.

"They have shed the blood of saints and prophets" (16:6): The angel continues his affirmation of God's justice in inflicting these judgments. He reveals that being forced to drink blood is an appropriate judgment for these rank unbelievers. After all, they were responsible for shedding the blood of God's people and God's prophets. The punishment thus perfectly fits the crime (see Isaiah 49:26). They took the lives of others, so their own lives were now being forfeit in judgment.

I heard the altar saying… "True and just are your judgments" (16:7):
As if to echo a hearty "amen" to the words just spoken by the angel,
John hears words from the altar. These words were apparently spoken
by the tribulation martyrs—those "under the altar" (Revelation 6:9).
They were among those whose blood was spilled by the evildoers still
on earth. These same martyrs earlier asked God, "O Sovereign Lord,
holy and true, how long before you will judge and avenge our blood
on those who dwell on the earth?" (Revelation 6:10). The wait is over.
Judgment is now falling.

The proclamation "true and just are your judgments" echoes what
we were told earlier in Revelation: "O Lord God the Almighty! Just
and true are your ways" (Revelation 15:3). Later in Revelation, we find
a reaffirmation that God's "judgments are true and just" (19:2). These
judgments are horrible, but they are truly just.

Revelation 16:8-9

The fourth angel poured out his bowl (16:8): Somehow, when the
fourth angel pours out his bowl on the sun, the intensity of the sun's
heat is greatly increased so that it scorches people (compare with Isaiah
24:6; 42:25; Malachi 4:1). Another possibility is that with all the other
judgments that have affected the environment during the tribulation
period, the ozone layer may become so depleted and thin that the sun's
rays become more intense. The combination of no fresh water to drink
and a scorching-hot sun will lead to immense misery.

This seems to be quite the opposite of the fourth trumpet judgment,
in which the sun was darkened (Revelation 8:12). The earth was created to be an ideal environment for humankind, but during the tribulation period it will become a hellish place.

*They were scorched…they cursed the name of God…they did not repent
(16:9)*: Instead of repenting and turning to God, the people who are
scorched on the earth will curse God's name. Just as Pharaoh's heart
became increasingly hardened as judgments fell against Egypt (Exodus
7:13-14,22; 8:15,19,32; 9:7,34-35; 13:15), so the people of the tribulation will become increasingly calloused against God (see Psalm 95:8;
Ephesians 4:18).

Major Themes

1. *Painful sores.* The painful sores of Revelation 16:1-2 are
   reminiscent of God's judgments in Old Testament times.
   During the Exodus account, for example, we read of "boils
   breaking out in sores on man and beast throughout all
   the land of Egypt" (Exodus 9:9). The Lord later warned
   His people of the dangers of disobedience: "The LORD
   will strike you with the boils of Egypt, and with tumors
   and scabs and itch, of which you cannot be healed"
   (Deuteronomy 28:27). Indeed, "The LORD will strike you
   on the knees and on the legs with grievous boils of which
   you cannot be healed, from the sole of your foot to the
   crown of your head" (Deuteronomy 28:35). The righteous
   Job suffered from such a malady at the hand of Satan:
   "Satan went out from the presence of the LORD and struck
   Job with loathsome sores from the sole of his foot to the
   crown of his head" (Job 2:7).

2. *Just judgments.* Have you noticed that people in the
   Bible often seem to receive punishments from God that
   perfectly fit their crimes? Pharaoh tried to arrange for all
   the Hebrew boys to be drowned, but instead Pharaoh's
   army drowned (see Exodus 1:22; 14:28). The evil Haman
   conspired to have Mordecai the Jew hanged, but instead
   he himself was hanged on the very gallows he had built for
   Mordecai (Esther 7:10; 9:6-10). Judgment was pronounced
   against the evil Joab, and the Lord brought "back his
   bloody deeds on his own head" (1 Kings 2:32). Adoni-
   bezek once said, "As I have done, so God has repaid me"
   (Judges 1:7).

Digging Deeper with Cross-References

Holy One—2 Kings 19:22; Job 6:10; Psalms 16:10; 71:22; 78:41;
   Proverbs 9:10; 30:3; Isaiah 1:4; 5:19; 40:25; 43:3,15; Luke
   4:34; Acts 2:27; Revelation 3:7.

Pour out—Psalm 69:24; Jeremiah 6:11; 10:25; Ezekiel 7:8; 14:19; 20:8,13,21; 21:31; Hosea 5:10.

Life Lessons

1. *Calloused hearts.* Even Christians can have calloused or hardened hearts. Psalm 95:8 exhorts God's people, "Do not harden your hearts." Picking up on this theme, Hebrews 3:8 warns, "Do not harden your hearts as in the rebellion, on the day of testing in the wilderness" (see verse 15). Hebrews 4:7 urges again: "Today, if you hear his voice, do not harden your hearts." Just as calloused skin is insensitive, so a calloused heart is insensitive to the things of God. That is a bad place to be in. The best way to avoid a calloused heart is to have regular exposure to God's Word (Psalm 119), be obedient to God (John 14:21; 1 John 5:3), and repent immediately whenever you fall into sin (Acts 3:19). Keep your heart sensitive to the things of God.

2. *Repentance brings relief.* In our text, the people of the earth refused to repent in the face of God's judgments. The truth is, repenting can actually bring relief from God's judgments and discipline. In Jeremiah 18:7-8 God Himself promises, "If at any time I declare concerning a nation or a kingdom, that I will pluck up and break down and destroy it, and if that nation, concerning which I have spoken, turns from its evil, I will relent of the disaster that I intended to do to it." However, if no repentance comes, continued judgment is righteous and just. Do you want to shorten God's disciplines in your life (Hebrews 12:5-11)? If so, develop a lifestyle of repentance.

Questions for Reflection and Discussion

1. Do you ever feel as though you may be insensitive to the things of God? If so, what have you learned in this study that can help you rectify this?

2. Would you say you are a quick responder when repentance is called for? Or do you have a tendency to lag for a while until God brings discipline?

The Fifth, Sixth, and Seventh Bowl Judgments

Revelation 16:10-21

Scripture Reading and Insights

Begin by reading Revelation 16:10-21 in your favorite Bible. As you read, remember that reading Scripture can strengthen your faith in God (Romans 10:17).

In the previous lesson, we learned about the first four bowl judgments. Now let's zero in on the fifth, sixth, and seventh bowl judgments. With your Bible still accessible, consider the following insights on the biblical text, verse by verse.

Revelation 16:10-11

The fifth angel poured out his bowl on the throne of the beast (16:10): The "throne of the beast" is the antichrist's dominion on earth.

Its kingdom was plunged into darkness (16:10): Darkness is associated with God's judgment in Isaiah 60:2; Joel 2:2; Mark 13:24-25.

People gnawed their tongues...cursed God...did not repent (16:10-11): The fresh water supply has been destroyed, the sun has become more intense, and now people affiliated with antichrist's kingdom gnaw their tongues and curse God. This is a picture of relentless misery. But despite the horror of these woes from the hand of God, people's hearts continue to harden, and they refuse to repent. They choose to continue their loyalty to the antichrist instead of turning to the one true God of heaven, who can bring relief. Their minds continue to be blinded by the power of Satan (2 Corinthians 4:4).

And yet there is always time to repent and turn to God. The gospel of the kingdom will be preached even in the midst of this pervasive rejection of God (Matthew 24:14).

Revelation 16:12-16

The sixth angel poured out his bowl on the great river Euphrates (16:12): The Euphrates River—the longest river of Western Asia at almost 1800 miles—begins in modern-day Turkey, heads toward the Mediterranean Sea, turns south and flows more than 1000 miles to eventually converge with the Tigris River, and then flows into the Persian Gulf. Many ancient cities, including Ur and Babylon, were on this river.

To prepare the way for the kings from the east (16:12): Here, at the unleashing of the sixth bowl judgment near the end of the tribulation period, the allied armies of the antichrist will gather for the final destruction of the Jews. The Euphrates River will be dried up, thereby making it easier for the kings of the east to assemble.

"Kings from the east" is more literally "kings from the rising of the sun." Who are these kings? A survey of 100 prophecy books reveals more than 50 different interpretations as to who they are. Some suggest they are the seven kings of Daniel 7 who have submitted to the authority of the antichrist. But prophecy scholar John F. Walvoord offers a different interpretation.

> The simplest and best explanation…is that this refers to kings or rulers from the Orient or East who will participate in the final world war. In the light of the context of this passage indicating the near approach of the second coming of Christ and the contemporary world situation in which the Orient today contains a large portion of the world's population with tremendous military potential, any interpretation other than a literal one does not make sense.[1]

This is what makes the Euphrates River so strategic. This river is the primary water boundary between the Holy Land and Asia to the east.

For this reason, theologian Charles Ryrie observes that "the armies of the nations of the Orient will be aided in their march toward Armageddon by the supernatural drying up of the Euphrates River."[2] (Compare with Isaiah 11:15.)

As for their motivation, these kings will be aware that their suffering is due to the God of Israel. In their perverted thinking, they may resolve that moving against the Jews (whom they view as God's people) will constitute a vengeful attack against God Himself.

I saw…three unclean spirits like frogs (16:13): The goal of the invading coalition will be to once and for all destroy the Jewish people. The entire satanic trinity—Satan (the dragon), the antichrist (the first beast), and the false prophet (the second beast)—will be involved. Demons (the three unclean spirits) who emerge at the behest of the satanic trinity (from their mouths) will summon the kings of the earth.

Why were these demons said to be like frogs? Frogs were ritually unclean (Leviticus 11:9-12,41). Many viewed them as vile, plague-inducing creatures. The demons are thus frog-like in the sense that they are vile and unclean.

They are demonic spirits, performing signs, who go abroad to the kings of the whole world (16:14): The signs performed by these demonic spirits are grade-B miracles (2 Thessalonians 2:9; see also Revelation 13:13-14). The unclean spirits will apparently need this limited miraculous power to cause the kings to journey to Palestine, for they will be thirsty (no fresh water), scorched (from the sun), and covered with sores (16:2). The journey will be painful, but the demons will use their miraculous powers to induce them to make the trek.

Battle on the great day of God the Almighty (16:14): This is another way of referring to the campaign of Armageddon.

"Behold, I am coming like a thief" (16:15): In the midst of judgment and chaos, we find a parenthetical call to surviving believers in Jesus to remain watchful and alert. After all, Christ will come when people least expect Him.

"Keeping his garments on, that he may not go about naked and be seen exposed" (16:15): The backdrop to this odd statement is that in biblical times, a guard who was caught sleeping on the job was stripped of

his clothing, leaving him naked so his disgrace would be evident to all around him. First-century readers would have understood this as a way of saying, "Be watchful and alert!" The one who does so will be blessed.

They assembled them at the place that in Hebrew is called Armageddon (16:16): The word "Armageddon" literally means "Mount of Megiddo" and refers to a location about 60 miles north of Jerusalem. This is the location of Barak's battle with the Canaanites (Judges 4) and Gideon's battle with the Midianites (Judges 7). This will be the site for the final horrific battles of humankind just prior to the second coming.

As we will see in the coming pages, a number of stages will comprise the campaign of Armageddon. It is therefore not one battle or a single event. Armageddon will involve an extended, escalating conflict, and it will be increasingly catastrophic.

Revelation 16:17-21

The seventh angel poured out his bowl...a loud voice (16:17): The loud voice is no doubt from God Himself. Recall that no other heavenly being (aside from God) was permitted to enter the heavenly temple "until the seven plagues of the seven angels were finished" (15:8).

The loud voice of God proclaims, "It is done!" This bowl judgment will at last complete God's wrath on the world. The original Greek carries the idea, "It is now done and will remain done." God's wrath will now be truly over.

There were flashes of lightning...and a great earthquake (16:18): This earthquake will be more severe than all previous earthquakes (see Haggai 2:6; Hebrews 12:26-27; Revelation 6:12; 8:5; 11:13,19). This final earthquake is much like an exclamation point on the previous destructive judgments.

The great city was split into three parts (16:19): Scholars debate whether the great city is Jerusalem or Babylon. Some note that in Revelation 11:8, Jerusalem is "the great city that symbolically is called Sodom and Egypt, where their Lord was crucified." If the great city is Jerusalem, this verse would coincide with Zechariah 14:4, which predicts that an earthquake will change its topography.

Other scholars say that the context in verse 19 seems to infer that the great city is Babylon. The latter part of the verse actually singles out Babylon as a prime target of God's wrath. The destruction of Babylon will be explained in detail in Revelation 17–18. God will act on His earlier promise that Babylon would fall and that the cup of His wrath would be poured out on it (Revelation 14:8,10).

Every island fled away (16:20): The landscape will change dramatically toward the end of the tribulation. This change in topography is apparently to prepare the earth for the millennial kingdom. As we read in Isaiah 40:4, "Every valley shall be lifted up, and every mountain and hill be made low; the uneven ground shall become level, and the rough places a plain."

Great hailstones...fell from heaven (16:21): With each hailstone weighing about a hundred pounds, the damage will be unfathomable. Very little will be left standing following the great earthquake and the apocalyptic hailstorm. Amazingly, despite the destruction, people still refuse to repent.

Major Themes

1. *Unclean spirits.* This is a common designation of demons in the New Testament (see Matthew 12:43; Mark 1:23). Luke 8:29 equates the two terms.

2. *Spirits are often not named.* Spirits are often identified in Scripture simply by their character. Our text refers to "unclean spirits." Scripture also refers to "evil spirits" (Luke 7:21; Acts 19:13) and "deceitful spirits" (1 Timothy 4:1). The Holy Spirit is also identified by His completely different character—holiness (John 14:26).

Digging Deeper with Cross-References

Always be ready—1 Thessalonians 5:2-4; 2 Peter 3:10; see also 1 John 2:28.

Cursing God—1 Kings 21:10,13; Job 1:5; 2:9.

Give God glory—Joshua 7:19; Isaiah 24:15; Jeremiah 13:16; Acts 12:23; Revelation 14:7.

Life Lessons

1. *Don't be unprepared.* God's people are called to be alert and watchful as the end times unfold. First Thessalonians 5:2 warns, "You yourselves are fully aware that the day of the Lord will come like a thief in the night." Verse 4 affirms, "You are not in darkness, brothers, for that day to surprise you like a thief." Second Peter 3:10 likewise affirms, "The day of the Lord will come like a thief." The rapture is imminent (Philippians 4:5), and we don't know the day it will occur. We ought always to be prepared by living righteously every moment.

2. *It is done.* In Revelation 16:17 we read, "It is done!" God's wrath against an unbelieving world is finally over. This reminds us of the wrath of God being poured out on Jesus for our sins at the cross of Calvary. Once Christ's saving work was complete, He uttered those famous words, "It is finished" (John 19:30), which can also be translated "paid in full." Jesus took our individual certificates of debt, listing all our sins, and nailed them to the cross. Our sins have been paid in full so we can be saved (see Colossians 2:14).

Questions for Reflection and Discussion

1. If the rapture were to happen in the next hour, would you be morally and spiritually prepared?

2. What steps can you take so that when He comes for us, you will not be ashamed? (See Luke 9:26; Philippians 1:20; 1 John 2:28.)

3. Your certificate of debt, listing all your sins for your entire life, was nailed to Christ's cross, and your debt was paid in full. How does this make you feel?

The Fall of Religious Babylon

Revelation 17

Scripture Reading and Insights

Begin by reading Revelation 17 in your favorite Bible. As you read, keep in mind that God desires you not only to hear His Word but also to do it (James 1:22).

In yesterday's reading, we witnessed the conclusion of the seven bowl judgments. In today's reading, we see the utter destruction of religious Babylon—the false religious system that will engulf the earth during the tribulation period. With your Bible still accessible, consider the following insights on the biblical text, verse by verse.

Revelation 17:1-6

One of the seven angels...said to me, "Come, I will show you the judgment of the great prostitute" (17:1-2): John wrote the book of Revelation in the order in which the truth was revealed to him. However, the events described are not necessarily all in chronological order. This is the case with Revelation 17, which depicts a scene from the first half of the tribulation.

Revelation 17 focuses on religious Babylon. Verses 1-7 provide a description of religious Babylon. Verses 8-18 interpret the description.

The term "Babylon" in Revelation 17–18 refers to both a literal city along the Euphrates River and a religious/commercial system. It is similar to the term Wall Street, which refers both to a literal street as well as a commercial system.

Why does Babylon represent false religion? In ancient times, the Babylonians believed in many false gods and goddesses and were deeply entrenched in paganism, idolatry, and divination. With such a history, it is not surprising that the false religious system of the tribulation period is identified with Babylon.

Verse 1 refers to a great prostitute. Prostitution is a common and graphic scriptural metaphor for unfaithfulness to God (see Jeremiah 3:6-9; Ezekiel 20:30). The great prostitute here symbolizes the apostate religious system of Babylon—probably apostate Christendom, embracing all those who were left behind at the rapture.

"Who is seated on many waters, with whom the kings of the earth have committed sexual immorality" (17:1-2): This symbolizes the false religion's control over various peoples, multitudes, nations, and languages. The fornication described here refers not to actual sexual sin but rather to idolatry, which is unfaithfulness to the true God (see Revelation 14:8).

"The dwellers on earth have become drunk" (17:2): Just as wine can intoxicate people, so people around the globe will become intoxicated by this false religion. Wine has a controlling influence on people, and this false religion will control people worldwide.

This false religious system apparently emerges into prominence during the first half of the tribulation period. But now, our text informs us, this religious system comes under judgment.

A woman sitting on a scarlet beast that was full of blasphemous names (17:3): The woman is the great prostitute mentioned in verses 1-2. This great prostitute (or blasphemous religion) sits on, or controls, the scarlet beast, who is the antichrist. The color scarlet points to the splendor of the antichrist. The beast's blasphemous names indicate its blasphemous character (see Psalm 74:18; Isaiah 52:5; Romans 2:24; Revelation 13:1,6; 16:9,11,21).

The woman was arrayed...holding in her hand a golden cup full of abominations (17:4): This imagery indicates that this false religious system will be wealthy and will have a glorious outer appearance. Note that in ancient times, prostitutes often dressed extravagantly to seduce men. This false religious system will be adorned so as to lure the people of the world into its religious web. This religious system will be outwardly attractive.

The woman has a golden cup, which on the outside is appealing. Regardless of how beautiful a cup looks on the outside, however, if it contains poison, it is deadly. This false religion will appear good on the outside, but on the inside it will be poisonous (see Deuteronomy 18:9; 29:17; 32:16; Jeremiah 51:7).

On her forehead was written... "Babylon the great, mother of prostitutes" (17:5): Prostitutes in ancient Rome typically wore a headband with their name on it (see Jeremiah 3:3).

I saw the woman, drunk with the blood of the saints (17:6): The woman—the false religious system—is drunk with the blood of the saints and Christian martyrs. This includes the blood of God's two prophetic witnesses (11:10) and all who refuse to receive the mark of the beast (13:15).

Revelation 17:7-18

The angel said... "I will tell you the mystery of the woman" (17:7): Recognizing that John was baffled by what he saw, the angel will provide more information about both the beast (verses 7-14) and the woman (see verses 15-18).

"The beast that you saw was, and is not, and is about to rise" (17:8): The antichrist was alive prior to his mortal wound. Then he was apparently mortally wounded, and now he "is about to rise from the bottomless pit" (see Revelation 13:3-4,12-14). How will the antichrist arise from the bottomless pit? As noted previously, while his body lies apparently mortally wounded, his spirit departs the body and goes to the abyss for a time, perhaps being further instructed by Satan. When the antichrist's physical wound is healed, his spirit ascends out of the bottomless pit and reunites with the supposedly resurrected body.

In this scenario, the antichrist will appear to be physically dead but will not really be dead. Once revived, people will assume that he was resurrected. Having encountered Satan in the bottomless pit, he is invigorated to carry out his anti-God purpose (see chapter 20).

"And go to destruction" (17:8): Fresh from the abyss, and empowered

by Satan, the antichrist will now take a destructive path in the final years of the tribulation period that will ultimately lead to eternal destruction in the lake of fire (see 2 Thessalonians 2:3; Revelation 19:20).

"The dwellers on earth whose names have not been written in the book of life" (17:8): These earth dwellers are characterized by the things of the earth. We might call them worldlings or worldly people. The book of life records the names of the redeemed who will inherit heaven (Revelation 3:5; 13:8; 20:12,15; 21:27; see also Luke 10:20; Philippians 4:3). The names of the worldlings are not in this book.

"Will marvel to see the beast, because it was and is not and is to come" (17:8): These worldlings marvel that the beast was alive, and then supposedly died, and then appeared to come to life again.

"The seven heads are seven mountains on which the woman is seated" (17:9): The seven mountains symbolize the seven kingdoms and their kings, as explained in the next verse. Mountains often symbolize kingdoms in Scripture (Psalms 30:7; 68:15-16; Isaiah 2:2; 41:15; Jeremiah 51:25; Daniel 2:35,44-45; Habakkuk 3:6,10; Zechariah 4:7).

These seven kingdoms are Egypt, Assyria, Babylon, Medo-Persia, Greece, Rome, and that of the antichrist. False paganized religion influenced all these empires—the woman was seated on them all.

"They are also seven kings" (17:10): The seven heads are identified as seven rulers over seven kingdoms—five of which have fallen, one still exists, and one is yet to come. At the time of John's writing, the Egyptian, Assyrian, Babylonian, Medo-Persian, and Greek empires had fallen. Rome still existed in his day. The antichrist's kingdom was yet to come.

He must remain only a little while (17:10): He will be "allowed to exercise authority for forty-two months" (Revelation 13:5)—the last half of the tribulation period.

"The beast...is an eighth but it belongs to the seven" (17:11): The antichrist is both the seventh and the eighth king. He is the seventh king prior to his mortal wound. He is the eighth king after his so-called resurrection. This eighth king "goes to destruction."

"The ten horns that you saw" (17:12): These ten kings who don't yet have power will receive delegated authority under the antichrist during

the tribulation. They will rule "for one hour"—a short time, as we might expect because the reign of the antichrist will also be short-lived (Revelation 13:5).

"These are of one mind" (17:13): These kings will be unanimously committed to serve under the antichrist.

"They will make war on the Lamb" (17:14): In making war against Jesus Christ, they follow the lead of the antichrist, who has always been against Jesus Christ. This war against the Lamb will be waged at Armageddon. It will be a futile endeavor, for the Lamb is the Lord of lords and King of kings. He is sovereign over all things (see 1 Timothy 6:15; Revelation 19:16; see also Deuteronomy 10:17; Psalm 136:3). None can defeat Him.

"The waters that you saw" (17:15): Water was a common symbol for people (Psalms 18:4,16; 124:4; Isaiah 8:7; Jeremiah 47:2). This imagery indicates that this single religious system will influence the entire world.

"The ten horns that you saw, they and the beast will hate the prostitute" (17:16): The antichrist will utilize the false religious system (the prostitute) to initially bring unity to the peoples of the world. Once he has accomplished this purpose, he no longer needs the false religion. He will hate it and dispose of it with the help of his ten lieutenants.

By the middle of the tribulation period, the antichrist now intends to be the sole object of worship. (See Daniel 9:27; 11:26-38; Matthew 24:15; 2 Thessalonians 2:4; and Revelation 13:8,15.)

"God has put it into their hearts to carry out his purpose" (17:17): Even though the antichrist and his ten lieutenants destroy the false religious system, God is actually bringing about His sovereign purposes through them. God will allow the antichrist to come into world dominion—but only for a short time.

"The woman that you saw" (17:18): As noted previously, just as Wall Street is a literal place as well as an economic system, so Babylon refers to both a real city and a false religious system. The woman personifies this false religious system.

Major Themes

1. *God's eternal purpose.* Human history in all its details, even

the most minute, is but the outworking of the eternal purposes of God. What has happened in the past, what is happening today, and what will happen in the future are all evidence of the unfolding of a purposeful plan devised by the wondrous personal God of the Bible (Ephesians 3:11; 2 Timothy 1:9).

2. *God is sovereign over evil.* God sovereignly uses the forces of evil to accomplish His supreme purposes. For example, He allows demonic spirits to gather the kings of the world to assemble for Armageddon (Revelation 16:13-16). He causes wicked armies to engage in friendly fire against each other to destroy them (see Judges 7:22; 1 Samuel 14:20; 2 Chronicles 20:23; Ezekiel 38:21). God's methods are inscrutable. In the end, evil will be defeated and all will be perfect (Revelation 21–22).

Digging Deeper with Cross-References

In the Spirit—Revelation 1:10; 4:2; 21:10.

Prostitution: a symbol of idolatry—Isaiah 23:15-17; Jeremiah 2:20-31; 13:27; Ezekiel 16:17-19; Hosea 2:5; 4:15; 5:3; 6:10; 9:1; Nahum 3:4.

Life Lessons

1. *You can trust Bible prophecy.* Revelation 17:17 affirms that the words of God will be fulfilled. Bible prophecy is trustworthy! The precedent has already been set. We have seen that more than 100 Old Testament prophecies were literally fulfilled in the first coming of Jesus (for example, Genesis 12:3; 49:10; Isaiah 7:14; 40:3; 53; Zechariah 12:10; Daniel 9:24-25; Micah 5:2). Likewise, all the prophecies dealing with the end times will be literally fulfilled.

2. *Called and chosen and faithful.* These three attributes describe believers in Revelation 17:14. You and I were called and chosen by God before the foundation of the

world (1 Peter 1:20). We are also called to be faithful (Proverbs 3:3; Matthew 25:23; Romans 12:12; Revelation 2:10).

Questions for Reflection and Discussion

1. We live in an age of prophetic agnosticism. Many seem unsure about Bible prophecy. In view of what you have learned in our study, do you trust Bible prophecy?

2. Many things in our culture can distract us from God. What steps can you take to beef up your spiritual defenses to ensure faithfulness to God in the face of such distractions?

The Fall of Commercial Babylon, Part 1

Revelation 18:1-8

Scripture Reading and Insights

Begin by reading Revelation 18:1-8 in your favorite Bible. As you read, keep in mind that God desires you not only to hear His Word but also to do it (James 1:22).

In yesterday's reading, we witnessed the destruction of religious Babylon. Now let's find out about the destruction of commercial Babylon—the antichrist's economic headquarters. With your Bible still accessible, consider the following insights on the biblical text, verse by verse.

Revelation 18:1-3

I saw another angel coming down (18:1): This portion of Revelation presents an interesting irony. While the antichrist is preparing his armies to attack Israel (the initial stages of the campaign of Armageddon), God judges and destroys the antichrist's economic headquarters in Babylon along the Euphrates River (see Isaiah 13:19; Jeremiah 50:11-27,40).

This destruction will come on Babylon as a direct, decisive judgment from the hand of God. Indeed, God will settle the score for Babylon's long history of standing against His people of Israel. Just as Babylon showed no mercy to its oppression against Israel in the past, so God will now show no mercy to Babylon during the tribulation. This judgment will apparently occur at the very end of the seven-year tribulation period.

In Revelation 18:1, the angel is said to have great authority, so we can surmise that an important judgment is about to be unleashed.

The earth was made bright with his glory (18:1): This does not necessarily mean that the angel has intrinsic glory. It is more likely that having just come from God's presence in heaven, the angel still shines forth the radiating glory of God. This is similar to what happened to Moses when receiving the two stone tablets of the law. On that occasion, "Moses did not know that the skin of his face shone because he had been talking with God" (Exodus 34:29).

"Fallen, fallen is Babylon the great" (18:2): The dual occurrence of the word "fallen" apparently indicates both the woeful condition of commercial/political Babylon as well as the certainty of judgment (compare with Isaiah 21:9; Jeremiah 51:8).

This is another proleptic announcement—a description of a future action as if it had already occurred. It emphasizes that God's triumph over evil Babylon is an accomplished fact even though its execution is actually yet future (in the seventh bowl judgment).

Religious Babylon is apparently destroyed about halfway through the tribulation period (Revelation 17), but the destruction of economic/political Babylon is apparently at the end of the seven-year period (Revelation 18). Revelation 18:2 describes the city of Babylon as it will be once God finally judges it at the end of the tribulation (see also Isaiah 13:21; 47:7-9; Jeremiah 50–51).

"She has become a dwelling place for demons, a haunt for every unclean spirit, a haunt for every unclean bird, a haunt for every unclean and detestable beast" (18:2): This demonstrates how horrific God's judgment will be. Babylon will become utterly desolate.

"All nations have drunk the wine of the passion of her sexual immorality" (18:3): The words of this verse are quite similar to those in Revelation 17:2. The earlier verse, however, dealt with religious Babylon (a false religious system), whereas our present verse deals with economic/political Babylon. Just as religious Babylon entices the people of the world into committing spiritual fornication (Revelation 17:2,4), so commercial/

political Babylon will entice the unbelieving world into anti-God materialism. In both cases, people will be utterly unfaithful to God.

The imagery seems to indicate that the anti-God political, economic, and commercial system of Babylon will influence everyone on earth—"all nations" and "the kings of the earth." The influence of Babylon will be universal. It will have an octopus-like reach around the world.

"The merchants of the earth have grown rich" (18:3): Because of the commercial success of this city, merchants around the world will become wealthy. Anti-God materialism will be rampant. The city and all that it represents will be ripe for judgment.

Revelation 18:4-8

Another voice… "Come out of her, my people" (18:4): John then hears another voice from heaven—perhaps an angel who speaks for God—urging the faithful to dissociate from Babylon. Otherwise, sin may result, and they may end up being on the receiving end of the plagues that will shortly fall on Babylon (see Isaiah 52:11; 2 Corinthians 6:14-17; 1 John 2:15-17).

If they separate, the implication is that they will receive God's protection (compare with Matthew 24:16; Revelation 12:14). Both Isaiah and Jeremiah called the people of God to leave Babylon (see Isaiah 48:20; Jeremiah 50:8; 51:6-9,45).

Prophecy scholars Thomas Ice and Timothy Demy provide this helpful explanation of how Jews are able to make it out of Babylon before judgment falls on the city:

> When Babylon is destroyed, the Antichrist will not be present in the city. He will be told of its destruction by messengers (Jeremiah 50:43; 51:31,32)…The attack will be swift, but there will be some warning or opportunity for Jews who are living in Babylon to flee from the city (Jeremiah 50:6-8,28; 51:5,6). Even in these last days, God will preserve a remnant of His people. These refugees are to go to Jerusalem and tell them of the city's destruction and their escape (Jeremiah 51:10,45,50; Revelation 18:4,5).[1]

"Her sins are heaped high as heaven" (18:5): Here is the reason why God's people must quickly exit Babylon. Babylon's sins are almost immeasurable. "God has remembered her iniquities"—His patience has now been exhausted. Judgment is about to fall. A righteous and holy God must judge such unrepentant evil.

"Pay her back…repay her double" (18:6): Here we find an echo of the *lex talionis*, the law of retaliation. As Matthew 7:2 put it, "With the judgment you pronounce you will be judged, and with the measure you use it will be measured to you." Galatians 6:7 tells us, "Whatever one sows, that will he also reap."

Babylon had sown evil and is now about to reap evil. Babylon will now receive the payment that it had paid out to others. It will now be on the receiving end of what it had dished out to others (such as the Jews throughout biblical history).

In fact, Babylon will be repaid double. This was a common judicial requirement in Old Testament law (see Exodus 22:4,7,9; Isaiah 40:2; 61:7; Jeremiah 16:18; 17:18; Zechariah 9:12). Babylon's judgment would be thorough, even overflowing.

Such judgment might seem harsh at first glance. One must keep in mind, however, that all the people associated with economic/political Babylon had fallen into such deep wickedness, with no repentance in view, that they were essentially beyond the point of no return in their moral choices. They seemed irrevocably committed to the person and program of the antichrist. They had permanently crossed the line, declaring allegiance for the antichrist and against God. Judgment was thus unavoidable.

"Give her a like measure of torment and mourning, since in her heart she says, 'I sit as a queen'" (18:7): What irony we see in this verse. Though Babylon had been proud, she will now be humbled. Though Babylon enjoyed glory and luxury, she will now be brought low in torment and mourning. Though Babylon had pretended to be a queen, she will now be brought low by the royal King of kings. Babylon had seemed superior in every way, but its moral inferiority will now be judged.

One cannot help but notice that the description of Babylon in this verse bears at least some resemblance to the Laodicean church. Christ said to this church: "You say, I am rich, I have prospered, and I need nothing, not realizing that you are wretched, pitiable, poor, blind, and naked" (Revelation 3:17). Self-delusion is a wretched state.

"Her plagues will come in a single day" (18:8): The people of God must make haste to separate themselves from the evil system of Babylon, for judgment will come suddenly in one day. There will be death and mourning and famine and fire. The collapse of the city will be stunning.

"Mighty is the Lord God who has judged her" (18:8): Babylon had thought itself to be mighty, but the Lord God is truly mighty.

Major Themes

1. *Sin: missing the target.* A key meaning of sin in the Bible is "to miss the target." Sin is failure to live up to God's standards. All of us miss the target. Not one person is capable of fulfilling all of God's laws at all times (Romans 3:23). Some people may be more righteous than others, but all of us fall short of God's infinitely perfect standards. When we sin, God desires repentance and confession (see 1 John 1:9). When people such as those associated with Babylon go deeper and deeper into sin, with no repentance in sight, they become ripe for judgment (see Psalms 9:7; 96:13; Ecclesiastes 3:17; Romans 2:1-5; 1 Thessalonians 5:2-3; 2 Peter 3:7).

2. *God's holiness and human sin.* Human sin shows up in the light of God's holiness (Romans 3:23). This is illustrated in the life of Isaiah. He was a relatively righteous man, but when he saw God in His infinite holiness, his own personal sin came into clear focus: "Woe is me! For I am lost; for I am a man of unclean lips, and I dwell in the midst of a people of unclean lips" (Isaiah 6:5). When we measure ourselves against other human beings, we may come out looking okay. But other human beings are not our moral measuring stick—God is. And as we measure ourselves against God in His infinite holiness and righteousness, our sin shows up in all of its ugliness. God's

judgments fall on unrepentant people in the tribulation period because their sin represents a calloused disregard for God in His holiness. They do not even care that they fall short of God's righteous standards.

Digging Deeper with Cross-References

Flee from evil Babylon—Genesis 19:12; Numbers 16:26; Isaiah 48:20; 52:11; Jeremiah 50:8; 51:6-9,45.

Materialism and riches—Proverbs 15:27; Ecclesiastes 5:10; Jeremiah 17:11; Matthew 6:19-21; 1 Timothy 6:10; James 5:3.

Life Lessons

1. *God forgets our sins.* Revelation 18:5 says that God remembers the sins of the Babylonians. But in the new covenant, God says of those who turn to Him, "I will forgive their iniquity, and I will remember their sin no more" (Jeremiah 31:34). In Hebrews 8:12 God promises, "I will be merciful toward their iniquities, and I will remember their sins no more." Psalm 103:12 proclaims: "As far as the east is from the west, so far does he remove our transgressions from us." It is a wondrous thing to be forgiven of our sins such that God no longer remembers them!

2. *Come out and be separate.* Christians today are called to separate themselves from that which is ungodly. The apostle Paul urges Timothy, "Do not...take part in the sins of others; keep yourself pure" (1 Timothy 5:22). To the Ephesians he writes, "Take no part in the unfruitful works of darkness, but instead expose them" (Ephesians 5:11). And he writes this to the church in Corinth:

   Do not be unequally yoked with unbelievers. For what partnership has righteousness with lawlessness? Or what fellowship has light with darkness? What

accord has Christ with Belial? Or what portion does
a believer share with an unbeliever? (2 Corinthians
6:14-15).

Questions for Reflection and Discussion

1. God has not only forgiven your sins but also forgotten
    them—all based on the work of Christ on the cross. Do
    you find that spiritually motivating? How does it affect
    your level of joy in life?

2. In view of the enticements of Western society, do you
    sometimes find it difficult to "come out and be separate"?
    In what ways?

3. Do you ever struggle with materialism?

DAY 31

The Fall of Commercial Babylon, Part 2

Revelation 18:9-24

Scripture Reading and Insights

Begin by reading Revelation 18:9-24 in your favorite Bible. As you read, stop and meditate on any verses that speak to your heart (Psalm 1:1-3; Joshua 1:8).

In the previous lesson, we saw the destruction of commercial Babylon. Now let's find out how this destruction affects the people of the earth. With your Bible still accessible, consider the following insights on the biblical text, verse by verse.

Revelation 18:9-20

The kings of the earth, who committed sexual immorality and lived in luxury with her, will weep and wail (18:9): The rulers of the earth, with their vested interest in the economic growth of their countries, will grieve and wail—literally, loudly lament—when they witness the collapse of the economic system that had enabled them to live so luxuriously. The collapse of Babylon will indicate to the rulers of the world that the sumptuous empire of the antichrist is utterly doomed. This is devastating news for them, for the antichrist is the source of their own power and wealth.

The "sexual immorality" of these leaders is not to be taken literally but is rather a graphic metaphor indicating that these leaders were intimately connected—prostituting themselves—with the anti-God

224

Babylonian system (see Ezekiel 26:16; 27:30-35). They will witness the smoke of Babylon burning, perhaps indicating that the primary instrument of judgment against Babylon will be fire (perhaps caused by nuclear detonations).

"You great city, you mighty city" (18:10): The world leaders will recognize that Babylon had been great and mighty, but more mighty than the city will be the mighty divine Judge—God Almighty—who brings the city to ruin. No wonder the world leaders will be in fear.

"In a single hour your judgment has come" (18:10): Babylon will fall rapidly. This means that the world leaders, watching from a distance (perhaps by live television and Internet feeds), will have no time to prepare for the calamity or make economic adjustments in order to save their own countries.

The merchants of the earth weep and mourn for her, since no one buys their cargo anymore (18:11): First we are told that world rulers will lament over the fall of Babylon. Now merchants join their lament. Business and government are so intertwined that what affects one affects the other.

Recall from Revelation 13 that no one on earth could buy or sell without having received the mark of the beast. In the chapters that follow in the book of Revelation, it becomes increasingly clear that economic Babylon, as a global system, became the heart and center of economic operations for the antichrist. Now, with the collapse of economic Babylon, the merchants of the earth are no longer able to buy or sell their goods. This means that they themselves become economically ruined.

There is an obvious irony here. Formerly the economic system of the antichrist was such that no one could buy or sell without having received the mark of the beast. Now, however, the economic system itself collapses, and all who are affiliated with this system can no longer buy or sell.

Cargo (18:12-13): The listing of multiple commercial products in verses 12-13 indicates that prior to the fall of economic Babylon, global trade will be extensive. These commercial products include precious metals and gems, clothing, furnishings, spices, food, animals, and even people.

Apparently slavery will continue into the end times. As horrible as it is to think about it, slavery even exists in our own day. In certain parts of the world, for example, young girls are abducted and forced into sexual servitude.

"The fruit for which your soul longed has gone" (18:14): These trade merchants will lose all the luxurious possessions that their eyes of avarice had longed for. Gone forever will be their culinary delicacies and their splendorous clothing. These items are "never to be found again." The Greek contains two double negatives, indicating the absolute certainty and finality of their loss of these items of wealth.

The merchants…will stand far off (18:15): These individuals will be in stunned disbelief at what has happened to Babylon. They are mentally and emotionally unprepared for this catastrophic turn of events, for it happens so very quickly.

"Fine linen, in purple and scarlet, adorned with gold, with jewels, and with pearls!" (18:16): Notice how Babylon as an economic system is described much like Babylon as a religious system was: "The woman was arrayed in purple and scarlet, and adorned with gold and jewels and pearls" (17:4). These words point to the "prostitute" dressing in such a way as to entice people into joining with her. Economic Babylon will likewise entice people to join with her in all of her splendor. But now Babylon is fallen, the splendor is gone, and the economy collapses.

"In a single hour all this wealth has been laid waste" (18:17): The sudden nature of Babylon's fall is reiterated. Babylon is devastated. It will be far worse than the collapse of the stock market in 1929. This event will catastrophically and permanently devastate the global economy and world trade.

Four categories of sea people are affected by this dire turn of events: shipmasters, seafaring men, sailors, and all whose trade is on the sea (such as fishermen and pearl divers). These individuals mourn over what has happened to Babylon. Perhaps the shipmasters, seafaring men, and sailors mourn because they are all involved in the transport and distribution of the merchandise of those affiliated with economic Babylon. Perhaps those "whose trade is on the sea" (such as fishermen and pearl divers) mourn because, like everything else, their goods will no longer be purchased, so they too will fall to economic ruin.

They threw dust on their heads (18:19): In Old Testament times, putting dust on one's head was a common means of expressing great grief. For example, when Job's friends beheld Job's suffering, they put dust on their heads (see Job 2:12). Those who made their living on or in the sea are brimming with grief over the sudden, fatal demise of Babylon. Babylon had been flattened—laid waste—"in a single hour."

"Rejoice over her, O heaven…God has given judgment for you against her" (18:20): Here we witness a change of scenery from earth's perspective to heaven's perspective. In contrast to the grief-ridden earth dwellers, God's people in heaven will respond with exuberant joy when economic Babylon collapses. It is interesting to observe that heaven also rejoiced when ancient Babylon fell (Jeremiah 51:48-49). The times may change, but heaven always rejoices when sin is overthrown. God's people rejoice that God's righteousness and justice prevail.

Notice in our verse that there are three categories of the redeemed in heaven—saints, apostles, and prophets. The word "saints" refers to all believers. All who have become born again are saints (see Philippians 1:1). God's apostles and prophets are in a special category of saints, for they were the instruments of God's revelation to humankind. All of these believers collectively rejoice at the collapse of economic Babylon. God had earlier pronounced His verdict, and now His verdict is executed against Babylon.

Revelation 18:21-24

A mighty angel took up a stone…and threw it into the sea, saying, "So will Babylon the great city be thrown down with violence" (18:21-22): This graphically symbolizes the demise of Babylon in judgment (see Exodus 15:5; Nehemiah 9:11; Jeremiah 51:63-64; Matthew 18:6). In Bible times, millstones were huge, weighing thousands of pounds. They were used to grind grain. When such large and weighty stones are thrown into the sea, they can never be recovered. Similarly, once

Babylon falls in judgment, it will never rise again. Babylon's destruction will be permanent.

Our text includes images that emphasize how completely Babylon is destroyed. Musicians, craftsmen, mills, lamps, bridegrooms…all are gone. The constant hum of a busy city will now be replaced with a deathly silence.

Such judgment against Babylon is justified, for all the nations of the earth had been seduced by its economic system. The seduction is rooted in materialism, the philosophy that wealth and luxury provide meaning in life. God is left entirely out of the picture. Now the city that represents materialism will be materially destroyed.

"In her was found the blood of prophets and of saints" (18:24): Our passage closes with a reason for God's judgment and destruction of Babylon: This city was responsible for slaying God's prophets and His saints. God's people had been martyred because of their testimonies for Jesus. Those associated with Babylon shed the blood of God's witnesses, and now their own blood will be shed in response. God brings about His justice. Vengeance is His (Romans 12:19-21). Economic Babylon falls, and the second coming is imminent.

Major Themes

1. *Expressing grief.* In Bible times, people expressed grief by putting dust on their heads. Joshua and the elders, in fear of the people being destroyed by the Amorites, put "dust on their heads" (Joshua 7:6). When the Israelites were defeated in battle by the Philistines, a man put "dirt on his head," made his way to Shiloh, and informed the high priest Eli that his two sons had been killed (1 Samuel 4:12; see also 2 Samuel 1:2; 13:19; 15:32; Job 2:12; Lamentations 2:10). Some of those who witness Babylon fall during the tribulation period will do the same.

2. *Sudden destruction.* We often find sudden destruction falling on the wicked in the Bible. Proverbs 6:15 warns, "Therefore calamity will come upon him suddenly; in a

moment he will be broken beyond healing." Proverbs 24:22 warns that disaster "will arise suddenly." Isaiah 47:11 warns that "ruin shall come upon you suddenly, of which you know nothing." God affirms in Jeremiah 15:8, "I have made anguish and terror fall upon them suddenly." In 1 Thessalonians 5:3, the apostle Paul warns: "While people are saying, 'There is peace and security,' then sudden destruction will come upon them as labor pains come upon a pregnant woman, and they will not escape."

Digging Deeper with Cross-References

Great city—Revelation 11:8; 14:8; 16:19; 17:18.

Rising smoke—Genesis 19:28; Isaiah 34:10.

"Saints" in the book of Revelation—Revelation 5:8; 8:3-4; 11:18; 13:7,10; 14:12; 16:6; 17:6; 19:8; 20:9.

Life Lessons

1. *Wealth and luxury.* Scripture reveals that wealth is fleeting. We are told that "riches do not last forever" (Proverbs 27:24). All people die, and at death they "leave their wealth to others" (Psalm 49:10). King Solomon lamented, "I hated all my toil in which I toil under the sun, seeing that I must leave it to the man who will come after me" (Ecclesiastes 2:18). The apostle Paul affirms that "we brought nothing into the world, and we cannot take anything out of the world" (1 Timothy 6:7). Such factors ought to influence the way we think about wealth and luxury.

2. *Your citizenship.* The earth dwellers who live during the tribulation period will be "citizens of Babylon" even though they may not live in the actual city. They will be citizens there because they live according to its anti-God and materialistic values. You and I, even though we live in different cities on earth, are citizens of heaven. The apostle

Paul said, "Our citizenship is in heaven, and from it we await a Savior, the Lord Jesus Christ" (Philippians 3:20). Paul also said that we are "fellow citizens with the saints and members of the household of God" (Ephesians 2:19). We are pilgrims passing through on earth, on our way to another country, another land, another city (Hebrews 11:16). And we are to behave here below as citizens of that city above.

Questions for Reflection and Discussion

1. What is your attitude toward wealth and the possession of material things?

2. Can you possess wealth without wealth possessing you? If you suddenly lost your wealth, how would it affect you?

3. Do you live more like a citizen of earth or like a citizen of heaven?

Shouts of Hallelujah and the Marriage Supper of the Lamb

Revelation 19:1-10

Scripture Reading and Insights

Begin by reading Revelation 19:1-10 in your favorite Bible. As you read, stop and meditate on any verses that speak to your heart (Psalm 1:1-3; Joshua 1:8).

In the previous two readings, we witnessed the destruction of commercial Babylon and its effect on the entire earth. In today's reading, we focus on an outbreak of praise in heaven. With your Bible still accessible, consider the following insights on the biblical text, verse by verse.

Revelation 19:1-3

After this I heard...a great multitude in heaven, crying out, "Hallelujah" (19:1): The phrase "after this" tells us that what now takes place follows the destruction of Babylon, just prior to the second coming of Christ.

John hears a "loud voice" of a great multitude offering praise in heaven (see Revelation 7:9-10). The imminent second coming of Christ may be among the reasons for this eruption of praise.

"His judgments are true and just" (19:2): This is another reason for the outbreak of praise in heaven. God's people yearn for God's holy and true judgments against sin and rebellion. Recall that in Revelation 6:10 the souls of the martyrs that were under God's altar cried out with a

loud voice, "O Sovereign Lord, holy and true, how long before you will judge and avenge our blood on those who dwell on the earth?" Now that God has brought about this just judgment, praise erupts in heaven.

Once more they cried out, "Hallelujah!" (19:3): The multitude exclaims again, for Babylon has justly been destroyed. The rising smoke represents the effects of the fire that will destroy Babylon (Revelation 17:16; 18:8-9,18). This smoke "goes up forever and ever," symbolizing that Babylon's destruction will be permanent. One of the more sobering aspects of Scripture is that the enemies of God will be punished forever and ever.

Revelation 19:4-5

The twenty-four elders and the four living creatures fell down and worshiped God (19:4): Recall that the 24 elders apparently represent the church. The four living creatures are apparently cherubim. Both groups now fall down and worship God on the throne. Cherubim often seem to be associated with worship in the book of Revelation (4:8,11; 5:9-12,14; 11:16-18).

From the throne came a voice saying, "Praise our God" (19:5): It is apparently a voice of an angel that calls out, inviting all who serve God—regardless of their rank, position, or heavenly status ("small or great")—to participate in praising God (compare with Psalms 113:1; 115:13).

Revelation 19:6-8

The voice of a great multitude, like the roar of many waters and like the sound of mighty peals of thunder (19:6): The proclamation sounds like Niagara Falls and a Texas thunderstorm.

"Hallelujah! For the Lord our God the Almighty reigns" (19:6): The term "Almighty" is a common title for God in the book of Revelation (1:8; 4:8; 11:17; 15:3; 16:7,14; 21:22).

The acclamation that God reigns should not be taken to mean that He has just started to reign. The verse simply means that God is now about to actively and sovereignly overthrow the thrones of earthly kings, the antichrist, and Satan. God's sovereign kingship is about to kick into high gear. God's will is now going to be done on earth as it has been in heaven!

Of course, a new aspect of God's reign will soon be established on earth. In Christ's millennial reign, He will rule from the actual throne of David in Jerusalem, in fulfillment of the Davidic covenant (2 Samuel 7:12-13). The whole planet will become a theocracy.

"Let us rejoice and exult...the marriage of the Lamb has come" (19:7): Heaven's inhabitants are now invited to rejoice and exult over the imminent marriage of the Lamb. Scripture often refers to the relationship between Christ and the church as a marriage (see Matthew 9:15; 22:2-14; 25:1-13; Mark 2:19-20; Luke 5:34-35; 14:15-24; John 3:29). The church is pictured as a virgin bride awaiting the coming of her heavenly Bridegroom (2 Corinthians 11:2; Ephesians 5:22-33). While she waits, she keeps herself faithful and pure, unstained from the world.

This wedding metaphor plays out in three parts. First, the Hebrew bride is betrothed to the bridegroom. This is certainly true of the church's relationship to Jesus Christ. As individuals come to salvation today, they become a part of the church, the bride of Christ, betrothed to Christ the Bridegroom.

In the second part of the wedding metaphor, the Hebrew bridegroom comes to claim his bride. Jesus the Bridegroom will come to claim His bride at the rapture, at which time He takes His bride to heaven, the Father's house, where He has prepared a place to live (John 14:1-3). The marriage of Christ and the church will take place in heaven sometime after the church has been raptured, prior to the second coming. (I will discuss the third part of the wedding metaphor shortly.)

"It was granted her to clothe herself with fine linen" (19:8): Arnold Fruchtenbaum suggests that the marriage ceremony takes place after the judgment seat of Christ, for the bride is portrayed as wearing white linen.

> The marriage...must take place after the judgment seat of Messiah...for the bride is viewed as being dressed in white linen...Thus, following the rapture of the church in which the Bridegroom brings the bride with Him to His home,

and following the judgment seat of Messiah which results
in the bride having the white linen garments, the wedding
ceremony takes place.[1]

The brightness of the fine linen indicates divine glory. Its purity
indicates that all remnants of sin are now gone. The bride is utterly
pure. Believers in their glorified resurrection bodies will no longer have
a sin nature, so the church is dressed appropriately in "fine linen, bright
and pure." The garment will be positively dazzling.

"The fine linen is the righteous deeds of the saints" (19:8): This does
not refer to the imputed righteousness of Christ that is given to Christians at the moment of conversion (Romans 3:28; 5:1-2; Galatians
2:16). Rather, it refers to the acts that grow out of that imputed righteousness (Ephesians 2:10; 2 Corinthians 5:10; James 2:17-18). That is,
believers on earth will engage in external righteous acts that reflect an
inner transformation. The white garments thus signify that the church
faithfully and habitually does righteous works in dependence on the
Holy Spirit (see Galatians 5:22-23) and thus is worthy of reward at the
judgment seat of Christ.

Revelation 19:9-10

"Blessed are those invited to the marriage supper of the Lamb" (19:9):
The third part of the Hebrew wedding metaphor is the marriage supper, which was a feast that lasted several days. The marriage supper of
the Lamb—yet future from the vantage point of this verse—apparently
takes place on earth after the tribulation period but before the millennial kingdom. (Daniel 12:11 reveals that there will be a 75-day interim
period between the end of the tribulation period and the beginning of
the millennial kingdom.)

The guests of the marriage supper of the Lamb are blessed. What a
wondrous privilege it will be. The guests will include all believers who
were saved prior to the day of Pentecost (the day the church was born).
Like the church (the bride of Christ), these believers will be given glorified resurrection bodies and will participate in Christ's millennial rule.
Also included among the guests are those who become believers during

the tribulation and were not killed. They will enter into Christ's millennial kingdom in their mortal bodies. (These will be given resurrection bodies following the millennial kingdom.)

"These are the true words of God" (19:9): Biblical prophecy can be trusted! Whatever is recorded in the pages of the Bible will surely come to pass. The Bible is the Word of God, so what the Bible says, God says.

"Worship God" (19:10): John was so overwhelmed by the glorious angel that spoke to him, his natural inclination was to bow down and worship it. The angel promptly instructed John not to worship him. To worship any person or object other than God is a form of idolatry (Exodus 20:3-5). The angel told John to worship God alone.

Angels are indeed glorious and awesome-looking creatures, far more so than anything humans are accustomed to seeing on earth. When Daniel saw an angel, he was left without strength (Daniel 10:8). Zechariah was gripped with fear when an angel appeared to him while he was in the temple (Luke 1:12). The shepherds in the field were very afraid when an angel appeared to them (Luke 2:9). The Roman soldiers trembled with fear and became as dead men when an angel appeared and rolled back the stone blocking Jesus' tomb (Matthew 28:2-4).

Angelic appearances in biblical times were so awesome and so glorious, people naturally responded with fear, trembling, and sometimes even worship. However, Scripture consistently emphasizes that humans are never to worship God's angels.

Apparently the church at Colossae had fallen into this error, because when the apostle Paul wrote to them, he included a prohibition against the worship of angels (Colossians 2:18). God's holy angels themselves refuse worship and affirm that God alone is worthy of such honor (see Revelation 22:8-9). Of course, God explicitly commands that only He is to be worshiped.

The testimony of Jesus is the spirit of prophecy (19:10): The verse indicates that the very nature or purpose of prophecy is to testify of Jesus Christ and to bring glory to Him. The Bible is a Jesus book. The entire Old Testament prophetically anticipates Jesus Christ. The four Gospels speak of the actual manifestation of Jesus Christ. The epistles speak of how the church is to live in view of Jesus Christ. The book of Revelation prophesies of the second coming and reign of Jesus Christ. The Spirit of Christ is involved in the actual proclamation of prophecy (see 1 Peter 1:12).

Major Themes

1. *Praise.* Like the redeemed humans and angels in heaven, we should always have praise for God on our lips (Psalm 34:1). We should praise God in the depths of our heart (Psalm 103:1-5,20-22) and continually "offer up a sacrifice of praise to God" (Hebrews 13:15). One means of praising God is through spiritual songs (Psalm 69:30).

2. *Worship.* We ought to always bow down in worship before the Lord our Maker (Psalm 95:6). We are to "worship him who made the heaven and earth, the sea and the springs of water" (Revelation 14:7). We should worship Him with "reverence and awe" (Hebrews 12:28) and worship Him alone (Deuteronomy 5:7).

Digging Deeper with Cross-References

Praise in the book of Revelation—Revelation 4:8,11; 5:9-14; 7:10-17; 11:15-18; 15:3-4; 16:5-7.

God's judgments and believers' petitions—Revelation 5:8; 6:9-11; 8:3-5; 14:18; 16:7; 19:2.

The bride purifies herself—Matthew 25:14-23; 2 Corinthians 7:1; 1 John 3:3; Jude 21.

Life Lessons

1. *Betrothed to Christ.* Today, the church is betrothed, or engaged, to Jesus Christ. Just as betrothed brides in Bible times kept themselves pure and faithful until the marriage ceremony, so you and I as members of the church ought to seek purity and faithfulness as we await our divine

Bridegroom from heaven (see Titus 2:11-14; see John 14:1–6; 1 Thessalonians 4:13-18).

2. *Hallelujah.* "Hallelujah" literally means "praise Yahweh." It is an exclamation of exuberant praise to the one true God (see the first verse of Psalms 106; 111; 112; 113; 117; 135; 146). The word often occurs in contexts where God delivers His people from their enemies, when God is meting out justice, and when God judges rebellion. Its appearance in the book of Revelation is thus appropriate.

Questions for Reflection and Discussion

1. Is your lifestyle befitting a bride who is awaiting the soon appearance of her Bridegroom?

2. Is the word "hallelujah" a part of your daily vocabulary? If not, what's holding you back?

The Second Coming of Christ

Revelation 19:11-16

Scripture Reading and Insights

Begin by reading Revelation 19:11-16 in your favorite Bible. As you read, notice how the Word of God is purifying your life (John 17:17-18).

In yesterday's reading, we witnessed an outbreak of praise in heaven, perhaps due to the anticipation of Christ's second coming. Now let's zero in on this glorious appearing of Christ. With your Bible still accessible, consider the following insights on the biblical text, verse by verse.

Revelation 19:11

I saw heaven opened (19:11): At His first coming, Jesus came as the Lamb of God to take away the sins of the world. Now, at His second coming, He comes as King of kings and Lord of lords.

John's words recall Jesus' baptism, when "the heavens were opened, and the Holy Spirit descended on him in bodily form" (Luke 3:21-22). Just as the heavens opened for the coming of the Holy Spirit on Jesus, so now the heavens open for the second coming of Jesus.

Behold, a white horse (19:11): In biblical times, generals in the Roman army rode white horses. Christ on a white horse will be the glorious commander in chief of the armies of heaven. This signifies His coming triumph over the forces of wickedness in the world, the details of which follow. This is in noted contrast to the lowly colt Jesus rode during His first coming (see Zechariah 9:9).

The one sitting on it is called Faithful and True (19:11): Names and titles in biblical times revealed a person's character, and Christ's character is here revealed as faithful and true in all things. Perhaps Jesus is called Faithful and True in this context because He is returning to earth in glory just as He promised He would (Matthew 24:27-31).

Note the obvious contrast between Christ and the antichrist. The antichrist is unfaithful (he breaks the covenant he made with Israel). He is also false (he consistently disseminates falsehood and deception).

In righteousness he judges and makes war (19:11): Unlike the antichrist, who will rule and judge over the world in unrighteousness, Jesus Christ rules and judges in righteousness (see Revelation 20:11-15).

Christ will be Victor. All who oppose Him in this war will be instantly slain. This war will be an expression of God's holy wrath against the antichrist and unrepentant sinners. In Revelation 13:4, the whole earth asked who could possibly fight against the beast. Christ will definitively answer that question at His second coming.

Revelation 19:12

His eyes are like a flame of fire (19:12): This description points not only to Christ's absolute holiness but also to His penetrating scrutiny in seeing all things as they truly are (see Revelation 1:14). At the second coming, no one will be able to escape His omniscient gaze.

On his head are many diadems (19:12): The many diadems, or crowns, represent total sovereignty and royal kingship. No one will be able to challenge Christ's kingly authority.

He has a name written that no one knows but himself (19:12): Perhaps this will be the same name that Christ will write on overcomers (see Revelation 2:17; 3:12).

Revelation 19:13

He is clothed in a robe dipped in blood (19:13): Some Bible expositors suggest the blood may speak of Christ's redemptive death on the cross. Others say the blood is likely that of the enemies Christ slays at the close of Armageddon (verse 15). Still others deny this, for Christ's enemies are not slain at this moment (Christ hasn't yet arrived on the earth from the perspective of this verse). Some thus conclude that perhaps the blood relates to Christ's previous battles against sin, Satan, death, and God's enemies.

The name by which he is called is The Word of God (19:13): This recalls John 1:1: "In the beginning was the Word, and the Word was with God, and the Word was God." The Greek noun for "Word" in John 1:1 is *logos*. In John's theology, Christ the Logos is the preexistent, eternal being—God. The Logos is the Creator of the universe (John 1:3).

In the Old Testament, God's Word is an active and effective agent for accomplishing God's will (see Isaiah 55:11).

Another aspect of the Jewish understanding of "the Word" is evident in the Jewish Targums (simplified paraphrases of the Old Testament Scriptures). Here the Jews, out of reverence for God, sometimes substituted the phrase the "Word of God" in place of the word "God." The Jews were fearful of breaking the third commandment about taking God's name in vain (Exodus 20:7). So, for example, where our Bible says, "Then Moses brought the people out of the camp to meet God" (Exodus 19:17), the Targum reads, "to meet the Word of God."

When we come to John's Gospel, the Word is a divine person who has come into the world to reveal another person (the Father—see John 1:14,18). For John, the Logos is a living being—the second person of the Trinity, the source of all life, and nothing less than God Himself (John 1:1).

Revelation 19:14

The armies of heaven, arrayed in fine linen, white and pure, were following him (19:14): We know that one of the armies is made up of redeemed human beings because of the "fine linen, white and pure." These are the very words used to describe the wedding gown of the bride of Christ, which is the church (verse 8). Some Bible expositors believe that Christ's human army will also include Old Testament saints (Jude 14; Daniel 12:1-2) and tribulation martyrs (Revelation 7:13).

The other army that accompanies Christ is angelic. Matthew 16:27 says, "The Son of Man is going to come with his angels in the glory of his Father." Matthew 25:31 affirms, "When the Son of Man comes in his glory, and all the angels with him, then he will sit on his glorious throne" (see also 2 Thessalonians 1:7).

Note that Christ does not need the help of these armies in battle. Christ alone—omnipotent God, King of kings and Lord of lords—engages in battle against all the enemies of God. Rather, the heavenly armies accompany Christ to participate in events that *follow* the second coming, including the establishment of Christ's millennial kingdom (see 1 Corinthians 6:2; 2 Timothy 2:12; Revelation 20:4).

Revelation 19:15

From his mouth comes a sharp sword with which to strike down the nations (19:15): The sharp sword is a symbol of Christ's omnipotent power to execute His enemies (compare with Isaiah 11:4). Because the sword comes out of His mouth, Christ likely accomplishes His victory over His enemies by the power of His spoken word, just as He created the universe by His spoken word (Psalm 33:6; Colossians 1:16; John 1:1-3).

Christ strikes down the nations (the forces of the antichrist) at Armageddon because they attacked Israel (Joel 3:2; Zechariah 12:2-3). At the end of the tribulation, the Israelites will be acutely aware that the forces of antichrist have gathered to destroy them. In this dire situation, they will finally see that Jesus really is the promised Messiah. Their spiritual blindness will be removed, and the Jewish remnant will experience national regeneration. This will be in fulfillment of Joel 2:28-29, which promises a spiritual awakening of the Jewish remnant. This will also be a fulfillment of the apostle Paul's prophecy of the Jews in Romans 11:25-27.

As the forces of antichrist advance, the Israelites will plead for their newly found Messiah to return and deliver them (Zechariah 12:10; Matthew 23:37-39), at which point their deliverance will surely come (see Romans 10:13-14). As we see in the next verse, Jesus subsequently comes and strikes down the hostile nations.

He will tread the winepress of the fury of the wrath of God the Almighty (19:15): Treading on grapes is a common metaphor for judgment. Instead of grape juice flowing, however, the blood of unbelievers will flow when Christ slays them.

Revelation 19:16

He has a name written, King of kings and Lord of lords (19:16): This title means that Jesus is the One who is absolutely supreme and sovereign over all earthly rulers and angelic powers (1 Timothy 6:15; see also Deuteronomy 10:17; Psalm 136:3). The long-awaited messianic King has now finally arrived.

Major Themes

1. *Christ the King.* The kingship of Jesus Christ is a common theme in Scripture. Genesis 49:10 prophesied that the Messiah would come from the tribe of Judah and reign as a king. The Davidic covenant in 2 Samuel 7:16 promised a Messiah who would have a dynasty, a people over whom He would rule, and an eternal throne (see also Luke 1:32-33). In Psalm 2:6, God the Father announces the installation of God the Son as King in Jerusalem. Psalm 110 affirms that the Messiah will subjugate His enemies and rule over them. Daniel 7:13-14 tells us that the Messiah-King will have an everlasting dominion.

2. *Angelic armies.* In Scripture, angels are often collectively called God's heavenly host. Micaiah the prophet, for example, said, "I saw the Lord sitting on his throne, and all the host of heaven standing on his right hand and on his left" (2 Chronicles 18:18). The term "host" has a distinctive military ring to it. The angels may be viewed as a celestial military force that accomplishes God's will. The Bible often calls God Himself "Lord of hosts"—the sovereign commander of the great heavenly army (see 1 Samuel 17:45; Psalm 89:6,8).

Digging Deeper with Cross-References

Christ's wondrous names—Isaiah 9:6; Luke 1:31; Philippians 2:9-11.

Christ judges in righteousness—Matthew 25:31-46; John 5:25-30; Acts 17:31; Revelation 20:11-15.

Rod of iron—Psalm 2:9; Revelation 2:27; 12:5.

Life Lessons

1. *Christ is Faithful and True (Revelation 19:11)*. We've seen before that Christ is Faithful and True, but the book of Revelation keeps reaffirming this, so we will as well. Because Christ is Faithful and True, you can trust all the prophecies, promises, and spiritual truths in the Bible. You can also trust that He'll save you—just as He promised!

2. *Jesus is King of kings and Lord of lords (Revelation 19:16)*. Christ sovereignly oversees all that comes into our lives. Regardless of what we may encounter, and regardless of whether we understand why certain things happen in life, the knowledge that our sovereign King of kings is in control anchors us in the midst of life's storms.

3. *Jesus' eyes are like a flame of fire*. Jesus is all-seeing and all-knowing (Revelation 19:12). Therefore, He already knows everything about us. He won't suddenly discover something He didn't know before that will cause Him to change His mind about us being in His family (see John 13:18-19,38). What an awesome Savior!

Questions for Reflection and Discussion

1. Christ is Faithful and True. What does that mean to you personally? Does it give you confidence in your salvation?

2. Are you facing any difficult circumstances that you would like to completely and unreservedly entrust to our sovereign King of kings?

3. Christ knows everything about you—including all your sins of yesterday, today, and all the tomorrows in the future—and still loves you. How does that make you feel?

The Campaign of Armageddon

Revelation 19:17-21

Scripture Reading and Insights

Begin by reading Revelation 19:17-21 in your favorite Bible. As you read, notice how the Word of God is purifying your life (John 17:17-18).

In the previous lesson, we focused on the glorious appearing of Jesus Christ. Now let's find out about how Christ will conquer the armies that gather to wage war against Him. With your Bible still accessible, consider the following insights on the biblical text, verse by verse.

Revelation 19:17-18

"Come, gather for the great supper of God" (19:17): The main battle of Armageddon is now about to occur. An angel, therefore, invites birds to gather for a hearty feast. The angel is "standing in the sun," where birds could easily see him. He cries out with a loud voice so birds everywhere will hear him.

Jesus prophesied about Armageddon and mentioned that birds would have a feast on the battlefield: "Wherever the corpse is, there the vultures will gather" (Matthew 24:28; Luke 17:37). The scene is gruesome.

"To eat the flesh of kings, the flesh of captains, the flesh of mighty men" (19:18): The casualties of this judgment will be massive and broad. All who have resisted Jesus Christ will be targets of this judgment, regardless of their status in the world. Everyone will be included—free and slave, small and great.

Here we find another application of the *lex talionis*, or law of retaliation—that is, an "eye for an eye." Recall the bodies of God's two prophetic witnesses were not buried (Revelation 11:9-10). Likewise, those executed at Armageddon will not be buried, and the birds will have a feast.

Revelation 19:19-21

I saw the beast and the kings of the earth with their armies gathered to make war (19:19): The antichrist will not give up without a fight. A multinational anti-God force, comprised of the armies of the beast and the kings of the earth, will gather to engage in battle against Christ as they see Him coming in glory.

This brings up a question related to the actual duration of Christ's second coming. If the antichrist and his forces have sufficient time to gather and unite in preparing to fight Christ, this seems to imply that the second coming will not be an instantaneous event.

Revelation 1:7 says, "Behold, he is coming with the clouds, and every eye will see him, even those who pierced him, and all the tribes of the earth will wail on account of him." Matthew 24:30 likewise tells us, "Then will appear in heaven the sign of the Son of Man, and then all the tribes of the earth will mourn, and they will see the Son of Man coming on the clouds of heaven with power and great glory."

If every eye will witness the second coming, the whole world may be able to see a majestic military processional en route from heaven to earth. As they witness this glorious entourage, they gather forces to do battle against Christ. If this processional takes a day or longer, then as the earth revolves, people all over the world will be able to witness the event firsthand. Of course, there will also be live television and Internet feeds.

The beast was captured, and with it the false prophet... These two were thrown alive into the lake of fire (19:20): The battle will instantly be over. None can thwart the King of kings. The Lord Jesus will promptly cast the antichrist and the false prophet alive into the lake of fire. Their punishment is just, for this diabolical duo will have deceived multitudes of people.

The Scriptures assure us that the lake of fire (hell) is a real place. But hell was not part of God's original creation, which He called good. Hell was created later to accommodate the banishment of Satan and his fallen angels, who rebelled against God (Matthew 25:41). Human beings who reject Christ will join Satan and his fallen angels in this infernal place of suffering. The Scriptures use a variety of words to describe the horrors of hell.

> the fiery furnace (Matthew 13:42)
>
> unquenchable fire (Mark 9:47-48)
>
> the lake of fire (Revelation 20:15)
>
> eternal fire (Matthew 18:8)
>
> eternal punishment (Matthew 25:46)
>
> destruction (Matthew 7:13)
>
> eternal destruction (2 Thessalonians 1:8-9)
>
> the place of weeping and gnashing of teeth (Matthew 13:42)
>
> the second death (Revelation 20:14)

The antichrist and false prophet will be consigned to this place before Christ's millennial kingdom.

Scripture describes degrees of punishment in hell. Christ's justice is perfect, and this requires that extremely evil persons (such as the antichrist and the false prophet) will experience much greater punishment than, for example, a non-Christian moralist. Theologians generally appeal to the following verses in support of the idea that there are degrees of punishment in hell: Matthew 10:15; 16:27; Luke 12:47-48; Revelation 20:12-13; 22:12. The suffering of the antichrist and the false prophet will be eternal (see Matthew 25:46; Revelation 14:11; 20:10).

The rest were slain by the sword (19:21): God's judgment is universal and comprehensive. All the rest of Christ's enemies will die in an instant as Christ speaks the word of judgment. The antichrist and the false prophet are cast into the lake of fire, but wicked humans are cast into Hades, a temporary abode of punishment where people await the great white throne judgment, after which they will be consigned to the lake of fire for all eternity (see 2 Peter 2:9). (More on this later in the book.)

C.S. Lewis once said that in the end, there are two groups of people. One group of people says to God, "Thy will be done." These are people who recognize that they are sinners, and they trust in Christ for salvation. The other group of people are those to whom God says, "Thy will be done." These are people who have refused to turn to Christ for salvation, thus ensuring their own destiny in hell forever.

A 75-Day Interim Period

Though the book of Revelation does not directly speak of it, other prophetic verses describe a 75-day interval between the end of the tribulation period and the beginning of the millennial kingdom. During this brief interim, a number of significant events transpire.

For example, the image of the antichrist that had caused the abomination of desolation at the midpoint in the tribulation will be removed from the temple after 30 days. Daniel 12:11 tells us, "From the time that the regular burnt offering is taken away and the abomination that makes desolate is set up, there shall be 1,290 days." The last half of the tribulation lasts only 1260 days (or three and a half years). So the abomination that makes desolate is removed from the Jewish temple 30 days after the tribulation ends.

An additional 45 days must also be added into the prophetic timetable. Daniel 12:12 states, "Blessed is he who waits and arrives at the 1,335 days." (The 1335 days minus the 1290 days means another 45 days are added into the mix.) Apparently the judgment of the nations, recorded in Matthew 25:31-46, takes place during this time. The Jewish survivors of the tribulation period will also be judged (Ezekiel 20).

Many theologians also believe that Old Testament saints will be resurrected from the dead during this interim period. "Your dead shall live; their bodies shall rise. You who dwell in the dust, awake and sing for joy! For your dew is a dew of light, and the earth will give birth to the dead" (Isaiah 26:19). "Many of those who sleep in the dust of the earth shall awake, some to everlasting life, and some to shame and ever-lasting contempt" (Daniel 12:2).

Finally, tribulation saints who died are resurrected from the dead. "I saw the souls of those who had been beheaded for the testimony of Jesus and for the word of God, and who had not worshiped the beast or its image and had not received its mark on their foreheads or their hands. They came to life and reigned with Christ for a thousand years" (Revelation 20:4).

The governmental structure of the coming millennial kingdom may also be set up during the extra 45 days. We have just read that the saints will reign with Christ in the millennial kingdom (see also 2 Timothy 2:12). After believers and unbelievers have been separated and the unbelievers are removed in judgment, some time will be required to appoint saints to different government positions and inform them of their various responsibilities.

The marriage feast of Christ—featuring the divine Bridegroom, Jesus Christ, and His bride, the church—may also take place at the close of the 75-day period. If so, it will be the highlight of those two and a half months. The invitation to the marriage feast, mentioned in Revelation 19:9, immediately precedes the second coming of Christ: "Blessed are those who are invited to the marriage supper of the Lamb." It would make good sense that the marriage feast would take place shortly thereafter.

Following the 75-day interval, Christ will set up His millennial kingdom (Isaiah 2:2-4; Ezekiel 37:1-14; 40–48; Micah 4:1-7; Revelation 20). (More on this in the next chapter.)

Major Themes

1. *Death of the body*. The term "flesh" in Revelation is used of the bodies of both humans and animals. Humans are made up of both a material part (the physical body) and an immaterial part (the soul or spirit). When human beings physically die, their immaterial part departs from the material body. The soul or spirit of Christians goes directly to heaven (2 Corinthians 5:8; Philippians 1:21-23). The

soul or spirit of unbelievers goes to a place of temporary punishment, where they await the great white throne judgment (see Luke 16:19-31; 2 Peter 2:9; Revelation 20:11-15).

2. *Birds feasting on the dead.* The Bible often graphically depicts judgment in terms of birds feasting on the dead. Deuteronomy 28:26 says, "Your dead body shall be food for all birds of the air and for the beasts of the earth, and there shall be no one to frighten them away" (compare with Psalm 79:2). Isaiah 18:6 says, "They shall all of them be left to the birds of prey of the mountains and to the beasts of the earth." Jeremiah 7:33 says, "The dead bodies of this people will be food for the birds of the air, and for the beasts of the earth, and none will frighten them away" (see also Jeremiah 16:4; 19:7; 34:20).

Digging Deeper with Cross-References

Eternal punishment—Matthew 13:40-42; 25:41; Mark 9:43-48; Luke 3:17; 12:47-48; Revelation 14:10-11.

Fire and brimstone—Revelation 14:10; 20:10; 21:8; see also Genesis 19:24; Psalm 11:6; Isaiah 30:33; Ezekiel 38:22; Luke 17:29.

Life Lessons

1. *The blessings of the second coming.* The judgment aspect of the second coming is a bit overwhelming. It's easy to lose sight of the greater significance of the blessings of the second coming for believers. Here are two: Christ will set up His own kingdom of perfect righteousness on earth, and you and I as resurrected believers will be with Christ not only during the millennial kingdom but throughout all eternity. How awesome it will be!

2. *Avoid prophetic apathy.* Some Christians seem to pay little attention to the second coming. One reason for this is

that there are many Christians who like to argue about the finer points of biblical prophecy, such as whether the rapture will happen before or after the tribulation period. For these Christians, prophecy has become a hot potato to be avoided. This is a tragic attitude because a significant part of the Bible is prophetic. A better policy is to regularly study Bible prophecy and become convinced in your own mind of what Scripture really teaches. On debated finer points, simply agree to disagree in an agreeable way.

Questions for Reflection and Discussion

1. Do you look forward to the second coming of Christ? Why or why not?

2. Do you ever feel tempted to pay less attention to matters related to end-times biblical prophecy because some Christians get a little too animated on the issue?

3. Has your study of biblical prophecy bolstered your faith in God and your confidence in the Bible? If so, how?

Christ's Millennial Kingdom

Revelation 20:1-6

Scripture Reading and Insights

Begin by reading Revelation 20:1-6 in your favorite Bible. As you read, notice how the Word of God is purifying your life (John 17:17-18).

In yesterday's reading, we focused on Christ's victory over the armies that gather to fight Him. In today's reading, we zero in on Christ's establishment of His millennial kingdom on earth. With your Bible still accessible, consider the following insights on the biblical text, verse by verse.

Revelation 20:1-3

I saw an angel coming down from heaven, holding in his hand the key to the bottomless pit and a great chain (20:1): The bottomless pit serves as the place of imprisonment of demonic spirits (Luke 8:31; 2 Peter 2:4).

He seized the dragon, that ancient serpent, who is the devil and Satan, and bound him for a thousand years (20:2): "Dragon" is an apt metaphor that points to the ferocity and cruelty of this evil spirit being. "Serpent" is apparently an allusion to Satan's first appearance in the Garden of Eden, where he deceived Eve (Genesis 3; 2 Corinthians 11:3; 1 Timothy 2:14).

"Devil" (see Matthew 4:1) carries the ideas of "adversary" and "slanderer." The devil was and is the adversary of Christ; he is the adversary of all who follow Christ. The word "Satan" also carries the idea of "adversary."

The devil—along with all demonic spirits—will be bound in the bottomless pit for 1000 years during Christ's millennial kingdom. ("Millennium" comes from two Latin words—*mille*, which means "thousand," and *annum*, which means "year.") This quarantine will effectively remove a powerful destructive and deceptive force in all areas of human life and thought during Christ's kingdom.

Christ's millennial kingdom will be wondrous. During this time, righteousness will flourish (Isaiah 11:3-5), peace will be universal (Isaiah 2:4), and the fruitfulness and productivity of the earth will be greatly increased (Isaiah 35:1-2).

The millennial kingdom is one of those doctrines that Christians seemingly love to debate. There are three primary theological views—premillennialism, amillennialism, and postmillennialism (see "Major Themes" below). I hold to premillennialism, the view that following the second coming, Christ will institute a kingdom of perfect peace and righteousness on earth that will last 1000 years. This view is based on a literal interpretation of prophecy.

The imprisonment of Satan and his host of fallen angels will greatly change the religious landscape during the millennial kingdom. Gone will be their deception, their destructive influence, their temptations to sin and rebel against God, their continued stance against the purposes of God, and the guilt they inflict on the consciences of Christians.

Threw him into the pit, and shut it and sealed it over him, so that he might not deceive the nations any longer (20:3): After the angel casts Satan into the bottomless pit, he seals it to prevent escape. He thereby ensures that Satan will be unable to deceive people during Christ's millennial kingdom.

After that he must be released for a little while (20:3): Satan is released after the millennial kingdom to allow him one last attempt to lead some of earth's people astray. But who are these people?

Scripture reveals that only believers enter into the millennial kingdom in their mortal bodies (for example, Matthew 25:34), but some of their descendants will not be believers. These are the people Satan will seek to gather against God in one final rebellion.

Christ will quickly and decisively crush this rebellion. Following the millennial kingdom, the great white throne judgment—which is the judgment of the wicked—will take place, and the lake of fire will be populated (Revelation 20:11-15). Those who participate in Satan's rebellion will be among the inhabitants of the lake of fire. (More on this in the next chapter.)

Revelation 20:4-6

I saw thrones (20:4): Many have wondered who occupies these thrones because we are not told. There are two popular views. One is that they are the 12 disciples. Luke 22:30 refers to the disciples sitting "on thrones judging the twelve tribes of Israel." The other popular view is that they represent the church. First Corinthians 6:2 tells us that the saints will judge the world. As well, 2 Timothy 2:12 affirms, "If we endure, we will also reign with him." Both these views are viable.

I saw the souls of those who had been beheaded for the testimony of Jesus and for the word of God (20:4): The souls who had been beheaded are the martyrs of the tribulation period (see Revelation 6:9; 18:24; 19:2).

They came to life and reigned with Christ for a thousand years (20:4): The idea of reigning with Christ is confirmed throughout the book of Revelation. For example, Revelation 5:10 reveals that believers have been made "a kingdom and priests to our God, and they shall reign on the earth." Revelation 20:6 adds this: "Blessed and holy is the one who shares in the first resurrection! Over such the second death has no power, but they will be priests of God and of Christ, and they will reign with him for a thousand years." Finally, Revelation 22:5 tells us, "They will reign forever and ever." The saints' privilege of reigning with Christ continues even beyond the millennial kingdom.

The rest of the dead did not come to life until the thousand years were ended (20:5): This refers to the resurrection of the wicked dead, who will be raised to face Christ at the great white throne judgment following the millennial kingdom (discussed in verses 11-15). This will be a somber event.

This is the first resurrection (20:5): We can easily get confused by this verse, so some explanation is in order.

The original Hebrew and Greek manuscripts of the Bible did not have chapter and verse numbers. People inserted these later to make for easier navigation in the Bible. In the great majority of cases, the chapter and verse divisions are very helpful. In a very few instances, such as Revelation 20:5, they can be misleading.

Bible expositors are in essential agreement that the last part of verse 5—"This is the first resurrection"—fits into the flow of verses 4 and 6. But the first half of verse 5 is a parenthetical truth. The resurrection of the wicked dead is *not* a part of the first resurrection. Rather, the first resurrection involves the resurrection of the righteous, as other verses on the first resurrection make clear.

Scripture mentions two types of resurrections. The first is appropriately called the "first resurrection," as in this verse. This is also called the "resurrection of life" (John 5:29), the "resurrection of the just" (Luke 14:14), and the "better life" (Hebrews 11:35).

The second resurrection is the last resurrection (Revelation 20:5a,11-15). It is appropriately called the resurrection of judgment (John 5:29; see also Daniel 12:2; Acts 24:15).

To be even more specific, the term "the first resurrection" refers to *all* the resurrections of the righteous even though they are widely separated in time. There is one resurrection of the righteous at the rapture (before the tribulation—1 Thessalonians 4:13-17), another during the tribulation (the two witnesses—Revelation 11:3,11), another at the end of the tribulation (the martyred dead—Revelation 20:4-5), and apparently another at the end of the 1000-year millennial kingdom (not recorded in Scripture). They all are "first" in the sense of being before the second (final) resurrection, in which the wicked dead are raised. Accordingly, the term "first resurrection" applies to all the resurrections of the saints regardless of when they occur, including the resurrection of Christ Himself (the "firstfruits"—see 1 Corinthians 15:23).

The second resurrection, or last resurrection, is an awful spectacle. All the unsaved of all time will be resurrected at the end of Christ's millennial kingdom, judged at the great white throne judgment, and then cast alive into the lake of fire (Revelation 20:11-15). People will be given resurrection bodies that will last forever, but these bodies will be subject to pain and suffering. They will exist eternally in the lake of fire.

Blessed and holy is the one who shares in the first resurrection! (20:6): Those who share in the first resurrection are blessed because they will have unfettered access to the presence of God forever. They will dwell with God (and Christ) face to face. Can there be any higher privilege and blessing than for the creature to dwell face to face with his Creator?

Those who share in the first resurrection are also called holy because they are set apart from all sin. In the glorified state, the sin nature is obliterated, for "we shall be like him" (1 John 3:2). Christ "will transform our lowly body to be like his glorious body" (Philippians 3:21).

Over such the second death has no power (20:6): The first death is physical death—that is, the separation of the spirit or soul from the body (for example, see Genesis 35:18). Virtually all people—except those Christians alive on earth when the rapture occurs—will experience the first death (1 Corinthians 15:50-55; 1 Thessalonians 4:13-17).

The "second death," which is for unbelievers only, entails eternal separation from God in the lake of fire, or eternal hell. "Their portion will be in the lake that burns with fire and sulfur, which is the second death" (Revelation 21:8). The lake of fire will be populated immediately following the great white throne judgment, which is the judgment of the wicked dead (Revelation 20:11-15).

They will be priests of God and of Christ (20:6): Priests do not need go-betweens to relate to God. Priests have direct access to God. Those who participate in the first resurrection (that's you and me) will have direct access to God forever and ever.

Major Themes

1. *Premillennialism*. This view teaches that following the second coming, Christ will institute a kingdom of perfect peace and righteousness on earth that will last for 1000 years. After this reign of true peace, the eternal state begins (Revelation 20:1-7; see also Isaiah 65:17-25; Ezekiel 37:21-28; Zechariah 8:1-17). I subscribe to this view because it takes a literal approach, recognizing that Old Testament prophecies of Christ's first coming were also literally fulfilled.

2. *Amillennialism.* This is a spiritualized view that teaches that when Christ comes, the eternal state will begin with no prior literal 1000-year reign on earth. The 1000-year reign is understood metaphorically of Christ's present spiritual reign from heaven over a long time.

3. *Postmillennialism.* This is another spiritualized view. It teaches that through the church's progressive influence, the world will eventually be "Christianized" before Christ returns. Following this return, the eternal state will begin (there will be no 1000-year kingdom). A practical problem for this view is that the world seems to be getting progressively worse instead of being "Christianized."

Digging Deeper with Cross-References

The Old Testament basis for the millennial kingdom—Psalm 2:6-9; Isaiah 65:18-23; Jeremiah 31:12-14,31-37; Ezekiel 34:25-29; 37:1-13; 40–48; Daniel 2:35; 7:13-14; Joel 2:21-27; Amos 9:13-14; Micah 4:1-7; Zephaniah 3:9-20.

The work of Satan—Genesis 3:1-5; John 8:44; Acts 5:3; 1 Corinthians 7:5; 2 Corinthians 11:14; 1 Timothy 3:6; 1 Peter 5:8; Revelation 12:10.

Life Lessons

1. *Satan is on a leash.* Our passage graphically illustrates that God puts boundaries around Satan and his host of fallen angels. Satan is not free to do anything he wants to you. All Satan's activities have divinely imposed parameters beyond which he cannot go (see this in Job 1:12 and 2:6). We ought all to be thankful for this protective ministry of God (compare with Psalm 91:1-12).

2. *Our wondrous resurrection bodies.* In 1 Corinthians 15:42-43 the apostle Paul describes the resurrection: "What is sown is perishable; what is raised is imperishable. It is sown in dishonor; it is raised in glory. It is sown in weakness; it is

raised in power." Our present bodies will wear out, but our resurrection bodies will be glorious, never again subject to aging, decay, death, or burial. How awesome!

Questions for Reflection and Discussion

1. Do you worry about attacks from the devil and demons? We should definitely have a healthy respect for the powers of darkness (2 Corinthians 2:11), resist them (James 4:7), and wear our spiritual armor (Ephesians 6:10-18). But let's keep our eyes focused on Jesus (Hebrews 12:2).

2. Do you struggle with any bodily ailments? As each year passes, do you become increasingly aware of the frailty of the human body? Rejoice! We've got a fantastic body upgrade coming!

Day 36

Satan's Final Rebellion and the Great White Throne

Revelation 20:7-15

Scripture Reading and Insights

Begin by reading Revelation 20:7-15 in your favorite Bible. As you read, notice how the Word of God is purifying your life (John 17:17-18).

In the previous lesson, we focused on Christ's establishment of His glorious millennial kingdom on earth. In today's lesson, we read of His final defeat of Satan after the millennial kingdom. With your Bible still accessible, consider the following insights on the biblical text, verse by verse.

Revelation 20:7-10

When the thousand years are ended, Satan will be released (20:7): We have seen that the bottomless pit serves as a prison for demonic spirits (Luke 8:31; 2 Peter 2:4). The devil and all demonic spirits will be bound here for the 1000 years of Christ's millennial kingdom (Revelation 20:1-3). This quarantine will effectively remove a powerful destructive and deceptive force in all areas of human life and thought during Christ's kingdom.

At the end of the 1000 years, Satan will be loosed from the bottomless pit. He will have one last opportunity to deceive the nations. God's purpose seems to be to prove once and for all that the heart of every human being is desperately wicked. Even in the best of environments

(Christ's kingdom), the fallen human heart still has a great propensity to sin.

To deceive the nations... to gather them for battle; their number is like the sand of the sea (20:8): Believers who survive the tribulation will physically enter into Christ's millennial kingdom (Matthew 25:31-46; Ezekiel 20:34-38). Longevity will characterize the millennial kingdom (see Isaiah 65:20), but both Jews and Gentiles will continue to age and die. Married couples among both groups will also continue to have children throughout the millennium. Apparently, some of the children of the saints (and grandchildren, great-grandchildren, and so forth) will not be believers. They are nevertheless permitted to live in Christ's kingdom so long as they do not rebel. When Satan is released at the end of the millennium, he will lead many of these unbelievers in a massive rebellion against Christ. This will represent Satan's last stand.

Gog and Magog (20:8): These terms relate to a military coalition made up of Russia, Iran, Sudan, Turkey, and a number of other Muslim nations who will attack Israel, either prior to the tribulation period or at the very beginning of it (see Ezekiel 38–39). God will destroy these invaders. In this verse, John apparently uses Gog and Magog as a metaphor for evil invaders, much like we today use Wall Street as a metaphor for the stock market. In other words, Satan and his human rebels will launch a Gog-and-Magog-like invasion against Christ and His people.

Surrounded the camp of the saints and the beloved city (20:9): Jerusalem will be the headquarters of Christ's government throughout the millennium (Isaiah 2:1-5). This beloved city—with believers camped around and about—will be the target city of this satanic revolt.

Fire came down from heaven and consumed them (20:9): The revolt is a suicide mission. Christ quickly and decisively crushes this rebellion.

The devil... was thrown into the lake of fire (20:10): All three persons of the satanic trinity—Satan, the antichrist, and the false prophet—suffer the same dire destiny. The antichrist and the false prophet had been thrown into the lake of fire after the tribulation period and before the millennial kingdom (Revelation 19:20). Now Satan joins them. All three will burn for all eternity. Demons too will be judged and cast into the lake of fire (see Matthew 25:41).

On page 246 I listed some of the Bible's other descriptive names for the lake of fire.

Revelation 20:11-15

I saw a great white throne and him who was seated on it (20:11): Thrones are mentioned almost 50 times in Revelation (see, for example, Revelation 4:2-3,9; 5:1,7,13; 6:16; 7:10,15). The throne of Revelation 20:11 is a judgment throne, where Jesus Christ sits as Judge of the wicked dead.

In his vision, John witnessed the earth and sky flee from the presence of the divine Judge. John saw a universe contaminated by sin and Satan vanish out of existence. Peter described this in more detail in 2 Peter 3:10-13.

> The heavens will pass away with a roar, and the heavenly bodies will be burned up and dissolved, and the earth and the works that are done on it will be exposed…The heavens will be set on fire and dissolved, and the heavenly bodies will melt as they burn! But according to his promise we are waiting for new heavens and a new earth in which righteousness dwells.

The dead were judged (20:12): All the wicked dead, both great and small, are forcefully brought before the divine tribunal. A strong sense of dread will be pervasive.

Books were opened (20:12): These books detail the lives of the unsaved. These books will provide the evidence to substantiate the divine verdict of a destiny in the lake of fire. Their works that will be judged will include their actions (Matthew 16:27), their words (Matthew 12:37), and even their thoughts and motives (Luke 8:17; Romans 2:16). These books will also be used to determine degrees of eternal suffering in the lake of fire (see Matthew 10:14-15; 11:22; Mark 12:38-40; Luke 12:47-48; Hebrews 10:29).

The book of life will also be there. As noted previously, this book contains the names of all of God's redeemed (see Philippians 4:3; Revelation 21:27). No unsaved person's name will be in the Lamb's book of life (Luke 10:20).

Those who participate in the great white throne judgment will be resurrected in order to face judgment (see John 5:28-29). They stand before this throne of judgment in much the same way that a criminal stands in a court of law as the judge reads a sentence. Warren Wiersbe notes some significant differences from a normal court scene: "There will be a Judge but no jury, a prosecution but no defense, a sentence but no appeal. No one will be able to defend himself or accuse God of unrighteousness."[1]

These individuals appear at this judgment because they are already unsaved. This judgment will not separate believers from unbelievers, for all who will experience it will have already made the choice during their lifetimes to reject God. They have a horrible destiny ahead:

> weeping and gnashing of teeth (Matthew 13:41-42)
>
> condemnation (Matthew 12:36-37)
>
> destruction (Philippians 1:28)
>
> eternal punishment (Matthew 25:46)
>
> separation from God's presence (2 Thessalonians 1:8-9)
>
> trouble and distress (Romans 2:9)

The sea gave up the dead who were in it, Death and Hades gave up the dead who were in them (20:13): Virtually every possible location and place will yield the bodies and souls of the unrighteous dead—the sea, Death, and Hades. Each of the wicked will receive a resurrection body capable of suffering forever (John 5:28-29).

Hades is a New Testament term that refers to the temporary place of the dead (Luke 16:19-31). The spirits or souls of the wicked dead are held captive there (2 Peter 2:9). On that future day, wicked evildoers will be raised from the dead—their spirits being reunited with resurrection bodies—and they will be judged at the great white throne judgment. Following this, their permanent place of suffering will be the lake of fire.

Death and Hades were thrown into the lake of fire (20:14): The apostle Paul affirmed that "the last enemy to be destroyed is death" (1 Corinthians 15:26). Finally, after all this time during which death has reigned supreme, this last enemy is destroyed. Death and Hades (the abode of death) are tossed into the lake of fire. This is the "second death."

We saw that the first death is physical death, or the separation of the spirit or soul from the body (Genesis 35:18). Virtually all people will experience the first death. The exceptions are those Christians who are alive on earth at the rapture of the church and those who are alive at the end of the millennial kingdom. These two groups will instantly receive glorified bodies (1 Corinthians 15:50-55; 1 Thessalonians 4:13-17).

The term "second death" refers to eternal separation from God in the lake of fire, which is eternal hell. No believer will experience the second death.

If anyone's name was not found written in the book of life (20:15): When Christ opens the book of life, no name of anyone present at the great white throne judgment is in it. Their names do not appear in the book of life because they have rejected the source of life—Jesus Christ. And because they rejected the source of life, they are cast into the lake of fire, which constitutes the second death.

Major Themes

1. *Fallen angels.* Some fallen angels are already confined, awaiting future judgment. Jude 6 affirms, "The angels who did not stay within their own position of authority, but left their proper dwelling, he has kept in eternal chains under gloomy darkness until the judgment of the great day." Peter writes, "God did not spare angels when they sinned, but cast them into hell and committed them to chains of gloomy darkness to be kept until the judgment" (2 Peter 2:4). Other demonic spirits remain free to continue their attacks on Christians (for example, Matthew 12:43; Mark 1:23,26; 3:30; 5:2,8; 7:25; 9:25; Luke 4:33; 8:29; 9:42; 11:24).

2. *The last of Satan's six judgments.* The Bible notes six distinct judgments against Satan:

- cast out of heaven (Ezekiel 28:16)

- cursed in the Garden of Eden (Genesis 3:14-15)

- defeated at the cross (John 12:31; Colossians 2:15; Hebrews 2:14)

- cast out of heaven in the middle of the tribulation (Revelation 12:13)

- confined in the abyss during the millennial kingdom (Revelation 20:2)

- cast into the lake of fire after the millennial kingdom (Matthew 25:41; Revelation 20:10)

Digging Deeper with Cross-References

Fire of judgment—Genesis 19:24; Exodus 9:23-24; Leviticus 9:24; 10:2; Numbers 11:1; 16:35; 26:10; 1 Kings 18:38; 2 Kings 1:10-14; Psalm 11:6.

The judgment of the wicked—Psalm 62:12; Proverbs 24:12; Matthew 16:27; Romans 2:6; Revelation 2:23.

Life Lessons

1. *No infants at the great white throne.* Many Christian parents who have lost infants and young children in death ask for assurance that they are saved. I am firmly convinced they are saved. Infants and young children are not morally responsible and therefore cannot possibly be called before the great white throne judgment (Deuteronomy 1:39; Isaiah 7:15-16; Romans 9:11). Jesus expressed great love for little children (see Matthew 18:3). David certainly knew he would be with his dead child in heaven (2 Samuel 12:22-23).

2. *The depths of human sin.* The rebellion at the end of Christ's millennial kingdom demonstrates the depth of human

sin. You and I are thoroughly contaminated. Jesus often spoke of sin in metaphors that illustrate the havoc sin can wreak. He described sin as blindness (Matthew 23:16-26), sickness (Matthew 9:12), bondage (John 8:34), and darkness (John 8:12; 12:35-46). Jesus also taught that both inner thoughts and external acts render a person guilty (Matthew 5:28; Mark 7:21-23). We can be delivered from the power of sin by depending on the Holy Spirit (see Galatians 5:16-25) and being rooted in Jesus (John 15:1-11).

Questions for Reflection and Discussion

1. Have you or someone you know lost an infant or young child in death? Have you thought much about Scriptures that may relate to their salvation? Meditate a few moments on Matthew 18:1-10.

2. Many spiritual leaders have commented that the more they mature as Christians, the more they become aware of the depth of sin in their lives (see Romans 7:15-20). Have you noticed the same thing? Have you noticed that the closer you get to God and His light, the more clearly you notice the darkness? Truly, none of us could be saved apart from God's grace (Ephesians 2:8-9).

The Descent of the New Jerusalem

Revelation 21:1-8

Scripture Reading and Insights

Begin by reading Revelation 21:1-8 in your favorite Bible. As you read, keep in mind that the Word of God brings spiritual maturity (1 Corinthians 3:1-2; Hebrews 5:12-14).

In yesterday's reading, we focused on Christ's final victory over Satan after the millennial kingdom. In today's reading, we zero in on God's creation of a new heaven and a new earth. The new Jerusalem—a heavenly city—will come down to rest on the new earth. With your Bible still accessible, consider the following insights on the biblical text, verse by verse.

Revelation 21:1

I saw a new heaven and a new earth (21:1): Notice that the Bible begins in paradise, but it is quickly lost. The Bible ends with paradise restored! In the Garden of Eden, Adam and Eve sinned against God. God subsequently cursed the earth (Genesis 3:17-18; Romans 8:20-22). So before the eternal kingdom can appear, God must deal with this cursed earth.

Satan has also long carried out his evil schemes on earth (see Ephesians 2:2), so the earth must be purged of all stains resulting from his extended presence. In short, the earth—along with the first and second heavens (the earth's atmosphere and the stellar universe)—must be renewed. The old must make room for the new.

The Scriptures often speak of the passing of the old heavens and earth (Psalm 102:25-26; Isaiah 51:6; Matthew 24:35). Indeed, the present earth and heavens (earth's atmosphere and the stellar universe) will be destroyed by fire in preparation for the new heavens and new earth (2 Peter 3:7-13).

After the universe is cleansed, God will create a new heaven and a new earth. All vestiges of the curse and Satan's presence will be utterly and forever removed. There will be no more curse, no more germs, and no more sickness, sorrow, tears, or death.

Scripture reveals that even while Christians are on the new earth, they will also be in heaven. The new earth will be subsumed in the heavenly existence. Peter speaks of this glorious future reality in 2 Peter 3:13. Heaven and earth will unite in a glory that exceeds the imaginative capabilities of the finite human brain (see Isaiah 65:17).

There will be geological changes in the new earth, for there will be no more sea (Revelation 21:1). Our present environment is water-based (our blood, for example, is 90 percent water). The environment in the new heavens and new earth, by contrast, will not be water-based. It will rather be based on a different life principle, a life principle that certainly includes the "water of life" (Revelation 22:1,17). Glorified humanity will inhabit a glorified earth re-created and adapted to eternal conditions.

Revelation 21:2

I saw the holy city, new Jerusalem, coming down out of heaven (21:2): The new Jerusalem—the eternal city that you and I will one day inhabit—is a holy city, for it will contain no sin or unrighteousness of any kind.

The new Jerusalem is portrayed as a real city, not some kind of an ethereal twilight zone. This is important because you and I will have real, physically resurrected bodies. As real persons with real bodies, we would naturally live forever in a real city—the new Jerusalem.

John witnessed the city coming down out of heaven. This means the city is actually being constructed (perhaps even now by Jesus

Christ—see John 14:1-3) in heaven. Eventually the new Jerusalem will come down and rest on the new earth. (More on this in the next chapter.)

Prepared as a bride (21:2): This metaphorical bride of Christ, the new Jerusalem, will include two previous brides of Christ: redeemed Israelites who had lived in Old Testament times (Isaiah 62:5; Jeremiah 2:2; 3:20; Ezekiel 16:8; Hosea 2:19-20) and the New Testament church (2 Corinthians 11:2; Revelation 19:7). The habitat is identified according to its inhabitants.

Revelation 21:3-4

"Behold, the dwelling place of God is with man" (21:3): God will now live directly with redeemed humankind (compare with Leviticus 26:11-12; Deuteronomy 12:5). Here at last we find unfettered companionship between the Creator and His creation.

He will wipe away every tear from their eyes, and death shall be no more (21:4): The Old Testament promises that in the heavenly state, death will be swallowed up forever (Isaiah 25:8). This is in contrast to the ancient Hebrew belief that death has a nasty habit of swallowing up the living. Paul speaks of this same reality as it relates to the future resurrection: "When the perishable puts on the imperishable, and the mortal puts on immortality, then shall come to pass the saying that is written: 'Death is swallowed up in victory'" (1 Corinthians 15:54).

There will be no more disease, no more weakness, no more decay, no more coffins, no more funerals, and no more graves. There will be no reason for tears. Life in the eternal city will be painless, tearless, and deathless.

It is not that we will be sad in heaven and need to be cheered. We will not start crying and then need to have our crying eased. Rather, tears will be utterly foreign to the whole setting. It will be a time of rejoicing in the grace of God. There will be nothing to cry about!

Bible expositor Albert Barnes reflects on the absolute absence of mourning in heaven: "How innumerable are the sources of sorrow here; how constant is it on the earth...How different, therefore, will heaven be when we shall have the assurance that henceforward grief shall be at an end!"[1]

Revelation 21:5-7

"Behold, I am making all things new" (21:5): There are two primary views as to how everything will be made new.

The replacement view holds that the universe will be annihilated and replaced with a brand-new, second universe created *ex nihilo* ("out of nothing"). It will be an entirely different and entirely new earth and universe. In favor of this view is Peter's affirmation that the present heavens and earth will be destroyed by fire (2 Peter 3:10-13).

On the other hand, according to the renewal view (my personal view), the new heavens and new earth will be our present universe, but it will be purified by fire of all evil, sin, suffering, and death. The Greek word for "new" in Revelation 21 does not mean "new in origin," but rather "new in quality." Our future cosmos will stand in continuity with the present cosmos, but it will be utterly renewed and renovated. It will be gloriously rejuvenated.

This means that a resurrected people will live in a resurrected universe! John Piper put it this way: "What happens to our bodies and what happens to the creation go together. And what happens to our bodies is not annihilation but redemption...Our bodies will be redeemed, restored, made new, not thrown away. And so it is with the heavens and the earth."[2]

"Write this down, for these words are trustworthy and true" (21:5): God's revelation about the future can be trusted because God always faithfully speaks the truth (see Revelation 3:14; 19:11).

"It is done" (21:6): This is a statement of divine finality. It represents a promise from God Almighty that what He has created for humankind's eternal state will indeed last forever and ever. It is an accomplished fact.

"I am the Alpha and the Omega, the beginning and the end" (21:6): God restates His name, as if to put an exclamation point on the reality that "it is done." As we have seen, this name expresses eternality and omnipotence.

"To the thirsty I will give from the spring of the water of life without payment" (21:6): Jesus gives the water of life, which eternally satisfies (see Revelation 7:17; 22:1,17; see also Isaiah 55:1-2; John 4:13-14; 7:37-38). This water cannot be earned. It is a grace-gift, given without payment.

"The one who conquers...I will be his God and he will be my son" (21:7): The one who conquers or overcomes seems to be the one who places saving faith in Jesus Christ. "Everyone who has been born of God overcomes the world. And this is the victory that has overcome the world—our faith. Who is it that overcomes the world except the one who believes that Jesus is the Son of God?" (1 John 5:4-5).

The one who overcomes—or trusts in Christ for salvation—is fortunate indeed, for he or she will dwell with God in a parent-child relationship. This will be the heritage or the inheritance of the believer as a child of God (see 1 Peter 1:4).

Revelation 21:8

As for the cowardly, the faithless, the detestable...their portion will be in the lake that burns with fire and sulfur (21:8): In this midst of all this glorious news for believers is a somber warning for unbelievers. Indeed, their inheritance will be an eternity in the lake of fire. This is the second death—eternal separation from God.

Major Themes

1. *God dwelling among us.* In the Garden of Eden, God walked with Adam and Eve. Once sin entered the world, God dwelt among the Israelites by means of the tabernacle (Exodus 40:34) and later the temple (2 Samuel 22:7). In New Testament times, God "tabernacled" among us in the person of Jesus (John 1:14). Today, Christians are the temple of the Holy Spirit (1 Corinthians 3:16; 6:19). In the new Jerusalem, God will dwell with His people face to face (Revelation 22:4).

2. *A better country.* Heaven is not only called a city but also "a

better country" (Hebrews 11:13-16). And what a glorious country it is, as eighteenth-century Bible expositor John Gill wrote:

> [The heavenly country] is full of light and glory; having the delightful breezes of divine love, and the comfortable gales of the blessed Spirit…Many are the liberties and privileges here enjoyed; here is a freedom from a body subject to diseases and death, from a body of sin and death, from Satan's temptations, from all doubts, fears, and unbelief, and from all sorrows and afflictions.[3]

Digging Deeper with Cross-References

Adopted into God's eternal family—Romans 8:14,29; Galatians 3:26; 4:5; Ephesians 1:5; 2:19; 3:6; Philippians 2:15; Hebrews 12:6-9; 1 John 3:1.

Christians' inheritance in heaven—Matthew 5:5; 19:29; 25:34; Hebrews 1:14; 9:15; 1 Peter 1:4.

Life Lessons

1. *How can we be happy in heaven when people are suffering in hell?* Some theologians believe God may purge our memories so that they do not retain memories of those in hell. In Isaiah 65:17-19, God speaks of the new heavens and a new earth: "Behold, I create new heavens and a new earth, and the former things shall not be remembered or come into mind…no more shall be heard in it the sound of weeping and the cry of distress."

2. *Recognition in heaven.* Scripture reveals that we will recognize our Christian loved ones in the new Jerusalem. The Thessalonian Christians were concerned about their Christian loved ones who had died. Paul responds that they will be reunited in heaven, implying that they'll recognize each other (1 Thessalonians 4:13-17). David

knew he'd be reunited with his deceased son in heaven and had no doubt about recognizing him (2 Samuel 12:23). Lazarus, Abraham, and the rich man all recognized each other in the afterlife (Luke 16:19-31).

Questions for Reflection and Discussion

1. Think about being reunited with some of your Christian loved ones who are now in heaven. Does this put wind in your spiritual sails?

2. You have been adopted into God's eternal family, and you have a family inheritance awaiting you in heaven. What do those things mean to you personally?

A Description of the New Jerusalem

Revelation 21:9-27

Scripture Reading and Insights

Begin by reading Revelation 21:9-27 in your favorite Bible. As you read, keep in mind that the Word of God brings spiritual maturity (1 Corinthians 3:1-2; Hebrews 5:12-14).

In the previous lesson, we focused on God's creation of a new heaven and a new earth. Now let's discover more about the new Jerusalem, the glorious heavenly city that will rest on the new earth. With your Bible still accessible, consider the following insights on the biblical text, verse by verse.

Revelation 21:9-21

"Come, I will show you the Bride, the wife of the Lamb" (21:9): In this context, the bride is the new Jerusalem.

The holy city Jerusalem coming down out of heaven (21:10): As John was carried away in the spirit to a high mountain (a perfect vantage point), he witnessed firsthand the eternal city—the new Jerusalem—coming down out of heaven from God.

Physically resurrected believers will live in this physical city (1 Corinthians 15:35-53). Jesus in John 14:1-3 describes this eternal abode using such words as "house," "rooms," and "a place," thereby indicating physicality. Today's passage describes the new Jerusalem as having walls, gates, foundations, a street, river, trees, and more.

Having the glory of God (21:11): John's words no doubt represent a human attempt to describe the utterly indescribable. George Marsden, author of *Jonathan Edwards: A Life*, explained Edwards's view:

> However wonderful it might be to imagine these things, earthly images are not really adequate...These biblical images, he explained, are "very faint shadows" that represent the joys of heaven humans are intended to enjoy.[1]

The heavenly city will be far more wondrous than we can possibly imagine.

The city is designed to reflect and manifest the incredible glory of God (it is "clear as crystal"). The transparency within the city distributes the glory of God throughout the city without hindrance. The human imagination is incapable of fathoming the immeasurably resplendent glory of God that will be perpetually manifest in the eternal city. This is especially so when one considers that all manner of precious stones will be built into the eternal city. This is a scene of indescribable beauty with the glory of God shining through a variety of multicolored stones. No wonder heaven is described as the paradise of God (2 Corinthians 12:3; Revelation 2:7).

Twelve gates...twelve angels...twelve tribes (21:12): Angels are positioned at each of the 12 gates, not only as guardians but also to minister to the heirs of salvation (Hebrews 1:14). The names of the 12 tribes of Israel are written on the gates, perhaps to remind us that "salvation is of the Jews" (John 4:22).

Twelve foundations...twelve apostles (21:14): Perhaps the names of the apostles appear on the foundations of the city in order to remind us that the church was built on these men of God (Ephesians 2:20). (What was John's reaction when he saw his own name inscribed on one of the foundations?)

Perhaps the inclusion of the names of the 12 tribes of Israel and the 12 apostles indicates that Jewish and Gentile believers will both be in God's eternal family. The heavenly city includes the redeemed—both Jew and Gentile—of all ages.

The one who spoke with me had a measuring rod of gold...He measured the city with his rod (21:15-16): The heavenly city measures 12,000 stadia on each side, meaning that the city is approximately 1400 miles by 1400 miles by 1400 miles. Though some interpret these big numbers symbolically, I think the dimensions are intended to be interpreted literally.

The eternal city is so huge that it would measure approximately the distance from Canada to Mexico, or from the Atlantic Ocean to the Rockies. The city is tall enough to reach about one-twentieth of the way from the earth to the moon. If the city has stories, each being 12 feet high, then the city would have more than 500,000 stories.

The eternal city could either be cube-shaped or pyramid-shaped—and there are good Christian scholars on both sides of the debate. Some prefer to consider it shaped as a pyramid, for this would explain how the river of the water of life could flow down its sides as pictured in Revelation 22:1-2.

Others prefer to consider it shaped as a cube. After all, the Most Holy Place in Solomon's temple was cube shaped (1 Kings 6:20). The eternal city could be likened to an eternal Most Holy Place.

Every kind of jewel (21:18-21): The mention of beautiful, diverse, multicolored jewels is an attempt to describe the indescribable, to depict that which is perfect with imperfect language, to portray that which is infinite and eternal with language that is finite and temporal. Such beautiful jewels provide only a faint analogy of the awesome beauty of heaven.

The colors of these various jewels include white, gold, blood red, bright red, orange-red, blue, sky blue, greenish blue, sea green, yellow green, apple green, and purple. All these jewels are transparent, so God's glory shining throughout the city will be an awesome thing to behold. The entire city will glisten.

Revelation 21:22-27

I saw no temple in the city, for its temple is the Lord (21:22): The temple in the eternal state is not a building but is rather God Himself (compare with John 2:19,21). This communicates the idea that one need not go to a specific place or location to encounter the Lord. Rather, the presence of God will permeate the entire new heaven and new earth (see Revelation 21:3). God's presence will be limitless. Fellowship with God will be unbroken.

The city has no need of sun or moon to shine on it, for the glory of God gives it light, and its lamp is the Lamb (21:23): This is in keeping with the prophecy in Isaiah 60:19: "The sun shall be no more your light by day, nor for brightness shall the moon give you light; but the LORD will be your everlasting light, and your God will be your glory." Dr. Lehman Strauss's comments on the Lamb's glory are worthy of meditation:

> In that city which Christ has prepared for His own there will be no created light, simply because Christ Himself, who is the uncreated light (John 8:12), will be there…The created lights of God and of men are as darkness when compared with our Blessed Lord. The light He defuses throughout eternity is the unclouded, undimmed glory of His own Holy presence. In consequence of the fullness of that light, there shall be no night.[2]

Related to this, Colossians 1:12 refers to heaven as "the inheritance of the saints in light." Christ, of course, is the light of the world (John 8:12). The eternal kingdom thus takes on the character of the King.

By its light will the nations walk (21:24): The nations are the redeemed people from every nation and tribe and people. All races of man blend into God's eternal family on the new earth. There will be no racial divisions among human beings!

The kings of the earth will bring their glory into it (21:24): All these kings will be believers. They have glory only by the grace of God, who sovereignly institutes kings (Romans 13:1).

Its gates will never be shut by day—and there will be no night there (21:25): In ancient times, city gates were closed at night for protection against invaders. Gates were part of the city's security. In the eternal city, however, there will never be any external threat to those who dwell within. Satan, demons, and unbelievers will be in eternal quarantine in hell. Besides, God Himself will dwell within the city. Who would dare attack it?

They will bring into it the glory and the honor of the nations (21:26): In Jewish worship in biblical times, Gentiles were not allowed to enter into the holy precincts. Recall the riotous stir some Jews caused by accusing the apostle Paul of bringing a Gentile into the temple (Acts 21:28-29). Gentiles were considered unclean. But no believing Gentiles will be unwelcome in the holy precincts in heaven!

Nothing unclean will ever enter it (21:27): The city will be characterized by absolute perfection. No more sin. No more Satan. No more demons. No more antichrist. No more false prophet. The environment of heaven will be righteous, pure, and clean.

Only those whose names are written in the Lamb's book of life are within the city. All others—the wicked dead of all ages, along with Satan and all fallen angels—are eternally quarantined in the lake of fire.

What an awesome city! Because you and I are so accustomed to living in a fallen world that has been viciously marred by sin and corruption, we cannot imagine life in a heavenly habitat (see 1 Corinthians 2:9). From birth to death, we are confronted with imperfection on every level. But in the eternal city, we will experience nothing but perfection.

Major Themes

1. *The number 12.* The number 12 surfaces often in Revelation 21–22. There are 12 gates, angels, tribes, foundations, apostles, pearls, fruits, and months. As well, the side of the city measured 12,000 stadia. The wall measured 144 cubits (12 times 12).

2. *The perfection of heaven.* Heaven will be perfect in every way, as A.T. Pierson notes:

> There shall be no more curse—perfect restoration. The throne of God and of the Lamb shall be in it—perfect administration. His servants shall serve him—perfect subordination. And they shall see his face—perfect transformation. And his name shall be on their foreheads—perfect identification. And

there shall be no night there; and they need no can-
dle, neither light of the sun; for the Lord giveth them
light—perfect illumination. And they shall reign forever and ever—perfect exultation.[3]

Digging Deeper with Cross-References

The glory of God—Exodus 24:17; 40:34; 1 Kings 8:11; Psalms 8:1;
19:1; Ezekiel 10:4; Luke 2:9; Acts 7:55; 2 Corinthians 3:18.
Unclean—Leviticus 11; 22:8; Deuteronomy 14:3-20; Judges
13:4,14; Acts 10:14,28.

Life Lessons

1. *A top-down perspective.* Gary R. Habermas and J.P.
   Moreland speak of the necessity of maintaining a top-
   down perspective (see Matthew 6:19-34): "The God of
   the universe invites us to view life and death from his
   eternal vantage point. And if we do, we will see how
   readily it can revolutionize our lives."[4] The more we keep
   our eyes focused on the realities of heaven, the better our
   perspective on temporal, earthly things (Colossians 3:1-2).

2. *Living clean.* Our text tells us that nothing unclean will
   enter into the eternal city, the new Jerusalem. Today, we
   ought to allow nothing unclean to enter our lives. We
   ought to be pure. As James 4:8 puts it, "Cleanse your
   hands, you sinners, and purify your hearts, you double-
   minded" (see also 1 Peter 1:22; 1 John 3:3).

Questions for Reflection and Discussion

1. Do you make a habit of maintaining a top-down
   perspective? How might this practice help you to
   keep earthly problems and difficult circumstances in
   perspective?

2. Is any part of your present lifestyle interfering with clean
   living?

The Delights of the New Jerusalem

Revelation 22:1-5

Scripture Reading and Insights

Begin by reading Revelation 22:1-5 in your favorite Bible. As you read, remember that the Word of God can help you be spiritually fruitful (Psalm 1:1-3).

In the previous two readings, we were introduced to the new Jerusalem, God's heavenly city that will rest on the new earth. Now let's find out more about the wondrous delights of the new Jerusalem. With your Bible still accessible, consider the following insights on the biblical text, verse by verse.

Revelation 22:1-2

The river of the water of life (22:1): This pure river of life, though it may be a real and material river, is likely also symbolic of the abundance of spiritual life that will characterize those who are living in the eternal city. The stream seems to symbolize the perpetual outflow of spiritual blessing to the redeemed of all ages, now basking in the full glow of eternal life. What spiritual blessedness the eternal state will bring.

From the throne of God and of the Lamb (22:1): God Himself is the source of this wondrous water and the wondrous blessing that accompanies it. Notice that the Lamb and God the Father are on the throne. This is as it should be, for Christ is absolute deity (John 1:1; 8:58; 10:30; 20:28) as well as King of kings and Lord of lords (Revelation 17:14; 19:16).

The tree of life with its twelve kinds of fruit (22:2): The tree of life is first seen bestowing continuing life in the Garden of Eden (see Genesis 2:9; 3:22-24). When Adam and Eve sinned, death entered the universe, and God assigned cherubim to guard the tree of life so that Adam and Eve could no longer partake of it.

This, of course, was an act of God's grace. How awful it would have been for Adam and Eve to eat of the tree of life and live forever in a state of fallenness and sin. Death was a blessing in disguise, for it limited the time God allowed His fallen creatures to suffer in a state of sin.

In any event, paradise was lost. In the book of Revelation, however, paradise is restored, and we again witness the tree of life in the glorious eternal state. The leaves on the tree are for the healing of nations. This should not be taken to mean that sickness and disease will be a part of the eternal state (see 21:4). The Greek word for healing (*therapeia*) carries the idea of "health-giving." It is from this Greek word that we get the English words "therapy" and "therapeutic." The leaves on the tree promote health and have a therapeutic effect.

Revelation 22:3-5

No longer will there be anything accursed (22:3): In the Garden of Eden, Adam and Eve sinned against God, thereby bringing a curse on all humanity (see Genesis 3:16-19). All such curses will be gone forever in the eternal state. Never again will God have to judge sin. All will forever be well and blessed.

The throne of God and of the Lamb will be in it, and his servants will worship him (22:3): There will be unbroken and unfettered fellowship between redeemed humans and God.

Notice that even though verse 3 speaks of both God the Father and God the Son, the singular pronoun "him" is used. This points to the essential oneness of the Trinity (see Matthew 28:19; 2 Corinthians 13:14). As Jesus said in John 10:30, "I and the Father are one."

They will see his face (22:4): The apostle Paul affirmed, "Now we see in a mirror dimly, but then face to face. Now I know in part; then I shall know fully, even as I have been fully known" (1 Corinthians 13:12). The psalmist wrote, "As for me, I shall behold your face in righteousness"

(Psalm 17:15). John affirmed, "We know that when he appears we shall be like him, because we shall see him as he is" (1 John 3:2).

Can there be anything more sublime and more utterly satisfying for the Christian than to enjoy the sheer delight of unbroken fellowship with God and immediate and unobstructed access to the divine glory? (See John 14:3; 2 Corinthians 5:6-8; Philippians 1:23; 1 Thessalonians 4:17.) We will gaze on His countenance and behold His resplendent beauty forever.

God "who alone has immortality, who dwells in unapproachable light" (1 Timothy 6:16) will reside intimately among His own. "They will be his people, and God himself will be with them" (Revelation 21:3). No wonder the psalmist exults, "In your presence there is fullness of joy; at your right hand are pleasures forevermore" (Psalm 16:11).

In the afterlife, fellowship with the Lord will no longer be intermittent and blighted by sin and defeat. Instead, there will be continuous fellowship. The sin problem will no longer exist. When we enter into glory we will no longer have the sin nature within us (Philippians 3:21; 1 John 3:2). Sin will be banished from our very being. All things will be made new!

To fellowship with God is the essence of heavenly life, the fount and source of all blessing. We may be confident that the crowning wonder of our experience in the eternal city will be the perpetual and endless exploration of the unutterable beauty, majesty, love, holiness, power, joy, and grace of God Himself.

When our beloved Christ was born on earth, He was called Immanuel, which means "God with us" (see Matthew 1:23). Throughout the entire eternal state, Jesus will be with us in the closest possible sense, face to face. In the old hymn "Face to Face with Christ, My Savior," we read words worthy of meditation:

> Face to face with Christ, my Savior,
> Face to face—what will it be—
> When with rapture I behold Him,
> Jesus Christ who died for me?
>
> Face to face—O blissful moment!

Face to face—to see and know;
Face to face with my Redeemer,
Jesus Christ who loves me so.

Face to face I shall behold Him,
Far beyond the starry sky.
Face to face in all His glory,
I shall see Him by and by.

Some theologians speak of "beatific vision" when addressing the wondrous reality that we will be in the direct presence of God throughout the rest of eternity. The term comes from three Latin words that carry the meaning, "a happy-making sight."

The idea is that seeing God brings perpetual happiness and joy. Randy Alcorn says that "our primary joy in Heaven will be knowing and seeing God."[1] Barry Morrow suggests that "this contemplation of God will not be a static, boring experience of simply staring at God but rather a dynamic, unending exploration of God and His attributes."[2] Because God's attributes are perfect, one could spend an eternity contemplating them.

One further fact is worthy of mention here. In biblical times, no human could see God's face and live (Exodus 33:20-23). In heaven, however, Christians will have new resurrection bodies that will enable us to live directly in God's presence. The apostle Paul affirmed, "This perishable body must put on the imperishable, and this mortal body must put on immortality" (1 Corinthians 15:53). Once that happens, we can live with God face to face.

Believers will also have God's name on their foreheads (Revelation 22:4). This seems to be in obvious contrast to unbelievers who received the mark of the beast during the tribulation period (Revelation 13:16-17). This also represents the fulfillment of God's promise to the faithful believers at the church of Philadelphia: "I will write on him the name of my God" (Revelation 3:12).

Night will be no more (22:5): This is obvious because the glory of God will light up the eternal city (compare with Isaiah 60:19). Night cannot fall where God's glory is perpetually present.

They will reign forever and ever (22:5): God's faithful believers will be involved in some capacity in the heavenly government. Perhaps one aspect of this will involve judging the angels somehow. "Do you not know that the saints will judge the world?...Do you not know that we are to judge angels?" (1 Corinthians 6:2-3).

This is noteworthy because humanity at present is lower than the angels (see Psalm 8:5). The situation will be reversed in the eternal state. Angels will be lower than redeemed human beings in heaven.

Finally, the purposes of God are fulfilled. God's plan of salvation, conceived in eternity past, is now brought into full fruition, as Wilbur Smith exults:

> All the glorious purposes of God, ordained from the foundation of the world, have now been attained. The rebellion of angels and mankind is finally subdued, as the King of kings assumes his rightful sovereignty. Absolute and unchangeable holiness characterizes all within the universal kingdom of God. The redeemed, made so by the blood of the Lamb, are in resurrection and eternal glory. Life is everywhere—and death will never intrude again. The earth and the heavens both are renewed. Light, beauty, holiness, joy, the presence of God, the worship of God, service to Christ, likeness to Christ—all are now abiding realities.[3]

My friends, any way you look at it, the eternal city—the new Jerusalem—is going to be absolutely wonderful, far more so than any human mind could possibly fathom or even begin to imagine. Christians are merely pilgrims en route to the final frontier of the new Jerusalem, just passing through this brief dot of time on earth.

Major Themes

1. *Serving God and Christ in heaven.* Scripture indicates that we will be busy in our service to God (Revelation 1:5-6), but this service will be invigorating and fulfilling, not toilsome or draining. It will not be tedious, but joyous, fully meeting our hearts' every desire. We will find

immeasurable satisfaction in serving God. There will be no time demands, no frustrations, no fear of failure, and no exhaustion.

2. *Jesus and the water of life.* We noted previously that Jesus gives the water of life, which eternally satisfies (see John 4:13-14; 7:37-38; compare with Isaiah 55:1-2). This is likely the backdrop to the affirmation that the river of the water of life flows from the throne of God and of the Lamb (Revelation 22:1). God is the source!

Digging Deeper with Cross-References

God's throne—Psalms 9:7; 45:6; 47:8; 93:2; 103:19; Isaiah 6:1; 66:1; Hebrews 1:8.

Worship of God—Exodus 20:3-5; Deuteronomy 5:7; Psalms 29:2; 95:6; 100:2; Hebrews 12:28.

Life Lessons

1. *Jesus' parable in Luke 19:11-27.* Our faithfulness in serving Christ during our mortal state here on earth will in part determine our service in the eternal state. In Jesus' parable of the ten minas, the master affirmed to one of the servants, "Because you have been faithful in a very little, you shall have authority over ten cities." The idea seems to be that if we are faithful in this life, Christ will entrust us with greater responsibility as we serve Him in the next life.

2. *The throne of grace.* Our passage speaks of the throne of God and of the Lamb (Revelation 22:3). The truth is, however, we don't have to wait until we get to heaven to approach God's throne. We can approach it today by faith. As Hebrews 4:16 exhorts us, "Let us then with confidence draw near to the throne of grace, that we may receive mercy and find grace to help in time of need." Do you have a need? God's throne of grace is available to you now!

Questions for Reflection and Discussion

1. Scripture reveals that if we are faithful in this life, Christ will entrust us with more in serving Him in the next life. What is your reaction to this truth?

2. God's throne is a "throne of grace" (Hebrews 4:16). What does that mean to you?

3. How do you need God's favor today? Go to the throne!

John's Epilogue

Revelation 22:6-21

Scripture Reading and Insights

Begin by reading Revelation 22:6-21 in your favorite Bible. As you read, remember that the Word of God can help you be spiritually fruitful (Psalm 1:1-3).

In the previous three readings, we discovered a great deal about the new Jerusalem. As John brings the book of Revelation to a close, he instills in us an eternal perspective. With your Bible still accessible, consider the following insights on the biblical text, verse by verse.

Revelation 22:6-11

"These words are trustworthy and true" (22:6): This is because they come from the One who is Faithful and True (Revelation 19:11). The trustworthy and true revelations contained in this book are intended to inform God's servants—believers in the Lord Jesus Christ—about what will take place in the future. This knowledge comforts us in our present tribulations.

"Behold, I am coming soon" (22:7): Jesus says this once in 3:11 and three times in this chapter (see verses 12,20). Almost 2000 years have transpired since Jesus said this. Scholars offer two primary suggestions as to what He might have meant.

Some suggest that from the human perspective, Jesus' return may not have come soon, but from the divine perspective, it will. We have been in the last days since the incarnation of Christ (Hebrews 1:2; James 5:3). Moreover, James 5:9 affirms that "the Judge is standing at the door." Romans 13:12 exhorts us that "the night is far gone; the day is at hand." First Peter 4:7 warns, "The end of all things is at hand." In view of such verses, Christ is coming soon from the divine perspective.

Other scholars suggest that perhaps Jesus meant He is coming soon from the perspective of the events described in the book of Revelation. In other words, from the vantage point of those living during the time of the tribulation period itself, Christ is coming soon.

Still others say that the main idea in these words is that the coming of Christ is imminent. This being the case, we must all be ready, for we do not know precisely when Christ will come.

Why has God seemingly delayed? Second Peter 3:9 affirms, "The Lord is not slow to fulfill his promise as some count slowness, but is patient toward you, not wishing that any should perish, but that all should reach repentance." God's delay is to allow people plenty of time to turn to Him. Of course, the time will come when the delay will end, after which there will be no further opportunity to turn to Him.

"Blessed is the one who keeps the words of the prophecy of this book" (22:7): We keep the sayings of the prophecy in the book of Revelation by protecting its contents from alteration and by being obedient to what we learn.

I fell down to worship at the feet of the angel (22:8): Angels are such awesomely glorious creatures that humans who see them are fearful and may even be tempted to worship them (compare with Daniel 10:8; Matthew 28:2-4; Luke 1:12; 2:9). John's response to the angel was inappropriate but understandable.

"You must not do that... Worship God" (22:9): To worship any person or object other than God is idolatry (Exodus 20:3-6). The apostle Paul explicitly condemned the worship of angels in Colossians 2:18.

"Do not seal up the words of the prophecy of this book, for the time is near" (22:10): The prophecies of Daniel were sealed because the time was not yet ready (Daniel 8:26; 12:4-10). Earlier in Revelation John had been commanded to seal up (or not write down) the utterances of the seven thunders (Revelation 10:4). Now, however, John is not to seal

up the words of the prophecy because the time of fulfillment is potentially drawing near.

"Let the evildoer still do evil…and the righteous still do right" (22:11): Following the second coming of Christ, people's destinies will be sealed. One's decision for or against Christ will become set in stone. Evil people will continue in their evil, just as the righteous will continue in their righteousness and the holy in their holiness.

Revelation 22:12-17

"Behold, I am coming soon" (22:12): The imminence of Christ's coming is emphasized. We do not know precisely when Christ is coming again, so we must always be ready (see Titus 2:13-14) and be busy doing good works, for which we will be rewarded. Our salvation is not rooted in good works, but the rewards we will receive from the Lord are rooted in good works.

"To repay each one for what he has done" (22:12): Believers will face Christ at His judgment seat (Romans 14:8-10; 1 Corinthians 3:11-15). Unbelievers, however, will face Christ at the great white throne judgment (Revelation 20:11-15).

"I am the Alpha and the Omega" (22:13): Christ is again called the Alpha and Omega. These words were intended to comfort and encourage Christians as they await their King. When used of God (or Christ), the first and last letters of the Greek alphabet express eternality and omnipotence.

The phrase "the first and the last" is used of God Almighty in the Old Testament (see Isaiah 44:6; 48:12). Christ's use of this title of Himself in this verse was undoubtedly intended to demonstrate His equality with God. And this is precisely what brings comfort and encouragement to Christ's followers. Christ wanted them to be absolutely assured that He is the all-powerful Sovereign, who will be victorious.

Blessed are those who wash their robes, so that they may have the right to the tree of life (22:14): Those who wash their robes are blessed because they have been cleansed by the blood of the Lamb (Hebrews 9:14; 1 Peter 1:18-19), so their sins have been forgiven. The redeemed will thus have access to the tree of life and will live forever in the new creation.

Outside are the dogs…and everyone who loves and practices falsehood (22:15): The term "dogs" was sometimes used as a metaphor for people of low character. Such people, along with sorcerers (who practice the magic arts), the sexually immoral (fornicators and adulterers), murderers (such as those who martyred God's people), and idolaters will be outside heaven. They will dwell forever in the lake of fire.

"I, Jesus, have sent my angel to testify" (22:16): This recalls Revelation 1:1, where we are told that Jesus' revelation was made known to John through an angel.

The apostle Paul affirmed that by Christ "all things were created… whether thrones or dominions or rulers or authorities—all things were created through him and for him" (Colossians 1:16). These are different orders of angels (see Romans 8:38; Ephesians 1:21; 3:10; 6:12; Colossians 2:15). All these angels—like all else in creation—were brought into being for Christ. All creation is intended to serve His will and to contribute to His glory. The angel mentioned in Revelation 1:1 and throughout chapter 22 is merely one of many angels at Christ's disposal.

"I am the root and the descendant of David, the bright morning star" (22:16): Christ is the root (or source) of David because Christ is the eternal Creator of all things (Colossians 1:16; John 1:3). At the same time, Christ is the offspring of David because He physically descended from David's line (2 Samuel 7:12-14).

The term "morning star" in this verse has a messianic sense related to Numbers 24:17: "A star shall come out of Jacob." The star had become a symbol of the coming messianic king, who was Jesus. The phrase "morning star" communicates that a spiritual dawn is right around the corner. The cold dark night of spiritual lethargy is nearly over with the coming of Jesus, the morning star.

Let the one who is thirsty come (22:17): The Holy Spirit and the bride (the church) extend an invitation to all who will listen. Those who hear the invitation are encouraged to extend the invitation to still others. Spread the word that salvation is entirely by grace. All who desire to have their thirsty souls satisfied are invited to come to Christ for the water of life.

Revelation 22:18-19

If anyone adds…if anyone takes away (22:18-19): Changing God's Word is a serious crime (see Deuteronomy 4:2; 12:32; Proverbs 30:6). It was customary in biblical times for writers to attach this type of warning at the end of their books. This served to dissuade copyists from tampering with what was written.

Of course, Scripture is much more important than a human book, for Scripture contains the Word of God. This is why such severe penalties are promised against those who add or take away from God's Word.

Revelation 22:20-21

He who testifies to these things says, "Surely I am coming soon" (22:20): Jesus is the faithful and true witness (Revelation 3:14; 19:11). A witness is one who testifies. Jesus testifies that His coming is imminent!

Come, Lord Jesus! (22:20): This phrase is rooted in the Aramaic term *maranatha,* which was a common greeting among New Testament saints. Believers often used the term because they greatly anticipated the soon coming of the Lord. Notice that as soon as the Lord affirms He is coming soon, the natural response is, "Amen. Come, Lord Jesus!" Christ's coming is the hope of the ages.

The grace of the Lord Jesus be with you all. Amen. (22:21): The book of Revelation begins and ends with a reference to the grace of God (see Revelation 1:4). The implication is clear: Any and all are urged to turn to Christ for the free gift of salvation.

Major Themes

1. *Grace.* The water of life is without price (Revelation 22:17). God gives it freely by His grace. The word "grace" literally means "unmerited favor." "Unmerited" means this favor cannot be earned. The apostle Paul wrote, "The free gift of God is eternal life in Christ Jesus our Lord" (Romans 6:23; see also Ephesians 2:8-9; Hebrews 4:16).

2. *Anticipating the second coming.* In 2 Timothy 4:8, the apostle Paul said, "There is laid up for me the crown of

righteousness, which the Lord, the righteous judge, will award to me on that Day, and not only to me but also to all who have loved his appearing." Presently we are "eagerly waiting for him" (Hebrews 9:28). We are "waiting for our blessed hope, the appearing of the glory of our great God and Savior Jesus Christ" (Titus 2:13). I can't wait!

Digging Deeper with Cross-References

The churches—Revelation 2–3.

Plagues in the book of Revelation—Revelation 9:18,20; 11:6; 15:1,6,8; 16:9,21; 18:4,8; 21:9.

Life Lessons

1. *Never predict dates.* It is unwise for Christians to predict dates regarding end-time events.

   • People who have predicted dates have been wrong every time.

   • Predicting dates may lead to harmful decisions, such as not saving for the future.

   • Failed predictions may damage one's faith in the Bible.

   • After failed predictions, prophecy might not motivate purity in daily life.

   • The timing of end-time events is in God's hands, not ours (Acts 1:7).

2. *Jesus' parable in Mark 13:33-37: Always be ready.* This parable indicates we ought always be ready:

   > Be on guard, keep awake. For you do not know when the time will come. It is like a man going on a journey, when he leaves home and puts his servants in charge, each with his work, and commands the doorkeeper to stay awake. Therefore stay awake—for you do not know when the master of the house will come,

in the evening, or at midnight, or when the rooster crows, or in the morning—lest he come suddenly and find you asleep. And what I say to you I say to all: Stay awake.

Questions for Reflection and Discussion

1. Have you ever been influenced by radio or TV preachers who have predicted or implied dates regarding end-time matters?

2. What lesson do you learn from Christ's parable in Mark 13:33-37?

Postscript

The Bible begins in paradise, but within a few chapters, paradise is lost, and pain, suffering, and death enter the human race (Genesis 1–3). The Bible ends with paradise restored. Pain, suffering, and death will be a thing of the past for the redeemed (Revelation 21–22). Meanwhile, we continue our sojourn on this fallen earth with the Bible in hand. This divine book informs us of what the future will look like.

As we close our journey through the book of Revelation, let's remember that our life on earth is ever so short. Theologian John Wenham once commented that "not only is it certain that this life will end, but it is certain that from the perspective of eternity it will be seen to have passed in a flash."[1] Christian writer Philip Yancey says our time on earth amounts to a mere "dot in eternity."[2]

This dot in eternity is quickly passing away. It will soon be over. Our destiny in heaven, by contrast, is an eternal destiny. We will live forever in a pain-free and death-free environment. A realization of our glorious future gives us much-needed strength today. This was true of the original recipients of the book of Revelation. It is just as true for us.

Consider the Puritans! They set an example for us. The Puritans saw themselves as "God's pilgrims, traveling home through rough country; God's warriors, battling the world, the flesh, and the devil; and God's servants, under orders to worship, fellowship, and do all the good they could as they went along."[3] We should have the same kind of attitude. John strategically engineered the book of Revelation to help Christians foster such an attitude.

I close with one of my favorite passages: "If then you have been raised with Christ, seek the things that are above, where Christ is, seated at the right hand of God. Set your minds on things that are above, not on things that are on earth" (Colossians 3:1-2). The original Greek of this passage is intense: "Diligently, actively, single-mindedly pursue the things above." It is also a present tense in the original Greek, carrying the idea, "perpetually keep on seeking the things above…Make it an ongoing process."

Let's remember that "our citizenship is in heaven, and from it we await a Savior, the Lord Jesus Christ" (Philippians 3:20). Meanwhile, we are "strangers and exiles on the earth" (Hebrews 11:13). We are pilgrims en route to a better country, a heavenly one (verse 16).

As we make our way to the heavenly country, may the book of Revelation be a continual source of spiritual strength and encouragement!

Bibliography

Barnhouse, Donald Grey. *Revelation: An Expository Commentary*. Grand Rapids: Zondervan, 1971.

Dyer, Charles. *The Rise of Babylon: Sign of the End Times*. Chicago: Moody, 2003.

Feinberg, Charles. *A Commentary on Revelation*. Winona Lake: BMH Books, 1985.

Fruchtenbaum, Arnold. *The Footsteps of the Messiah*. San Antonio: Ariel, 2004.

Heitzig, Skip. *You Can Understand the Book of Revelation*. Eugene: Harvest House, 2011.

Helyer, Larry, and Richard Wagner. *The Book of Revelation for Dummies*. Hoboken: Wylie, 2008.

Hindson, Ed. *Book of Revelation: Unlocking the Future*. Chattanooga: AMG, 2002.

Hitchcock, Mark. *The Complete Book of Bible Prophecy*. Wheaton: Tyndale House, 1999.

———. *The Coming Islamic Invasion of Israel*. Sisters: Multnomah, 2002.

———. *Iran: The Coming Crisis*. Sisters: Multnomah, 2006.

———. *Is America in Bible Prophecy?* Sisters: Multnomah, 2002.

———. *The Second Coming of Babylon*. Sisters: Multnomah, 2003.

Hoyt, Herman. *The End Times*. Chicago: Moody, 1969.

Ice, Thomas, and Timothy Demy. *Prophecy Watch*. Eugene: Harvest House, 1998.

Ice, Thomas, and Randall Price. *Ready to Rebuild: The Imminent Plan to Rebuild the Last Days Temple*. Eugene: Harvest House, 1992.

———. *When the Trumpet Sounds*. Eugene: Harvest House, 1995.

Ironside, H.A. *Revelation*. Grand Rapids: Kregel, 1978.

LaHaye, Tim. *The Beginning of the End*. Wheaton: Tyndale, 1991.

———. *The Coming Peace in the Middle East*. Grand Rapids: Zondervan, 1984.

———. *Revelation Illustrated and Made Plain*. Grand Rapids: Zondervan, 1975.

LaHaye, Tim, ed. *Prophecy Study Bible*. Chattanooga: AMG, 2001.

LaHaye, Tim, and Ed Hindson, eds. *The Popular Bible Prophecy Commentary*. Eugene: Harvest House, 2006.

———. *The Popular Encyclopedia of Bible Prophecy*. Eugene: Harvest House, 2004.

LaHaye, Tim, and Thomas Ice. *Charting the End Times*. Eugene: Harvest House, 2001.

LaHaye, Tim, and Jerry Jenkins. *Are We Living in the End Times?* Wheaton: Tyndale, 1999.

Lindsey, Hal. *There's a New World Coming: A Prophetic Odyssey*. Santa Ana: Vision House, 1973.

Newell, William. *Revelation Chapter-by-Chapter*. Grand Rapids: Kregel, 1994.

Pentecost, J. Dwight. *Things to Come*. Grand Rapids: Zondervan, 1964.

Phillips, John: *Exploring Revelation*. Grand Rapids: Kregel, 1974.

Pink, Arthur W. *The Antichrist: A Study of Satan's Christ*. Blacksburg: Wilder, 2008.

Price, Randall. *Jerusalem in Prophecy*. Eugene: Harvest House, 1998.

Price, Walter K. *The Coming Antichrist*. Neptune: Loizeaux Brothers, 1985.

Reid, T.R. *The United States of Europe: The New Superpower and the End of American Supremacy*. New York: Penguin, 2004.

Rhodes, Ron. *The Coming Oil Storm: The Imminent End of Oil…and Its Strategic Global Role in End-Times Prophecy*. Eugene: Harvest House, 2010.

———. *Five Views on the Rapture: What You Need to Know*. Eugene: Harvest House, 2011.

———. *Is America in Bible Prophecy?: What You Need to Know*. Eugene: Harvest House, 2011.

———. *The Middle East Conflict: What You Need to Know*. Eugene: Harvest House, 2009.

———. *Northern Storm Rising: Russia, Iran, and the Emerging End-Times Military Coalition Against Israel*. Eugene: Harvest House, 2008.

———. *The Popular Dictionary of Bible Prophecy*. Eugene: Harvest House, 2010.

———. *The Topical Handbook of Bible Prophecy*. Eugene: Harvest House, 2010.

———. *Unmasking the Antichrist*. Eugene: Harvest House, 2012.

Rosenberg, Joel. *Epicenter: Why Current Rumblings in the Middle East Will Change Your Future*. Carol Stream: Tyndale House, 2006.

Ryrie, Charles. *Ryrie Study Bible*. Chicago: Moody, 2011.

Stedman, Ray. *God's Final Word: Understanding Revelation*. Grand Rapids: Discovery House, 1991.

Swindoll, Charles. *Insights on Revelation*. Grand Rapids: Zondervan, 2011.

Unger, Merrill. *Beyond the Crystal Ball: What Occult Practices Cannot Tell You About Future Events*. Chicago: Moody, 1973.

Walvoord, John F. *End Times*. Nashville: Word, 1998.

———. *The Millennial Kingdom*. Grand Rapids: Zondervan, 1975.

———. *The Prophecy Knowledge Handbook*. Wheaton: Victor, 1990.

———. *The Return of the Lord*. Grand Rapids: Zondervan, 1979.

Walvoord, John F., and John E. Walvoord. *Armageddon, Oil, and the Middle East Crisis*. Grand Rapids: Zondervan, 1975.

Wiersbe, Warren. *Be Victorious*. Colorado Springs: David C. Cook, 1985.

Notes

Day 13: The Seventh Seal Judgment

1. Charles Swindoll, *Insights on Revelation* (Grand Rapids: Zondervan, 2011), p. 127.
2. Skip Heitzig, *You Can Understand the Book of Revelation* (Eugene: Harvest House, 2011), p. 90.
3. Ed Hindson, *The Book of Revelation: Unlocking the Future* (Chattanooga: AMG, 2002), p. 99.

Day 21: The Rise of the Antichrist

1. Walter K. Price, *The Coming Antichrist* (Neptune: Loizeaux Brothers, 1985), p. 145.
2. Mark Hitchcock, *The Complete Book of Bible Prophecy* (Wheaton: Tyndale House, 1999), pp. 199-200.

Day 23: The Rise of the False Prophet

1. David Reagan, "The Rise and Fall of the Antichrist," RaptureReady. www.raptureready.com/featured/reagan/dr33.html.
2. John F. Walvoord, "Revelation," in *The Bible Knowledge Commentary*.
3. John Phillips, *Exploring Revelation* (Grand Rapids: Kregel, 1987), p. 171.

Day 24: The False Prophet's Exaltation of the Antichrist

1. J. Hampton Keathley III, "The Beast and the False Prophet (Rev. 13:1-18)," Bible.org /seriespage/beast-and-false-prophet-rev-131-18.

Day 28: The Fifth, Sixth, and Seventh Bowl Judgments

1. John F. Walvoord, "Revelation," in *The Bible Knowledge Commentary*.
2. Charles Ryrie, *The Ryrie Study Bible* (Chicago: Moody Press, 2011).

Day 30: The Fall of Commercial Babylon, Part 1

1. Thomas Ice and Timothy Demy, *Prophecy Watch* (Eugene: Harvest House, 1998), p. 191.

Day 32: Shouts of Hallelujah and the Marriage Supper of the Lamb

1. Arnold Fruchtenbaum, *The Footsteps of the Messiah* (Tustin: Ariel Ministries, 2003), p. 597.

Day 36: Satan's Final Rebellion and the Great White Throne

1. Warren Wiersbe, *Be Victorious: Revelation* (Colorado Springs: David C. Cook, 2008), p. 176.

Day 37: The Descent of the New Jerusalem

1. Albert Barnes, "Revelation," in *Notes on the New Testament* (Grand Rapids: Baker, 1996), pp. 444-45.
2. Cited in Randy Alcorn, *Heaven* (Wheaton: Tyndale, 2004), p. 125.
3. John Gill, "Hebrews 11:13-16" in The Online Bible.

Day 38: A Description of the New Jerusalem

1. George Marsden, *Jonathan Edwards: A Life* (New Haven: Yale, 2003), p. 98.
2. Cited in Tim LaHaye, *Revelation: Illustrated and Made Plain* (Grand Rapids: Zondervan, 1975), p. 315.
3. Cited in John F. Walvoord, *The Revelation of Jesus Christ* (Chicago: Moody, 1966), p. 332.
4. Gary R. Habermas and J.P. Moreland, *Immortality: The Other Side of Death* (Nashville: Thomas Nelson, 1992), p. 185.

Day 39: The Delights of the New Jerusalem

1. Randy Alcorn, *Heaven* (Wheaton: Tyndale, 2004), pp. 169-70.
2. Barry Morrow, *Heaven Observed: Glimpses of Transcendence in Everyday Life* (Colorado Springs: NavPress, 2001), p. 324.
3. Cited in "Revelation," *Wycliffe Bible Commentary* (Chicago: Moody, 1960), p. 1524.

Postscript

1. John Wenham, *The Enigma of Evil: Can We Believe in the Goodness of God?* (Grand Rapids: Zondervan, 1985), p. 55.
2. Philip Yancey, *Where Is God When It Hurts?* (Grand Rapids: Zondervan, 1977), p. 176.
3. J.I. Packer, ed., *Alive to God: Studies in Spirituality* (Downers Grove: InterVarsity, 1992), p. 163.

Other Great Harvest House Books by Ron Rhodes

Books About the Bible

Bite-Size Bible® Answers
Bite-Size Bible® Charts
Bite-Size Bible® Definitions
Bite-Size Bible® Handbook
Commonly Misunderstood Bible Verses
Find It Fast in the Bible
Understanding the Bible from A to Z
What Does the Bible Say About…?

Books About the End Times

The Coming Oil Storm
Cyber Meltdown
The End Times in Chronological Order
Northern Storm Rising
The Topical Handbook of Bible Prophecy
Unmasking the Antichrist

Books About Other Important Topics

5-Minute Apologetics for Today
1001 Unforgettable Quotes About God, Faith, and the Bible
Angels Among Us
Answering the Objections of Atheists, Agnostics, and Skeptics
Christianity According to the Bible
The Complete Guide to Christian Denominations
Conviction Without Compromise
Find It Quick Handbook on Cults and New Religions
The Truth Behind Ghosts, Mediums, and Psychic Phenomena
Why Do Bad Things Happen If God Is Good?
The Wonder of Heaven